THE

CONVERSION OF INDIA

THE CONVERSION OF INDIA

FROM PANTAENUS TO THE PRESENT TIME

A.D. 193-1893

GEORGE SMITH, C.I.E., LL.D.

GYAN

Published by

GYAN

Gyan Publishing House
5, Ansari Road
Daryaganj, New Delhi-110002
Phone: 011-47034999, 9811692060
E-mail: books@gyanbooks.com

Distribution Network
gyanbooks.com
India, USA, Canada, UK, Australia, France

ISBN : 978-81-212-9218-4 (PB)
First Published, 1893

2nd Impression 2023

Printed at: Gyan Press, Delhi.

THE CONVERSION OF INDIA
Author: GEORGE SMITH

THE CONVERSION OF INDIA

THE

CONVERSION OF INDIA

FROM PANTÆNUS TO THE PRESENT TIME

A.D. 193–1893

By GEORGE SMITH, C.I.E., LL.D.

AUTHOR OF THE LIVES OF CAREY, OF HENRY MARTYN, OF DUFF, OF WILSON, OF HISLOP, OF SOMERVILLE, ETC.

WITH ILLUSTRATIONS

Δεήθητε

LONDON

JOHN MURRAY, ALBEMARLE STREET

1893

PREFACE

The first of the Churches of the Reformation to become missionary was that of the Netherlelands. The Dutch colony of New Netherlands, in North America, lasted from the year 1609 to 1664. In 1628 the first congregation was organised on Manhattan Island, now New York. That was the earliest to work among the Red Indians. The organization which is now known as the Reformed Church in America, has furthermore established one of the most remarkable missions in British India, the Arcot Mission. In 1888 one of the elders of that Church, Mr. Nathan F. Graves, of Syracuse, N. Y., wrote to the late L. W. V. B. Mabon, D.D., Professor in its Theological Seminary, New Brunswick, N. J.: "I understand there is no Seminary or Professorship of Missions in the United States." The result was the establishment, by that benefactor, of a foundation like the Boyle Lecture of England, on which, in 1864, the late Dean Merivale delivered in the Chapel Royal, Whitehall, eight lectures on the Conversion of the Roman Empire, and, in 1865, eight lectures on the Conversion of the Northern Nations.

The present writer chose as the subject of the fifth course of Graves' lectures, The Conversion of India. This volume contains a somewhat fuller treatment of that question, historically and practically, than was possible in the six lectures which he was appointed to deliver in the first fortnight of October 1893. But the book is only an outline of the past history and of the process which is going on before our eyes in India.

The previous courses, on the same foundation, were delivered, in 1889, by six distinguished American missionaries on their own missions: in 1890 by Rev. John Hall, D.D., LL.D., of New York, on Missions from Apostolic to Modern Times; in 1891 by Rev. Arthur T. Pierson, D.D., formerly of Philadelphia, on The Divine Enterprise of Missions; and in 1892 by Rev. A. J. Gordon, D.D., of Boston, on the Holy Spirit in Missions.

NAPIER ROAD, MERCHISTON,
EDINBURGH.

CONTENTS

PAGE

VII. THE UNITED STATES OF AMERICA'S CO-OPERATION—

VIII. THE METHODS OF THE EVANGELICAL MISSION TO INDIA—

Be these thy trophies, Queen of many Isles!
On these high Heaven shall shed indulgent smiles.
First by thy guardian voice to India led,
Shall Truth divine her tearless victories spread;
Wide and more wide the heaven-born light shall stream
New realms from thee shall catch the blissful theme,
Unwonted warmth the soften'd savage feel,
Strange chiefs admire, and turban'd warriors kneel,
The prostrate East submit her jewell'd pride,
And swarthy kings adore the Crucified.
Fam'd Ava's walls Messiah's name shall own,
Where haughty splendour guards the Burman throne.
Thy hills, Tibet, shall hear, and Ceylon's bowers,
And snow-white waves that circle Peking's towers,
Where, sheath'd in sullen pomp, the Tartar lord
Forgetful slumbers o'er his idle sword;
O'er all the plains where barbarous hordes afar
On panting steeds pursue the roving war,
Soft notes of joy th' eternal gloom shall cheer,
And smooth the terrors of the arctic year:
Till from the blazing line to polar snows,
Through varying realms, one tide of blessing flows.
Then shall thy breath, celestial Peace, unbind
The frozen heart, and mingle mind with mind;
With sudden youth shall slumb'ring Science start,
And call to life each long-forgotten art,
Retrace her ancient paths or new explore,
And breathe to wond'ring worlds her mystic lore.

Yes, it shall come! E'en now my eyes behold,
In distant view, the wish'd-for age unfold.
Lo, o'er the shadowy days that roll between,
A wand'ring gleam foretells th' ascending scene!
Oh, doom'd victorious from thy wounds to rise,
Dejected India, lift thy downcast eyes,

And mark the hour, whose faithful steps for thee
Through Time's press'd ranks bring on the jubilee!

Roll back, ye crowded Years, your thick array,
Greet the glad hour, and give the triumph way.
Hail First and Greatest, inexpressive name,
Substantial Wisdom, God with God the same!
O Light, which shades of fiercest glory veil,
O human Essence, mix'd with Godhead, hail!
Powers, Princedoms, Virtues, wait thy sovereign call,
And but for Thee exists this breathing all.
Then shake thy heavens, thou Mightiest, and descend
While Truth and Peace Thy radiant march attend.
With wearied hopes thy thousand empires groan,
Our aching eyes demand thy promis'd throne.
Oh cheer the realms from life and sunshine far!
Oh plant in Eastern skies thy sevenfold star!

Then, while transported ASIA kneels around,
With ancient arts and long-lost glories crown'd,
Some happier Bard, on Ganges' margin laid,
Where playful bamboos weave their fretted shade,
Shall to the strings a loftier tone impart,
And pour in rapturous verse his flowing heart.
Stamp'd in immortal light on future days,
Through all the strain his country's joys shall blaze;
The Sanscreet song be warm'd with heavenly fires,
And themes divine awake from Indian lyres.

CHARLES GRANT, M.A., *Fellow of Magdalen College, Cambridge*, 1805; *afterwards Lord Glenelg.*

ILLUSTRATIONS

THE CONVERSION OF INDIA

I

INTRODUCTION

THE greatest event in the history of the world is the conversion to Christ of the Roman Empire. The revolution occupied three centuries till it was completed,—externally, by the *coup d'état* of Constantine, the first Christian emperor; internally, by the Nicene theology. The immediate consequent and the richest result of this divine transformation was the conversion to Christ of the Northern Nations chiefly through Celtic and Saxon missionaries, whose representatives at the present hour are the English-speaking families of the British Empire and the United States of America. This movement required other twelve centuries, and ended in the reformation of the Church, which, historically, finished the conversion of Europe. The Christian revolution and the Church's reformation were confined to the West; the Eastern and North African Churches virtually abandoned Asia and Africa to the old heathen cults of Brahmanism, Buddhism, and demonolatry. These Churches even became so corrupt in life and doctrine that from their errors, working along with the imperfections of Judaism, there arose Mohammedanism, the greatest antagonist of Christianity to the present day.

The Reformed Churches of Europe and America, after a critical pause for two centuries more, during which they were unconsciously preparing the Word of God for the world-races, and were opening up new continents and islands to its sway, entered a century ago on the third spiritual revolution—the conversion of the East, of India and Southern Asia, to Christ. The conversion of Africa and the islands may be regarded as the work of the missionary century on which we are just entering. So far as Africa is under Mohammedan influence, the evangelising of that continent is really a part of the greater problem of Asia. Following up the two revolutions of the eighteen Christian centuries, the third, the conversion of India in the widest sense of that word, is the first and greatest mission to which Western Christendom is called. The fitful and mistaken attempts of the Early Church, the long neglect or cruel intolerance that succeeded these up to a century ago, have made Brahmanism, with its offspring, and Islam apparently more powerful enemies of Christ than even the classical paganism of Hellas and Imperial Rome. Hinduism and Islam once fairly grappled with, the millions of China and Japan, of Africa and Oceania, must follow willing captives in the triumphal train of the Christ.

We stand to-day at a point in the history of the human family almost as many years after the incarnation of Jesus Christ as His first and greatest forerunner lived before that central event. The nineteen Abrahamic centuries were the period of decentralisation, of scattering, of despair, but of silent preparation. The nineteen Christian centuries have been the time of unification, of elevation, of hope. Then the warring races and jarring civilisations, preying upon each other, groped about the old world around the Persian Gulf and the Mediterranean Sea, knowing little of their home or of physical law. Now, and especially in the last century, men have been taught by Christ the unity of their destiny in Him, and their consequent responsibility to each other. Science has revealed and almost surveyed the whole world, old and new. Colonisation has at last, after the struggles and the strifes of six thousand years, taken possession of the planet. One language, the English, transcending even the limits of races and nations and governments, as the Greek never did, has become the ever-growing depository of the highest civilisation and the fruitful medium of its unifying extension. The one faith of Christ Jesus, the Son of Man, who said that He came to seek and to save the lost, prompting science, guiding colonisation, and using English speech, is working out the realisation of the unity of mankind by the very modern enterprise of Foreign Missions.[1]

In this historical evolution of the human family through Christianity, the oldest, the most wonderful, and still the most fruitful and necessary portion, is that which is concerned with India and Southern Asia. In working out this process the Christians of the United States of America are allied and co-operate with those of the British Empire on almost equal terms. We together, 100 millions strong, in Europe and America, with the same origin, the same history, the same tongue, the same literature, the same faith, and therefore the same Christ-commanded duty and assured hope, are set over or over against the 300 millions of India in the providence of God. Our fathers, theirs and ours, dwelt together four thousand years ago when

[1] In 1852 David Livingstone, having explored as a medical missionary north to the Upper Zambesi, wrote thus to his directors—"You will see by the accompanying sketch-map what an immense region God in His grace has opened up." Again—"I never anticipated fame from the discovery of the lake (Ngami). I cared very little about it; but the sight of the rivers and countries beyond, all densely populated, awakened many and enthusiastic feelings. Consider the multitudes that in the providence of God have been brought to light; the probability that in our efforts to evangelise we shall put a stop to the slave trade in a large region, and by means of the highway into the north which we have discovered, bring unknown nations into the sympathies of the Christian world." The result is the difference between the Africa of 1853 and 1893, and the possibilities, amounting to certainties, of the future of the whole African peoples. The process is going on before our eyes.

the first missionary call from "the God of Glory" fell on the ears of Abraham in the ancestral land, and the first whisper of the missionary covenant was heard by "the father of a multitude." How has it come about that we have had committed to us so vast a task which we did not consciously seek, so splendid a trust from which again and again we have shrunk, and which sometimes even still we resent? What has been the attitude and what the action of the Christian Church to the peoples of India?

Since the first application of the comparative method of Philology to early history fifty years ago, no well-established advance has been made on the conclusion that, from the great plateau of Iran, between the Persian Gulf and the Caspian Sea, the Indo-European race, who called themselves Aryan or "noble," scattered south-east to the Indus and north-west to Europe, and ultimately to America.[1]

Of all the teachings of Science and of History there is none so important to the human race, and especially to the British and American peoples, as this evolution of Providence during the past four thousand years. It is the racial, the historical, the divine root of all Foreign Missions, alike in their spiritual and their civilising aspects. The Turanian is succeeded by the Semitic, and both prepare the way for the Aryan or Indo-European. Of the Aryans, the elder branches, Sanskritic and Persic, find a home in North India, and there from the nature-worship

[1] See pp. 8-10 of *Study of Comparative Grammar*, by George Smith, 1854. In his "Essay on the Geography of the Valley of the Oxus" (1872), prefixed to Captain John Wood's *Journey to the Source of the River Oxus*, the late Sir Henry Yule inclines to the interpretation of the sacred narrative of Genesis, which finds the Adamic paradise in the heart of Asia which gives birth to the Oxus, "the great physical and political watershed of the Old Continent." The high tableland of Pamir nearly realises the old pictures of Eden, which figure the four rivers as literally diverging from a central lake to the four quarters of the earth,—the Oxus towards Europe, the Yarkand river to the verge of China, the Jaxartes to the north-east, and the Indus to the south-west.

of their Vedic literature develop the Brahmanical system of Pantheism and caste and the Puranic idolatry. They utterly fail. The younger branches alone continue the slow work of preparation, first in the sunny lands of Greece and Italy, then in the Teutonic forests of Central Europe, in the Scandinavian snows of the north, and the Celtic islands of the far west. Receiving the doctrine of Jesus Christ, the Son of God and the Saviour of men, first the Celts through Patrick and Columba, and then the Saxons through Boniface, become missionaries to Germany. Scandinavia and all Europe, escaping the humanistic heresy of Arius, become Christian. But still Christendom itself needs at once reformation and expansion westward. The first is given to it by Wiclif and Luther, especially in the form of the Word of God in the vernaculars of the people. The expansion begins at the same time when, seeking for India, Christopher Columbus first finds America, and the blind absolutism of English statesmanship three hundred years after results in the independence of the United States.

Thus have the English-speaking Aryans been trained to become the rulers of India and the evangelisers of Asia. The younger, of Great Britain and America, have been prepared to serve the elder, of India, in the highest ministry of sacrifice, that through them the Hindus, Parsees, and Mohammedans may now receive Christ. Upon us, as upon all Christians, there rests the command to go and teach all nations. But the teaching of India is pre-eminently the first and the greatest duty of the English-speaking Aryans, who have been chosen as the servants of Jehovah for this end as truly as the great Cyrus was in the Old Testament, that the Jews might fulfil their preparatory mission to the world, and might in their turn bring in the fulness of the nations. Through Brahmanism the Hindus have been missionaries of evil to the aboriginal people of India, whose Dravidian demon-worship is not so far from the kingdom of Heaven as its caste-bound philosophy and ritual. Through Buddhism the Hindus were the most enthusiastic and successful missionaries of a pantheistic nihilism in faith and morals to the millions of China and Tibet, Burma and Ceylon. Thus the duty laid upon us to seek and save India first or above all regions, is accompanied by the assurance that when we open the door of Brahmanism to Christ we open it to the millions of China and Japan, of the Eastern Peninsula and Ceylon. India is the key to all South and Central Asia. The complete conquest of the Brahman and the Mohammedan of India by the Cross will be to all Asia what the submission of Constantine was to the Roman Empire—*in hoc signo vincimus.*

The historical or providential problem of missionary Christianity—the only true Christianity—to the outlines of the solution of which these Lectures are devoted, is to bring into the kingdom of Jesus Christ the elder branch of the great Indo-European family in India and Southern Asia. Daniel's vision of the Four Empires presented the universal problem, of which the Indian is the most important element after the European, under the figure of a colossal image, its four parts successively destroyed by what appeared to be a little stone cut out of the mountain without hands. The gold of Chaldæa and the silver of Medo-Persia had given place to the brass of Greece under Alexander and his successors, and that in turn was at once yielding to and subduing the iron empire of Rome, when, in the fulness of time, Jesus Christ was enrolled in the census taken under the decree of Cæsar Augustus. Then it was that there began the training of the future English-speaking peoples of the West to fit them for the mightiest work in their history, the Christianising of India and the dark races. If we prolong the vision of Daniel beyond the close of the iron empire, so distant from the prophet, we shall best represent the great missionary evolution, which is to end in the conversion of India to Christ as its fullest triumph, as a drama in these acts:

I. THE GREEK ATTEMPT, through the Nestorians, whose metaphysical religion misrepresented Christ.

II. THE ROMAN ATTEMPT, through the Jesuits, Franciscans, and Dominicans, whose compromise with heathenism resulted in the defeat, admitted by Abbé Dubois, in 1815.

III. THE DUTCH ATTEMPT, whose nominal converts vanished with the extinction of their power in India and Ceylon.

IV. THE BRITISH EAST INDIA COMPANY'S WORK OF PREPARATION, and its extinction in 1858.

V. GREAT BRITAIN'S ATTEMPT through the Evangelical Societies and Churches since 1793, and especially since 1858.

VI. THE UNITED STATES OF AMERICA'S CO-OPERATION in the English-speaking Mission.

VII. THE METHODS OF THE EVANGELICAL MISSION TO INDIA.

VIII. THE RESULTS AND THE PROSPECTS OF CHRISTIAN MISSIONS TO INDIA AND SOUTHERN ASIA.

II

THE GREEK ATTEMPT

"*Beware lest any man spoil you through philosophy and vain deceit, after the tradition of men, after the rudiments of the world, and not after Christ. For in Him dwelleth all the fulness of the Godhead bodily. And ye are complete in Him.*"—COL. ii. 8-10.

INDIA, like the Britain of our Celtic and savage forefathers, first received the gospel of Jesus Christ through commerce and colonisation, which are still the most rapid and wide-spreading carriers of divine truth. At the close of the first Christian century, when the Phœnicians were trafficking in Cornwall and Wales, and in India and Ceylon, "those who had seen the apostles," to use the words of Photius, were beginning to teach the nations alike of England and of the Indias, and to found Churches in both regions. The Jews, as widely dispersed as their Tyrian neighbours, with whom they had been partners since the days of Solomon and Hiram, and ever closely connected with Jerusalem, used the facilities of communication given by the Greek tongue and the Roman order to carry first their own Monotheism and Messianic hopes, and then the good news that Jesus Christ was the promised One, whereever trade penetrated. That apostolic Christianity was carried to what we now call India, and especially to its western coast between Barygaza or Broach, north of the modern island of Bombay, and Cranganor above Cape Comorin, by Jews, is a fact of intense spiritual interest.

Seventeen years after the atonement, the resurrection,

and the ascension of our Lord, when He had repeated His last charge to every believing disciple in all ages, the first great geographical and scientific discovery was made to which Christian missions owe their progress. In the year 50 A.D. the pilot Hippalus revealed the semi-annual reversal of the wind system of the Indian Ocean which is called by the Arabic word for "a season," *moussin* or monsoon. Hippalus sailed right across the open sea from the Arabian promontory of Syagros or Cape Fartask to Barygaza, Kalliena, Muziris or Mangalor, and Nelkynda or Cannanor, on the Malabar coast. The discovery was as momentous for India as the application of the constant nature of the trade winds by Columbus more than fourteen centuries afterwards proved to be, in the revealing of America. Up to the time of Hippalus the gold and spice and gem and cloth trade of India had been carried by land at least as far as the Persian Gulf; and even the Jews, such as those who went to Jerusalem at the Pentecostal feast, must have had their depôts on the Malabar coast and Ceylon. But a knowledge of the regularity of the trade winds gave the command of the trade thenceforth to the fleets of Egypt. Gradually Judæo-Christian disciples, who had received the arrow of conviction at Pentecost, and others who had been scattered abroad on the death of Stephen, found their way to the trading settlements of West and South India, according to their own traditions.

When the great catastrophe came to which Christ had in vain pointed the Jews of His day, and which His own apostles expected to be the end of the age—the fall of Jerusalem—the trading settlements of India formed refuges for not a few of the finally dispersed Jews. The traditions of the thirteen thousand Jews who still worship the God of their fathers chiefly at Bombay and Cochin, are recorded in the Hebrew tongue as handed down to them, and partly confirmed by titles engraved on two sides of a copper plate deposited by Claudius Buchanan in the University Library of Cambridge. The scroll of the White Jews of Cochin thus begins—"After the Second Temple was destroyed (which may God speedily rebuild!)

our fathers, dreading the conqueror's wrath, departed from Jerusalem, a numerous body of men, women, priests, and Levites, and came into this land." At that time, 70 A.D., South India was, and continued almost till the disastrous arrival of the Portuguese by the Cape of Good Hope to be, divided among independent native rulers, such as those of Pandya (Madura and Tinnevelli), Chola, Chera (Coimbator and Salem), and Kerala (Malabar),—men generally favourable to strangers who sought their protection and enriched them by trade. In the providence of God this Indian land seemed prepared to be an early nursery first of Old Testament psalm and prophecy, and then of primitive Christianity. All through the eighteen centuries since, Christianity and Judaism have found a home in the midst of the Brahmanical castes of Hinduism and the devil-worshipping aborigines, who never showed the intolerance of Romanist Portugal or the fanaticism of the Mohammedan rule of Aurangzeb and Tipu. At this day a fourth of the population of the native state of Cochin consists of Nazarani or Christian descendants of the apostolic and the Nestorian missionaries.

The patriarchates of Alexandria and of Antioch, from the former of which cities men were converted on the day of Pentecost, while at the latter they were first called Christians, became successively the great missionary centres[1] for Asia as well as North Africa. At each, through Ptolemy and Seleucus, the civilising energy of the great Alexander, on his return from the Punjab and Sindh through Baloochistan and by the Persian Gulf, had become concentrated and perpetuated. Alexandria was the first to send a Christian missionary to India, whose name and character we know. Antioch followed, as the seat of the Nestorian missionaries, to far Cathay as well as more distant Malabar.

[1] In his *Old Syriac Element in the Text of Codex Bezæ* (1893), Mr. F. H. Chase, B.D., shows that that most valuable of the ancient manuscripts on which Biblical criticism rests, had its origin at Antioch, as well as similar Syriacised texts,—a striking fact in the early history of Christian missions.

Pantænus, Greek Stoic and Principal of the Christian College of Alexandria, was the first historical missionary of Christ to the peoples of India. The traditions of local Churches claim Peter or Thomas or Bartholomew as their apostolic founder. But apart from the natural desire of the early Christians thus to link their origin with the apostles, the traditions can all be accounted for so far as India is concerned, when we remember the vagueness with which the name India was used from Homer to Columbus, and even sometimes in the present day. The India which captivated the imagination and excited the desire of classical and mediæval times was that half of the world which stretches from the east coast of Africa eastward to Japan. It consisted of, or rather the geographical idea contained, the Middle, the Greater, and the Lesser Indias. Ethiopia and South Arabia, with Sokotra, Zanzibar, and the other islands down to Madagascar, all formed Middle India. India proper and Ceylon, including much of what is now the Chinese Empire, was the Greater India. The Lesser or Farther India was composed of the Golden Peninsula of Malacca, and of the thousand spice islands which form a bridge almost to Japan. Marco Polo's personal travels gave consolidation to the geography of Aristotle, and led Columbus to his fruitful determination to find India by sailing westward to its Japanese extremity, and converting its idol-worshippers to Christ. This vast and magnificent India was washed by one Eastern Ocean, the periodicity of the monsoons and currents of which early came to be understood and used with wonderful skill. That ocean was to the eastern half of the ancient world what the Mediterranean was to the western. Traders and missionaries sailed its waters. It was to the Greater India, the India of us moderns, that Pantænus went, called thereto, like Paul a century before him to Macedonia and Malta, to Spain and Italy, in Mediterranean ships. What sort of a man was this whose name stands at the head of the golden book of Christ's missionaries to India, as Patrick's and Columba's among our British missionary forefathers?

Thanks to his own great disciples, Clement and Origen, to Jerome also and the historian Eusebius, we have little difficulty in realising the training, the character, and the influence of Pantænus, though none of his writings save a few pregnant extracts have survived. Is it not possible that some of his commentaries may yet be discovered in the Fayum of Egypt, which is proving so fertile in such treasures? Pantænus first comes before us as the earliest example of a Greek scholar who brought his philosophy to the feet of Christ, and humbly used his learning in the service of the Cross. Born in Athens, unless Clement's admiring reference to his industry and fertility as "the Sicilian bee" points to Sicily as the home of his youth, Pantænus was of the Stoic school, though, with the eclecticism of his age, he mastered the Platonism of Pythagoras. The one taught him "righteousness together with godly knowledge." According to Clement, the other gave him juster conceptions of God and of spiritual things. Both the duty and the faith thus imperfectly learned found their sanction and their completion in the Christ of the evangelists, in the testimony of Jesus, which is the spirit of the Old Testament, of the psalmists, and the prophets. Thus, as a learned thinker and master of the non-Christian philosophy of his day, Pantænus became fitted to be the first missionary to the Brahmans and the Buddhists, who at that time had most fully developed their systems. He was the appropriate predecessor of Carey and Martyn, of Duff and Wilson, of French and Caldwell, of Judson and Scudder. It does not appear whether Pantænus was called from Paganism by the forgiveness of sins as was Clement, who after studying under the greatest Christian teachers in Greece and Syria and Italy, settled in Egypt, because he there met with Pantænus, described by him as "a very great Gnosticus, who had penetrated most profoundly into the spirit of Scripture."

To consecrated learning and the mastery of his opponents' system of error, Pantænus added the second essential qualification of a missionary to the Brahmans—

he was the greatest teacher of his age, and exercised a fascination over the minds of his students. Appointed by the Bishop of Alexandria sole catechist of the School of the Catechumens, which had been established for the instruction of the heathen in the facts and the doctrines of Christianity, Pantænus made the Didaskaleion not only the nursery of men like Clement and Origen, but the training school of missionaries who went forth over North Africa, Ethiopia, Yemen, and Southern Asia. Of that college he was the famous principal certainly in or before the year 180 A.D., according to Eusebius. Fronted at that time by the great heathen institution, the Serapeum, as the modern missionary colleges are in the Egypt of this day by the Azhar Madrissa, and in India by the Government, the Hindu, and the Mohammedan colleges, the truth taught by Pantænus in time swept error away. The Greek Platonist, Dion Chrysostom, who died not long before the birth of Pantænus, writes of "Ethiopians, Arabians, Bactrians, Scythians, Persians, and Indians flocking to Alexandria." Even then the third of the three qualifications essential to a successful missionary of Christ was possessed by Pantænus in an unusual degree—he knew and he loved to expound the Word of God. This, indeed, came to take precedence of his Christian philosophy and to afford the vehicle for his learning. We find Eusebius, while he describes Clement as "a most excellent teacher and shining light of Christian philosophy," declaring that Pantænus "was distinguished as an expositor of the Word of God." In another place the same historian discriminates the latter as one who, in his literary works, "interpreted the treasures of the divine dogmas," while Jerome records that he left many commentaries on the Scriptures. Truly this missionary[1]

[1] Of Church historians Neander, as usual, and the eloquent French senator and pastor, Dr. E. de Pressensé, have alone done justice to Pantænus, of whose mission the latter writes :—"Happy is the age in which scientific theology is not severed from active and militant piety, in which a man gave his whole self to the cause and heroically carried into practice that which he eloquently taught in theory" (vol. ii. p. 271, cap. ii. of second book of *The Earlier Years of Christianity*).

had his message in the life-giving oracles of God with their self-evidencing power, as few of his later successors had till Wiclif and Luther gave the peoples of Christendom the Scriptures in their own tongues, and Carey began to do the same for the races of Southern Asia.

At some time between the years 180 and 190 the Bishop of Alexandria received an appeal from the Christians in India to send them a missionary. Probably the applicants were students of the catechetical school. What so natural as that Pantænus, himself a presbyter, whom long after, writing in the seventh century, Anastasius of Sinai describes as "priest of the Church of the Alexandrians," should be chosen? In one of his epistles Jerome writes that "Pantænus was sent to India that he might preach Christ among the Brahmans." He would be the less unwilling to go that Clement was ready to take his place during his absence. He would be the more eager to go that he might give to the churches founded by Jewish Hellenists fuller instruction in the new canonical writings, that he might make them missionary lights to all around, and that he might bring back with him new facts and followers whereby to quicken the zeal of the Alexandrian Church. We can picture him in those days sailing up the Nile to Coptos, and thence on an eleven days' journey crossing the Thebaid, then a highway now a desert, to the great port of Berenice, at which the treasures of India were received from the traders. Taking ship down the Red Sea at the beginning of September, to catch the trade winds, looking in on the Christians at Aden, tarrying a little to refit with those at Sokotra, and then spreading his sails for the south-west monsoon to carry him quickly, he would reach the coast of Malabar in forty days. How long he was there, how far inland he travelled, and when he returned, we know not. This characteristic fact, however, we have, that he found among them the Hebrew or Aramaic Gospel of St. Matthew, which formed the basis of our Greek evangel, said to have been taken to them by the apostle Bartholomew. All that this apostolic reference means is that the Jewish Christians in India were a colony from some place where Bartholomew had founded the Christian Church after Stephen's martyrdom. Pantænus went back to Alexandria, relieved Clement, and continued to preside over the College of the Catechumens, probably through the reign of the Emperor Severus, or till 211 A.D. Jerome places him even in the reign of his successor, and the Roman Martyrology commemorates the first great missionary to India on the 7th day of July every year.

Of the apostolic or earliest Christians in the Indian region we hear nothing for a century till about the time that Constantine established the Church. Then, according to the learned Arian historian, Philostorgius, there arrived in Europe from the island Diu or Sokotra one whom we would now describe as a missionary on furlough, Theophilus surnamed Indicus. From his native island he had visited India itself, where he found Christianity already planted. The statement that he "had only to correct certain things there" introduces us to the next missionary name of Nestorius. Evidently the Christian Churches of India had always looked to Persia as their origin. At the Council of Nicæa in 325, Johannes, the Metropolitan of Persia, signed also as "of the Great India." This probably implied little more than an episcopal claim to what had always, as in the Book of Esther, been considered a province of the Persian empire. But it shows, thus early, the ecclesiastical connection between Persia and India historically. So early as 334 Merv was an episcopal see.

The scene now shifts from Alexandria to Antioch, from the beginning of the third to that of the fifth century. The subjective, intuitive attitude of the Alexandrian writers to the person of Christ, which while dwelling on his Divinity ended in the Monophysite view, has given place to the rationalising of the Antiochene school, which, exalting the human side of the Lord, finally taught His double personality. The heresy of Arius had meanwhile arisen. While Pantænus stands at the head of the evangelicalism which has ever since carried to Asia the missionary message that *God is in Christ reconciling the world unto Himself*, Nestorius is the representative of those who preach a Christ less than Divine, and who have therefore ever failed to convert mankind. Nestorianism became such a compromise with heathenism as led to Mohammed's teaching; it supplanted in India the apostolic Churches confirmed by Pantænus, and it has ever since fossilised the Syrian Church there while making it powerless against the persecutions of Portuguese Catholicism. This fact of compromise must be remembered when we proceed to look at the otherwise bright missionary progress of Nestorian Christianity in Asia, Central, East, and South.

Let us take our stand in the city of Mesopotamian Edessa, to which Seleucus gave the name of the original seat of the Macedonian race that had conquered the world up to the Indus and the Jumna. There, on a northern affluent of the Euphrates, Eusebius the historian found a letter in the Syriac language, which the Church believed to have been written to its ruler Abgar by Christ Himself. However spurious the correspondence, the story marks the spot as the earliest region to receive the light of the gospel. It became gradually the greatest ecclesiastical school in Asia, rivalling that of Alexandria for the West, and ultimately supplanting it. It was to Edessa that Miesrob, the greatest Armenian Father and translator of the first complete vernacular version of the Bible in 410, sent Moses Chorenensis and his ablest followers. To Edessa students flocked from all Asiatic Christendom. When Nestorius and Cyril, like Arius and Athanasius, had buried their controversy in the grave, and the Council of Ephesus was over, the conflict broke out afresh in Edessa and the neighbouring school of Nisibis. It ended in the year 499 in the synod which fully accepted the Nestorian teaching, and added to that the right of the bishops and priests to marry. This return to apostolic liberty and example removed one great objection of the Zoroastrian fire-worshippers to the Christian Church. Nestorian Christianity became popular in Persia, became ready to influence and conciliate the new enemy which was about to burst forth from the sands of Arabia, to prove the scourge of the mediæval world and the tyrant of Asia to the present century. Like the Arian Ulfilas, however, and the Greek Church to this day, the Nestorian missionary Church, under the old impulse of Theodore of Antioch and Mopsuestia, was ever enthusiastic in expounding and spreading abroad the Word of God.

From the year 500[1] the missionaries of Edessa, Nisibis, and the metropolitan see of Seleucia-Ctesiphon, went everywhere abroad preaching the word. What an opportunity the Nestorian Church had! All Central, Southern and Eastern Asia was at its feet. The sixth century was a crisis in the history of Christianity and the human race, as the sixteenth and now the nineteenth have been. Mohammed was about to rise, and to add to the half truth of Nestorianism as to the nature and person of Jesus Christ the whole lie of his own call and inspiration. Not yet, however, were the unevangelised millions of Asia, from the Red Sea to the Pacific Ocean, to see Islam with the sword offered to them as the rival of Christ with the Cross of peace to sinners, purity to the forgiven, and life to the world. Christianity had at least a whole century's chance to reform its Church, and transform Asia for ever. But it failed, because its message was not the fulness of that proclaimed by the Christ of John's Gospel.

The settlements that had gone forth from Persia and Alexandria to India, holding apostolical truth and doubtless propagating it, seem to have been the earliest to conform to the Nestorian teaching and practice as fixed by the Synod of Seleucia. All around that province the savage Turanian peoples, whose descendants afterwards deluged Europe — Huns and Slavs, also within Persia Bactrians, Medes, Elamites, and Koords—received the missionary with his Bible. Before the Mohammedans had

[1] Arnobius (A.D. 300) writes of the Christian deeds done in India and among the Seres, Persians, and Medes. Nestorian monks brought the eggs of the silkworm to Constantinople in A.D. 551, and these had resided long in China.

burst out of Arabia Nestorians were preaching Christ in farthest China and even in the islands of Japan. Timotheus, who was Nestorian Patriarch from the year 778 to 820, was most active in sending forth missionaries. Two are especially named, Cardag and Jabdallaha, who reported such conversions that they were ordained bishops, and were instructed, if they were called on to ordain a native bishop in the distant savage lands which they evangelised, to associate with themselves one of the Gospels as the third bishop necessary for ordination. One David was ordained bishop for China. When the Arab traveller of the ninth century, Ibn-Wahab, was in China, he found in the Emperor's court figures of our Lord and of the apostles, and the Emperor had been so far instructed, that he said Christ had discharged the office of a teacher on earth for thirty months.

Fortunately for the annals of Christianity at the darkest period and in lands like India, where the first principles of historical evidence are unknown, we have written on living stone, and preserved to the present day, the records of the missionary enterprise of the Nestorians from Cape Comorin to far Cathay, and a statement of their missionary teaching. There are no epigraphic witnesses more genuine and reliable than the inscriptions on the Nestorian Tablet of Si-ngan-fu in North-Western China, and those around the three Persian crosses of St. Thomas's Mount, Madras, and the Kottayam church in Travankor. These, related to each other by the old Syriac characters known as Estrangelo, common to all four, are eloquent witnesses from so early a period as the year 635 A.D., and into the eighth century. We owe the rediscovery and preservation of the former, in recent times, to one of the most learned and cautious of American scholars, Edward E. Salisbury, Professor of Arabic and Sanskrit in Yale, New Haven.

In the year 1625 a Chinese labourer, digging the foundations of a house in the ruins of the old Tartar capital of Si-ngan-fu in Shen-si, unearthed a great slab, seven and a half feet high by three feet wide, and covered with Chinese characters surrounded by others then unknown in China. The Jesuit missionaries there, notably Alvarez Semedo, sent home an account of the treasure, which was first made known to Europe by Kircher in his *Prodromus Copticus* in 1636. Those who treated the inscription as a fabrication of the Jesuits he contemptuously answered in his *China Illustrata,* in which he published a copy of the original with a very imperfect Latin rendering (1667). It was clearly unlikely, indeed impossible, that the Jesuits should fabricate an inscription which reflected glory on their Nestorian predecessors, whom they persecuted and finally extinguished, except in South India, where the Dutch and the English saved a great remnant of them by destroying the Portuguese power. Semedo, who first reported the discovery, when moved to Cranganor, the old centre of the Nestorians on the Malabar coast of India, consulted his brethren there as to the strange characters surrounding the Chinese, and they at once recognised these as the old Syriac with which the Syrian Christians there are familiar. The Nestorian Tablet continued to excite the discussion of the learned without definite result, until the American Oriental Society, in 1853, put the facts to the test in the light of modern scholarship. While Voltaire had scoffed and Bishop Horne had doubted, the learned S. Assemanus, Mosheim in his *Historia Tartarorum,* Abel-Rémusat, and Klaproth accepted it. He who is still the greatest historian of the Christian Church, Neander, accordingly suspended his judgment.

In 1852, when the missionary Dr. Bridgman was on furlough in America, Professor Salisbury was induced by his conviction of the genuineness of the inscription to examine the whole subject anew. The result of the paper,[1] which he read on the 14th October 1852, was that the American Oriental Society addressed each of the missionaries of the United States then in China, requesting that the stone be visited again, and that a facsimile of

[1] *Journal of the American Oriental Society,* vol. iv. for 1853, pp. 401-419.

the inscription be taken by a competent person. Fortunately one of the greatest sinologues, Mr. A. Wylie,[1] was available, and to him the request was referred by Dr. Bridgman. The result in due time was the masterly article by Mr. Wylie, reprinted from the *North China Herald* in volume v. of the *Journal of the American Oriental Society*, which its committee of publication declared to be conclusive. Since that time the good work of Salisbury and Wylie has been carried farther by the Baron von Richthofen, of Berlin, who spent years in China, where he took an absolutely accurate "rubbing" of the inscriptions. That has been reproduced on a small scale and with exquisite accuracy by Sir Henry Yule in the second edition of his *Book of Ser Marco Polo, the Venetian*,[2] where he describes and comments on the Chinese and Syrian characters. The genuineness of this precious testimony is for ever established.

It is well that Professor Salisbury and the American Oriental Society moved when they did, for in the present year 1893, the latest missionary who has visited the spot reports the covering put up by the Chinese authorities to protect the monument as levelled, and the stone as laid low and part of the inscription as defaced. The local priests ascribe the ruin to a great wind, but it is believed to have been due to malicious hands.

Apart from the internal evidence of the inscription, which Mr. Wylie translates, he cites seventeen native (non-Christian) authors, each of whom treats it as both

[1] Alexander Wylie was of Scottish parents, educated in Scotland, a cabinetmaker, learnt Chinese, went out as agent of the Bible Society to print the Chinese Bible at Shanghai in 1847; travelled from St. Petersburg to Peking (the first to do so), in 1863; wandered in seventeen provinces of China (all but one of its eighteen); retired from the Bible Society service in 1877 from failing sight; died blind in 1887, aged 72. His *Bible in China*, 1868, is said to be "an interesting though brief account of Christian work, from the earliest times, going back to the Nestorians," etc. Sir Thos. Wade and Dr. Legge speak of him in highest terms as a Christian and a sinologue

[2] Vol. ii. page 22.

CHRISTIAN INSCRIPTION OF SI NGAN-FU IN CHINESE AND SYRIAC, REDUCED.

To face page 20

genuine and authentic while having something peculiar to record regarding it. The imperial proclamation of A.D. 746 which it contains is found in a contemporary book, and the fact that a foreign temple stood on the very spot indicated on the Tablet is recorded in the works of two dynasties. Mr. Wylie traces the influence of the three national religious sects in the phraseology of the inscription. The writer was evidently a convert well versed in Confucian lore. The tenets of the Christian faith are "clothed in an elegance of diction unobjectionable even to Chinese taste." The nomenclature of the various ecclesiastical institutions shows a Buddhist tendency. Taouist phraseology is conspicuous in the edict of toleration.

The main inscription, which is of great length and beautiful execution, consists of 1780 Chinese characters. Mr. Wylie's version of it deserves reproduction, with that of the ode which follows it, and that of the Syriac. The Alopan or Olopan mentioned is pronounced by Sir Henry Yule to be the Chinese form of the Syriac word for monk, "Rabban."

The Tablet, which describes itself as "eulogising the propagation of the Illustrious Religion in China, with a preface; composed by King-tsing, a priest of the Syrian Church," begins with an account of creation by "our eternal true Lord God, triune and mysterious in substance. He appointed the cross as the means for determining the four cardinal points. . . . He then made the first man pure and unostentatious, until Satan introduced the seeds of falsehood. . . . Thereupon our Trinity being divided in nature, the illustrious and honourable Messiah, veiling his true dignity, appeared in the world as a man; angelic powers promulgated the glad tidings, a virgin gave birth to the Holy One in Syria, a bright star announced the felicitous event, and Persians observing the splendour came to present tribute. The ancient dispensation as declared by the twenty-four holy men was then fulfilled, and He laid down great principles for the government of families and kingdoms; He established the new religion of the silent operation of the pure Spirit of the Triune, He rendered virtue subservient to direct faith. . . . Having thus completed the manifestation of His power in clear day He ascended to His true station. Twenty-seven sacred books have been left, which disseminate intelligence by unfolding the original transforming principles. By the rule for admission it is the custom to apply the water of baptism."

These extracts show the comparative purity of the teaching of the Nestorian missionaries as received by a Confucian, and expressed in old Chinese style. These historical facts follow that, in the time of the Emperor Tae-tsung, "among the holy men who arrived was the Most-virtuous Alopan from the court of Syria. . . . In the year A.D. 635 he arrived at Chang-gang. The sacred books were translated in the imperial library; the sovereign investigated the subject in his private apartments; when becoming deeply impressed with the rectitude and truth of the religion he gave special orders for its dissemination." Then follows his proclamation, which informed the millions of Cathay, "in the seventh month of the year A.D. 638," that Christianity "has taken its rise from the establishment of important truths; its ritual is free from perplexing expressions, its principles will survive when the framework is forgot, it is beneficial to all creatures, it is advantageous to mankind." The result is told, and the inscription continues: "While this doctrine pervaded every channel the state became enriched, and tranquillity abounded. Every city was full of churches." The closing passage tells how "our great benefactor E-sze . . . from the distant city of Rajagriha, came to visit China," and "practising the discipline of the illustrious religion he distributed his riches in deeds of benevolence." At the same time, we know that the Chinese pilgrim Hwen Tsang was visiting India to worship at its Buddhist shrines, Rajagriha among them. In Cathay, as in India, Buddhism and Brahmanism prevailed, while the Christians were persecuted by the Mohammedans, from their first conquest of Persia to the butcheries perpetrated by Timur, the sixth in descent from whom, Baber, founded in 1526 the Mogul dynasty at Delhi.

The Chinese portion of the Si-ngan-fu Tablet concludes with an ode, of which these two verses, as translated by Wylie, refer specially to Christianity, while the others record the prosperity of the successive emperors who professed the new faith.

"When the pure, bright, Illustrious religion
Was introduced to our Tang dynasty,
The Scriptures were translated and churches built,
And the vessel set in motion for the living and the dead;
Every kind of blessing was then obtained,
And all the kingdoms enjoyed a state of peace.

. . . .

The true doctrine how expansive!
Its responses are minute;
How difficult to name it!
To elucidate the Three in One."

The two lines of Syriac in the Estrangelo character, running down the right and left sides of the Chinese, are thus translated by Kircher—

"Adam, Deacon, Vicar-episcopal, and Pope of China,
In the time of the Father of Fathers, the Lord John Joshua, the Universal Patriarch."

In Syriac also, at the foot, is an account of Adam, his father, "priest of Balkh, a city of Turkestan," and his archdeacon. On the left-hand edge of the stone are the Syriac names of sixty-seven priests, and of sixty-one in Chinese.

The Tablet was next visited and described by Dr. Alexander Williamson in 1866, when on a tour for the National Bible Society of Scotland, in North China, Manchuria, and Eastern Mongolia. After preaching in the great city of Si-ngan-fu, to which his passport admitted him, he left it by the west gate, crossed a desolated tract, then a field of wheat, and leaping a ruined wall, he found the Tablet "perfect, with not a scratch on it, in a brick enclosure facing the south." "The preserving care of a wise Providence was the first thought in our minds, for this Tablet not only enumerates all the leading doctrines of our holy religion, but is a most important witness in favour of our faith in opposition both to the heathen and the Romanist." Since Mr. Wylie's visit, he found on the edge of the stone on the left side an inscription to the effect that, in the ninth year of Hiengfung (1859 A.D.), one Han-tai-wha, from Woo-lin, had found the characters and ornamentation perfect, and had rebuilt the brick covering. The stone is a coarse marble, and was then rebuilt in the brick wall where it had once stood outside the city. The Professor of Chinese at Yale College, S. Wells Williams, LL.D., in *The Middle Kingdom*, reproduces Wylie's translation as marked by "a fulness and a care which leaves little to be desired." [1]

We owe to the late Dr. Burnell, the most distinguished scholar of the Indian Civil Service in his day, the best account of the three Persian crosses of South India with their old Syriac inscriptions.[2] So early as 1802 Mr. F. Wredè, of the same service, wrote what is still the best account of the "St. Thomè Christians on the Coast of Malabar," in the *Asiatick Researches* [3] of the Bengal Society, founded by Sir William Jones, and the parent of all subsequent Oriental societies. He was the first to expose the legend of the arrival and martyrdom of the apostle Thomas in India, and in this all scholars now agree.[4] Dr. Burnell is inclined to substitute Mani and the Manichæans as probably the first preachers before 272 A.D., and he makes the Nestorians later, but on insufficient grounds. His service consists in bringing to notice the many Pahlavi[5] inscriptions which are known to have existed all over

[1] Vol. ii. p. 277 of the revised edition. London, 1883.

[2] *The Indian Antiquary* for November 1874, p. 308, then edited by Dr. Burgess C.I.E.

[3] Vol. vii. p 362.

[4] See *Syriac Documents Attributed to the First Three Centuries*, as translated in Messrs. T. and T. Clark's Ante-Nicene Christian Library 1871.

[5] The literary language of the Persians, or Perso-Sassanians.

Southern India, and prove the importance of the Perso-Christian settlements. He has reproduced the cross built into the wall behind the altar in a church on the Great Mount near Madras, and discovered during some Portuguese excavations about 1547. The slab was then accurately described as having on one face a cross in relief, with a bird like a dove over it with its wings expanded, as the Holy Ghost is usually represented when descending on our Lord. Two others are in the old church at Kottayam. The inscriptions belong to the seventh or eighth century, the period of the Si-ngan-fu stone. One of the Kottayam tablets has a Syriac[1] inscription, which Dr. Burnell believes to be later than the Pahlavi, and to have been added to make all orthodox according to Nestorian views. The result of repeated readings by himself and by Drs. Haug and E. W. West is this—

Syriac.

LET ME NOT GLORY EXCEPT IN THE CROSS OF OUR LORD JESUS CHRIST.

Pahlavi.

WHO IS THE TRUE MESSIAH AND GOD ALONE AND HOLY GHOST.

Dr. Burnell, holding to his theory, sees in this statement a desire to contradict the Manichæan doctrine, that the

[1] The close and frequent intercourse between Persia and India in the early Christian centuries finds a striking literary illustration in the mission of the good physician, Barzoi, sent by King Khosru Nushirvan (A.D. 531-579) to India to procure a copy of the earliest of all collections of stories with a moral. Barzoi, if not altogether then "almost" a Christian, translated into Pahlavi many of the Sanskrit books, but particularly the *Panchatantra,* or "five books," and three tales in the *Mahabharata* epic, forming the collection *Kalilah and Dimnah,* as told by Bidpai, the "Pilpay" of modern Europe, at his sovereign's request. The Pahlavi version was at once, in 570 A.D., translated into Syriac by an ecclesiastic named Bod, and into Arabic. The former has disappeared, but the latter version was translated into

crucified Messiah was the son of a poor widow and not Jesus Christ. Dr. Milne Rae[1] traces in this the Nestorian teaching of the incarnation of the Godhead, not of the Logos only—that each of the three Persons of the Holy Trinity was incarnate in the Christ. However this may be, all true Christians will rejoice in the evidence that links the earliest attempts at the conversion of India not only with the once doubting Thomas, but with the mighty apostle of the Gentiles, and his glorying in the crucified One (Galatians vi. 14). And we may note that the Syrian

Syriac again by a Christian priest in the tenth and eleventh centuries. This later Syriac version was rendered into English, with learned critical notes, by the Hon. I. G. N. Keith-Falconer, M.A., in 1885 (for the Syndics of Cambridge University Press). Two years after that devoted Christian scholar went to South Arabia to found the mission which, after his early death, bears his name.

[1] *The Syrian Church in India* (Edinburgh, 1892). For the recent history and present position of the Nazarani of Malabar, see that volume; also Collins's *Missionary Enterprise in the East*, and Whitehouse's *Syrian Church of Malabar*, both published in 1873. Dr. Germanns's *Die Kirche der Thomaschristen* (Gütersloh, 1877, 792 pp.) is a thorough history from St. Thomas to Mar Ignatius, the Jacobite Patriarch of Antioch, who appeared at the Brighton Church of England Congress in 1874 *en route* to Malabar, but of no critical value. It does not, however, refer to Captain Swanston's three invaluable papers—"Memoir of the Church of Malayâla" in the *Royal Asiatic Society's Journal* for 1834-35. The latest account of the Christians is the hopeful statement made by the Anglican clergy in Travankor and Cochin to Lord Wenlock, Governor of Madras, when in 1892, accompanied by Bishop Hodges, he visited Kottayam:—"Many abuses which shocked the early missionaries have been removed. Vernacular preaching by better educated Kattanars has become common; and the Syrian Christians, whether those calling themselves children of the Jacobite Patriarch of Antioch, or those following the Reforming Metrans, have one godly feature in common with the Anglican Church, namely, a growing appreciation and reverence for the Word of God in the vernacular. Furthermore, it is only due to the Syrian Church to say that the co-operation and assistance of the Anglican clergy is often welcomed, and it might be further developed but for the immediate charge of their own flocks, at present numbering over twenty-five thousand people"

THE OLDEST CHRISTIAN INSCRIPTION IN INDIA—SEVENTH CENTURY

To face page 25

characters added to the inscription in each case bring together the public confession of Christ by the Churches of Malabar and Coromandel, and that of the old capital of far Cathay.

In the Chaldæan Breviary of the Church of India in Malabar the office of St. Thomas thus commemorates its legendary origin: "By St. Thomas were the errors of idolatry banished from among the Indians. By St. Thomas were the Chinese and the Ethiopians converted to the truth." And this anthem further links together the three missionary conquests of the Nestorian Church: "*The Hindus and the Chinese and the Persians, and all the people of the isles of the sea, and they who dwell in Syria and Armenia, in Javan and Romania, call Thomas to remembrance and adore Thy Name, O Thou, our Redeemer.*" But the evidence, at once the saddest and the most overpowering, of the extent and the influence of the first missionary organisation in Asia is seen in its persecution by Shahpoor II. of Persia in 339, 340, who sought to extirpate it, when Constantine identified the Empire with the Christian Church. Nowhere is there such a record of suffering to the death for Christ, with occasional apostasy, as in the Syrian *Acts of Persian Martyrs.* The persecution lasted for forty years; but the Church was not suppressed even in its headquarters of Nisibis, which was twice besieged, nor was the Armenian Church destroyed. By the sixth century it covered the western coast of India and the island of Ceylon, by the seventh it was tolerated, and by the eighth—as we have seen—it was encouraged by imperial decree in China.

We have what may be most justly described as the first India Mission Report written in 547, or thirteen and a half centuries ago, by the man who comes next to Pantænus in the history of the Church of India—Cosmas, Indian navigator and monk. This work is the *Universal Christian Topography*, Χριστιανικὴ Τοπογραφία παντὸς κοσμοῦ, written at the request of his friend Pamphilus, at first in six books, and then gradually increased to twelve, of which the last alone is imperfect. Intending only, as Gibbon puts it, to confute the impious heresy of those who maintain that the earth is a globe and not a flat oblong table, as represented in the Scriptures, Cosmas, who was no less wise than the clerical assailants of geology a generation ago, left the most suggestive missionary and geographical treatise up to William Carey's *Enquiry* and David Livingstone's *Travels* in our own time. He was the classical precursor of Livingstone, indeed, as the traveller who was the first to make Geography, Commerce, and Industry the handmaids of Christian missions.

Cosmas was a merchant of Alexandria and frequent navigator to the East, in the reign of the Emperor Justinian. From the Mediterranean down the Red Sea to the Persian Gulf and the Bay of Bengal this Indicopleustes, as he was surnamed, pursued his adventurous calling. Nor was he content with the sea and the commercial settlements which dotted its coasts from the Pharos to far Taprobanè. Well educated, his observant eye and inquisitive mind investigated the history, the character, and the customs of the peoples of the East, and his ready pen recorded the results in many a work that has not survived. When, for instance, he had done his business at Adulè, the Red Sea port of Ethiopia, he found out and copied inscriptions, one of which describes the conquest of the Asiatic empire of the Seleucidæ by Ptolemy Euergetes, B.C. 247-222, which led scholars to inquire into and establish the history of the campaigns. Wearied with much globe-trotting, as it is now called, and an ardent student of Scripture, the Alexandrian merchant and sailor became a monk, and gave up the rest of his days to what so good a critic as Canon Venables describes as vivid descriptions of the countries he had visited, and the remarkable facts he had observed or learned. His *Christian Topography* is illustrated by sketches and diagrams from his own hand.

He represents the four gulfs as seas which enter the land from the ocean, then impossible to navigate on account of the multitude of the currents and fogs, as the Roman or Mediterranean, the Arabian or Erythræan, the Persian, and the Caspian or Hircanian. "I myself," he writes, "for purposes of trade have sailed on three out of those four gulfs: to wit, the Roman, the Arabian, and the Persian; and I have got accurate information about the different places on them from the natives as well as from seafaring men." The most precious passage of the whole work is the following, which surveys the preaching of the gospel throughout the world five centuries after our Lord's death. It might be mistaken for part of a modern missionary history:—

"So that I can speak with confidence of the truth of what I say, relating what I have myself seen and heard in many places that I have visited.

"Even in the Island of Taprobanè, in Farther India, where the Indian Sea is, there is a Church of Christians with clergy and a congregation of believers, though I know not if there be any Christians farther on in that direction; and such is also the case in the land called Malè, where the pepper grows. And in the place called Kalliana there is a bishop appointed from Persia as well as in the isle called the Isle of Dioscoris in the same Indian Sea. The inhabitants of that island speak Greek, having been originally settled there by the Ptolemies who ruled after Alexander of Macedon. There are clergy there also ordained and sent from Persia to minister among the people of the island and a multitude of Christians. We sailed past the island, but did not land. I met, however, with people from it who were on their way to Ethiopia, and they spoke Greek. And so likewise among the Bactrians, and Huns, and Persians, and the rest of the Indians, and among the Persarmenians, and Greeks, and Elamites, and throughout the whole land of Persia, there is an infinite number of churches with bishops and a vast multitude of Christian people, and they have many martyrs and recluses leading a monastic life. So also in Ethiopia and in Axum, and in all the country round about; among the Happy Arabians, who nowadays are called Homeritæ, and all through Arabia and Palestine, Phœnicia, and all Syria, and Antioch, and Mesopotamia, also among the Nubians and the Garamantes, in Egypt, Libya, and Pentapolis, and so through Africa and Mauritania as far as Southern Gades. In a very great number of places one found churches of Christians with bishops, martyrs, monks, and recluses, wherever, in fact, the gospel of Christ hath been proclaimed. So likewise, again, in Cilicia, Asia, Cappadocia, Laricè, and Pontus, and in the northern regions of the Scythians, Hyrcanians, Heruli, Bulgarians, Greeks and Illyrians, Dalmatians, Goths, Spaniards, Romans, Franks, and other nations, till you get to Ocean Gades."

"Southern Gades" was the equivalent then for the World's End, on the west coast of Africa. "Ocean Gades" may well include the British Isles which traded with it. Thus this merchant-missionary, in his survey of advancing Christendom from his central watch-tower in Alexandria, links on the Scoto-Irish Church of the saints with the Nestorian Church of Malabar and Ceylon, at the time when Justinian was building at Constantinople the great Basilica of Saint Sophia, and Columba was training in Iona the missionary band who were to flash the light once more on Saxon England, and, through Boniface, on still heathen Germany, and so to prepare both to light up the torch of truth in India.

Yet, in India, as all over Asia, the Nestorian missionaries failed to create self-propagating Christian Churches, when Rome took up the work, and summoned the nations of the East also to submit to its sway. At the present time the whole number of Syrian Christians[1] in India, chiefly in the feudatory state of Cochin, is 200,467, out of the 2,284,172 who returned themselves as Christians in the imperial census of 1891. This considerable remnant has survived first neglect, then the change from the Nestorian patriarchate of Babylon in 1665 to the Jacobite patriarchate of Antioch, the intolerance of Romanist Portugal, the indifference of the Dutch, the reforming efforts of the Church Missionary Society and successive Bishops of Calcutta, and the enlightenment diffused among its young men by such institutions as the Madras Christian College. Every eleventh Christian in India still lives on a theological past so dead as the middle of the fifth century, still holds a metaphysical religion. What Gibbon wrote, in his thirty-seventh chapter, of their fathers is still true of them: the Nestorian and Eutychian controversies which attempted to explain the mystery of the Incarnation, hastened the ruin of Christianity in her native land. Be-

[1] For the 200,000 Nestorians in their central seat in Koordistan and North Persia, to whom the Archbishop of Canterbury sends a mission, see Dean Maclean's book, *The Catholicos of the East and His People*, 1892. See also Gibbon's forty-seventh chapter.

cause their faith was weak, their message mutilated, their intellect darkened, and their life selfish, it was not possible for the colonies of Syrian and Persian Christians dispersed on its southern shores to bring India to Christ. Unpurged from the old leaven, it was not for them to leaven the whole lump.

III

THE ROMAN ATTEMPT

"*Not of works, lest any man should boast.*"—EPHESIANS ii. 9.

THE marvel is that Christianity, which in all the circumstances of its environment is Asiatic, did not permeate Asia first, did not bring in the elder Aryans of India, and then spread over Europe. The process was reversed. Taken by Paul from the martyr-teaching of Stephen, and the direct revelation of the Lord Himself, and of the Holy Spirit, the gospel sought Europe through Macedonia, Athens, and Corinth,—through Rome above all. It found our fathers as savages in the far West, and has gradually given the English-speaking peoples the combined power and duty of propagating it in Asia. Christianity transformed Europe first, because Europe remained true to the New Testament teaching of the Incarnation, and rejected the Arian heresy. Christianity in Asia yielded first to Buddhism, and then to Mohammedanism, which travestied its ritual, borrowed its ethics without the motive power, and opposed its root ideas, till the Christian became in India little more than an addition to the many Brahmanical castes.

Parallel in time with the missionary progress of Christianity in Europe, the Saracens carried the Koran and the sword of Mohammed all over Western Asia and Northern Africa, then threatened Europe itself up to Vienna, and from Spain into the heart of France. In 637 A.D. they seized Jerusalem; in 737 their devastating progress was arrested by Charles Martel at Tours, the whole breadth of two continents having been covered in a century. The answer of the Church of Rome was twofold. The six Crusades from 1096 to 1248 familiarised Europe with the missionary idea, but achieved no spiritual result, while their military failure only strengthened the power of Islam. The monastic brotherhoods increased in number and took up the missionary cry, "God wills it," some of them in a higher sense than the crusading hosts. The Italian Francis of Assisi, and the Spaniard Raymund Lull of Majorca, became the most devoted preachers to the Mohammedans Christendom had seen. The Castilian Dominic founded his order of preachers backed by the Inquisition, proclaiming the Pope or the sword.

But such men were exceptional. And the terror of Europe was soon turned from the advance of Islam to the rise of another power. At the head of his Mongol hordes, Chinghiz Khan (born in 1162, died 1227) conquered China, and then the whole of Western Asia from the Indies to the Caspian and European Russia. The Mongolian dynasty which he founded continued his conquests right into the heart of Europe, under Batu at Cracow and Breslau, Pesth, and Lignitz, defeating the chivalry of Christendom led by Prince Henry of Silesia on the 12th April 1241. With the Pope and the Emperor Frederic II. at enmity in those days, it seemed as if the end had come to the Church of Christ, when the Tartar host disappeared almost in one hour, recalled by a courier who announced the death of the Great Khan (Okkodai) in the depths of Asia.

The defeat near Lignitz thoroughly roused Christendom, so that in 1245 the Council of Lyons was summoned by Pope Innocent to devise measures for its protection against the Tartar enemy. There was also the under-current of feeling that the Mongolian hordes had been already so far influenced by the Nestorian missionaries as to be ready to accept the profession, at least, of Christianity, and Chinghiz Khan was by not a few identified with the mysterious

Prester John. Was this new people, whose Great Khan had beat down Mohammedans over so great a portion of Asia, not likely to unite with the West in friendly co-operation, and even to accept the spiritual teaching of its Church? At any rate the attempt was made. The new Asiatic empire had become tolerant, and it had by its very conquests made journeying at once secure and easy to the new capital of Cambaluc or Peking. Hence missionaries and travellers, ambassadors and traders, crossed and recrossed Asia with a facility impossible ever since, and least of all, at the close of this nineteenth century. One chronicler invites the grateful remembrance of all Christian people, because "just at the time when God sent forth into the eastern parts of the world the Tartars to slay and be slain, He also sent forth in the west his faithful and blessed servants, Dominic and Francis, to enlighten, instruct, and build up in the faith."

Then, in Cathay as in Africa in the present day, the missionaries of Rome were more diplomatists than evangelists. Thus early did failure begin to mark their mission as it had vitiated that of their predecessors the Nestorians, whose churches and followers they frequently met with. Their message was imperfect, their methods were more of this world than those of Christ Himself, their motives were mixed. The first monkish envoy from the Pope, sent forth from Lyons in 1245, was an Italian, John of Plano Carpini, and he returned from North China in 1247 with a haughty reply. His narrative tells of Cathayans, on the sea-shore of China, with the Christian books, churches, and worship, but unbaptized, evidently of Nestorian origin. He was succeeded in 1256 by William de Rubruquis, who professed himself a pure missionary, but who carried letters from Louis IX. of France, and he is the first accurately to describe the Chinese hieroglyphic writing. Immediately after him Hayton I., king of little Armenia, sent his brother to the Khan to do homage as a vassal, and he was absent for four years. In a letter to the king and queen of Cyprus, sent from Samarkand, the prince writes of Tangut, in

Cathay, as the land from which the three kings went to Bethlehem to worship Jesus Christ, and adds—"I tell you that we have found many Christians scattered all over the East, and many fine churches, lofty, ancient, and of good architecture, which have been spoiled by the Turks." He records how the conquests of the Khans had delivered from the cruelty of the Mohammedans a certain Christian king in the land of India. King Hayton himself went to the Great Khan's court, and gives a rough account of Buddhism.

By the end of the thirteenth century it seemed to depend on an accident whether the prevailing religion in Asia might not be Christianity, nominally, at least, like Vladimir's in Russia. The Khans, described as "deists," had gradually come to accept the policy of uniting with the Christian Powers of Europe against the Musalmans, as formulated at Lyons. Kublai Khan, the greatest of them, was willing to study Latin Christianity, but he was denied the opportunity for which he sought. It is Marco Polo who records the facts, and no part of his marvellous book is so interesting as that record.

When Nicolas and Maffeo Polo, the father and uncle of the great Venetian, first visited his court as teachers, Kublai examined them "about the ways of the Latins," and sent them back as his envoys to the Pope. In his letter, copies of which, dated a century later from the Khan of Persia to the King of France, are preserved in the French archives, Kublai asked for a hundred Christians, "intelligent men acquainted with the seven arts," well qualified to enter into controversy, and able clearly to prove by force of argument to idolaters and other kinds of folk that the law of Christ was best, and that all other religions were false and naught; and that if they would prove this he and all under him would become Christians and the Church's liegemen." This is a remarkable document. When we remember the circumstances of the Christian nations of Europe and our own Saxon forefathers, we may say that virtually the fate of Asia as to prevailing religious belief hung upon it. But what was the result? On their return the two Polos found that Pope Clement IV. had just died. Such were the factions among the cardinals that no successor was elected for three years. When Gregory was chosen in 1271, he selected Nicolas of Vicenza and William of Tripoli, preaching friars and "unquestionably as learned churchmen as were to be found in that day," to accompany the Polos, now joined by their young nephew, Marco, to the Great Khan. But, alas for the missionary zeal of the friars! they fled back from Layas port in the Levant. The three Venetians in due time reached the Khan, who, instead of a hundred learned and zealous Christians, had to be content with "oil from the sepulchre" at Jerusalem. Thus an opportunity was lost for Christianising Asia, similar to that which Europe was allowed in the persons of Constantine and Clovis, Vladimir and our own Æthelbert.

The Book of Ser Marco Polo, the Venetian, concerning the Kingdoms and Marvels of the East, as newly translated and edited with learned notes by the late Colonel Sir Henry Yule, LL.D. (2nd edition, 1875), gives a most vivid, detailed, and accurate picture of the progress and the position of Nestorian and Roman Christianity towards the close of the thirteenth century under the tolerant sway of the Great Khan of Cathay and of the Hindu sovereigns of India. As one of Kublai Khan's governors or envoys Marco Polo twice visited India. On the first occasion he approached it from the Chinese side of Yunan, and spent some time in the province of Bangala, which was probably the modern Burma then ruled by a Bengal dynasty, and included modern Assam and Bengal up to its later Musalman capital of Murshidabad. At a later time he not only visited but dwelt in several of the cities and countries of Southern India, regarding which, their Brahmans and their Christians, he gives us wonderfully correct information. Finally, when he, his father, and uncle were reluctantly permitted by the Great Khan to leave Cathay in charge of a bride for Arghun, Khan of Persia, he touched at Ceylon and the extreme south of India again. On his way to

Hormuz and at the head of the Persian Gulf he became acquainted with the Malabar coast and Western India as far as Mekran, to say nothing of Madagascar, Sokotra, the east coast of Africa up to Abyssinia, and the islands of the Indian Ocean. The port from which he started in 1292 was Zayton, now Chin Chan in Fokien, which has given to our language the word Satin. He tells us of eleven countries, in most of which he describes Christian churches, using such a sentence as this—"The people are idolaters, but there are also some Christians and some Jews." The eleven, in their proper geographical order and present names, are these, following the coast of the Indian peninsula from east to west, from the Bay of Bengal to the Persian Gulf:—Telingana, Madras, Tanjor, Tinnevelli, Comorin, Quilon, Cannanor, Bombay, Cambay, Somnath, and Mekran. Marco Polo tells also the same story of the diamonds of Golconda guarded by serpents, and obtained by throwing down pieces of flesh which are carried off by eagles, that has become well known through the *Arabian Nights.* The earliest mention of this legend is by St. Epiphanius, Bishop of Salamis in Cyprus, who tells it of the jacinth in his account of the twelve jewels in the breastplate of the Jewish high priest.

The rivalry of the Romanist and Nestorian Churches, which began in India soon after Marco Polo's visit, and the gradual apostasy of not a few communities abandoned by the mother Church and without spiritual life, is seen in his account of the Island of Sokotra. There, eleven centuries before, Pantænus had found earnest disciples of the apostolic school, and had confirmed them in the faith. Now the Venetian traveller writes, "Their archbishop has nothing to do with the Pope of Rome, but is subject to the great Archbishop who lives at Baudas (Baghdad). He rules over the bishop of that island, and many other bishops in those regions of the world, just as our Pope does in these." Piracy and witchcraft prevailed, and Islam followed. By the middle of the seventeenth century a Carmelite who visited the people found them still professing to be Christians, but following rites in which the cross, circumcision, and sacrifices to the moon, were horribly jumbled without knowledge. Now the only trace of Christian influence in the savage Mohammedan island protected by the British Empire, is found in the name of the village Colesseah, which is believed to embody the Greek *ekklesia.* Sokotra is at once a living example of the failure of a false or imperfect Christianity to regenerate a people, and a warning to the evangelical Church to bear and have patience, and for the Name's sake to labour and not to faint, as our Lord declared to Ephesus, and again to Laodicea—"be zealous and repent."

The first half of the fourteenth century was, alike in India and Cathay, a time of Franciscan and Dominican missionary enterprise and Latin commercial activity. The Mongol domination kept Islam in check, and promoted toleration all over Asia. Marco Polo's spirit and example, the wealth he brought, and the stories he told, stirred up many followers. John of Monte Corvino was, after him, the first of a band of missionaries eager to win the Buddhist, Mohammedan, and Nestorian alike to allegiance to the Pope, who made him Archbishop of Peking and Patriarch of a wide region, with the approval of the Great Khan. He was the first to begin Roman Catholic missions in India. From the crowd of monkish annalists and adventurous travellers, who have left narratives of their experience, two missionaries stand out, Friar Jordanus and Friar Odoricus, in the century which transferred the command of the commerce and the Christianity of the people of India from the illustrious republics of Italy to the maritime enterprise and fanatical intolerance of Portugal.

Jordanus, a Dominican born at Séverac, near Toulouse, was twice in India. He wrote the *Mirabilia Descripta, or the Wonders of the East*, translated by Sir Henry Yule, with a commentary, for the Hakluyt Society. We have also two of his Latin letters. The first was addressed to his Dominican brethren and to Franciscan missionaries then at Tabreez and two other cities in North Persia, since made famous by the hardships of Henry Martyn and the toils of the American missionaries on the plain east of Lake

Ooroomia. He urges the despatch of missionaries to the three cities in Western and Southern India—of Supéra or Surat, Paroco or Broach, and Columbum or Quilon. Thereupon the Dominican Nicolaus Romanus at once left Persia for India. The second letter, written three years after, describes his own journey from Tabreez and voyage to Quilon, reversing the route followed by Henry Martyn five centuries later, when he took the Word of God to the Persians. After a year at Columbum or Quilon Jordanus seems to have returned, and to have been sent out again as Bishop of Columbum in 1430. The bull of Pope John XXII. commends the new prelate to the goodwill of the Christians, and invites the Nascarine or Nazarani, the name of the Syrian Christians to this day, to abjure their schism and enter the unity of the (R.) Catholic Church. On the way out Jordanus was entrusted with the pallium for the Archbishop of Sultania, between Tabreez and Tehran, the old Persian capital to which ecclesiastically Columbum was subject, and the ruined camp at which, we may add, the dying Martyn in vain sought audience of the Shah that he might present his Persian New Testament.

Jordanus was a true missionary, as appears from the whole tone of his curious book. He describes the Parsees, the casteless aborigines, the Hindu worship of idols, and the iconoclasm of the Mohammedan invaders from Mahmood of Ghazni's time. He is the first to note the instinctive apprehension called prophecy and fully realised by England in the Mutiny of 1857, thus—"The pagans of this India have prophecies of their own that we Latins are to subjugate the whole world." After his survey of the non-Christian peoples, closing with the words, "'Tis grief to hear and woe to see," Jordanus goes on, "In this India there is a scattered people, one here another there, who call themselves Christians, but are not so, nor have they baptism, nor do they know anything else about the faith; nay, they believe St. Thomas the Great to be Christ! There I baptized and brought into the faith about three hundred souls, of whom many were idolaters and Saracens.

And let me tell you that among the idolaters a man may with safety expound the Word of the Lord, nor is any one among the idolaters hindered from being baptized throughout all the East." The conclusion to which the zealous missionary comes is this, that while there is no land equal to Christendom, "and above all we have the true faith though it be ill kept," "as God is my witness, ten times better Christians and more charitable withal be those who be converted by the preaching and Minor friars to our faith than our own folk here, as experience hath taught me."

Jordanus was full of loyalty to the Master's command, of faith in His promise, and love to the souls for whom He died, presenting in all this a delightful contrast to the Abbé Dubois of the same Church and region a century ago. The friar's closing words are a summons to all Christians—"Of the conversion of those nations of India I say this, that if there were two or three hundred good friars who would faithfully and fervently preach the Catholic faith, there is not a year which would not see more than X. thousand persons converted to the Christian faith. For whilst I was among those schismatics and unbelievers, I believe that more than X. thousand or thereabout were converted to our faith; and because we, being few in number, could not occupy or even visit many parts of the land, many souls (wo is me!) have perished, and exceeding many do perish for lack of preachers of the word of the Lord." Then after describing that contemporary burst of proselytising zeal which carried the Koran to Sumâtra and Java,—Mohammedan ever since,—Jordanus relates how he had been four times cast into prison by the Mohammedans. "How many times I have had my hair plucked out and been scourged and been stoned God Himself knoweth and I, who had to bear all this for my sins, yet have not attained to end my life as a martyr for the faith as did four of my brethren! Nay, five preaching friars and four Minors were there in my time cruelly slain for the Catholic faith. Wo is me that I was not with them there!"

This introduces us to the story of the Four Martyrs

of Thana, near Bombay, which is the brightest episode in the generally dark history of early Romanist missions in India, after allowing for the legendary allegorical language in which it has been preserved to us. We find the details in a chronicle of the fourteenth century purporting to have been written by Jordanus, and the main facts are vouched for not only by his acknowledged work, but by his contemporary Odoricus and successor John de Marignola.

Sent by the Pope, then residing at Avignon, Jordanus and his band of missionaries preached their way through Persia, departed from Hormuz, landed at Diu off the north coast of Bombay, and thence sailed to Thana in 1321. They found the Mohammedan fury at its height. In the absence of Jordanus on a preaching tour to the north, the four missionaries, who were Franciscans,—Thomas, James, Demetrius, and Peter,—were accused by one Yusuf before the governor, and boldly defended the doctrine of the divine Sonship of the Lord Jesus Christ, so obnoxious to the unitarians of Islam. They were sentenced to death by fire. The youngest, James of Padua, to quote the chronicler, "a young wrestler for Christ, incontinently went into the fire and abode in it until it was well-nigh spent, rejoicing and uttering praise, and without any burning of his hair even, or of the cloth of his gown." Stripped of his garment which, according to the Mussulman tradition, was that of Abraham, who when cast into the flames at Chaldæa took no hurt, the young confessor was again thrown into the furnace, but without harm. The four were then set free, but were the night following despatched to the joys of heaven. Hastily returning to Thana, Jordanus, helped by a Genoese merchant there, removed the precious remains to old Surat, and buried them in a church there. Odoric, the Bohemian, a wandering saint, accompanied by an Irishman, Friar James, arrived at Surat a year after, and carried off the ashes of the four martyrs on his fourteen years voyaging to Peking, and through Central Asia to Padua, where he told his long story, as translated by Sir Henry Yule. To the expressed annoyance of that great scholar and good Christian, Odoric was made a beatus or semi-saint of the Church of Rome, although he showed little of the self-consecration of John of Monte Corvino and Jordanus. A quaint bas-relief at his shrine at Udine represents a friar of sixty with a Socratic countenance preaching to the people of India, while a cherub pours a cataract of water on the adoring crowd.

We may pass over the not infrequent references to Christianity in India by Ibn Batuta, of Tangier, the remarkable Mohammedan traveller in 1324; by Nicolo Conti, the Venetian, who apostatised to save his life in 1419-1440; by Abd-er-Ruzzak, at the same time, who found a Christian as vizier of the sultan of Vijayanagar; by the Russian Nikitin (1468-1474), who recorded that he had already passed the fourth great day in a Musalman country and had not renounced Christianity; by the Genoese merchant Hicronomo di Santo Stefano (1494-1499), and by the Bolognese Ludovico Varthema (1503-1508), who witnessed the decadence of the Syrian and the advent of the Romanist power of Portugal. From west and east India is about to be approached by sea. Columbus and Da Gama are at hand.

Hitherto we have traced the failure of missionary Christianity because of its giving forth an uncertain or a false sound on the central message of Jesus Christ, or because of its using political methods and unspiritual weapons which our Lord Himself denounced. Buddhism and Islam prevailed in Asia accordingly. Now we come to the first example in history of the union of the gospel with science, or the use of scientific discovery and ascertained truth by Christianity. In the historical providence of God, geography and the gospel have worked together in a holy and fruitful alliance all through the three centuries from Prince Henry the Navigator and Christopher Columbus to Walter Raleigh, the Pilgrim Fathers, William Carey, and David Livingstone. In these men we see Scripture and science united sincerely and reverently to bring the world to Christ. Of them all are the words of Henry Yule, that great Christian officer and geographer, true—their genius and lofty enthusiasm, their ardent and justified previsions mark them as "lights of the human race." To the landing of Carey, son of the English wool-weaver, at Calcutta on the 10th November 1793, as to that of Columbus, son of the Genoese wool-weaver, on the (West) Indian Island of Guanahani three centuries before, we may apply the words in which the "Christ-carrier" closed the letter reporting his first voyage —"Our Redeemer hath granted this victory . . . an event of such high importance in which all Christendom ought to rejoice, and which it ought to celebrate with great festivals and the offering of solemn thanks to the Holy Trinity, with many solemn prayers both for the great exaltation which may accrue . . . . in turning many nations to our holy faith, and also for the temporal benefits which will bring great refreshment and gain . . . . to all Christians."

To that noble Prince of Portugal, Henry the Navigator (great-grandson of Edward III. of England), who chose as his motto, "Talent de Bien Faire," or "the desire to do good," we owe the discovery of the Cape route to India. When Cape Bojador was passed—the first step in the history of African and Indian discovery by the east—Prince Henry besought the Virgin that she "would guide and set forth the doings in this discovery to the praise and glory of God, and to the increase of His holy faith." Columbus, as the servant of Spain after His own Genoa had refused his offer—Henry VII. of England having sent his favourable answer too late—determined, with a fanatical resolution, to reach India by the west, beginning with his countryman Marco Polo's islands of Chipangu (Japan) and Antilla. These were represented in the chart of his learned correspondent, Toscanelli of Florence, as midway between the coasts of Europe and Africa on the east and the coasts of Asia on the west. Marco Polo had written of these people as idolaters, and "concerning the fashion of the idols," the deeds ascribed to which are "such a parcel of devilries as it is best not to tell." Columbus burned to convert them to Christ, and he took with him a letter as ambassador from Spain to the Grand Khan of Cathay with this object.[1] The illustrious admiral sailed under the green cross, a banner of his own device; he took possession of new lands with "immense thanksgivings to Almighty God," with solemn services and an immediate effort to instruct the natives; he carried home to Ferdinand and Isabella nine of the native Indians for baptism.

Christopher Columbus, in truth, was the first and greatest Christian missionary in action, as his contemporary, Erasmus, was in writing and in translating the New Testament. But he was as sternly and narrowly a member of the Church of Rome as the missionary bishop Las Casas, whose father sailed with him, and who ecclesiastically followed him. By their discoveries through Portugal and Spain, Prince Henry and Columbus began the counter-reformation which the Society of Jesus was soon after chartered by the Pope Paul III. to carry on, along with the older monastic orders. For the three centuries, from Columbus to Carey, foreign missions were identified with the intolerant and sacramentarian form of Christianity, if we except the small Moravian society of Germany in the later years of that period. According to the teaching and practical action of the great discoverers, not to be in the Church was to be without the only true and saving faith, was to be certain of hell. Even Columbus, who was so pious that "for fasting and saying all the divine office he might be thought professed in some religious order," who wrote Latin prayers, and used as his cipher a seven-lettered device based on his name Christopher, reported it as the drawback of his distant voyages, that he was so far away from the holy sacraments of the Holy Church as to be out of salvation if he were to die. "Weep for me, ye that are charitable to me or just," he wrote.

This ritualistic conviction became the source of, as it

[1] Let due record be given to the name of the monk, Antonio de Marchena, who, in the seclusion of La Rabida, first fired Columbus with the missionary idea at the time when the Mohammedans and the Jews were being expelled from Spain. See the *Life of Columbus* (the best) by Clements Markham, C.B. (1892).

was the apology for, every form of intolerance and even crime at the hands of otherwise good men. Like Saul, the early explorers verily thought they did God service when they persecuted the dark races. He who had called the first island he discovered San Salvador, and had reported that its people "would easily be converted to Christianity," became unconsciously, but not the less really, the originator of the slave-trade. "To the first island that I found I gave the name San Salvador, in remembrance of His High Majesty, who hath marvellously brought all these things to pass." Of the natives he wrote: "I gave away a thousand good and pretty articles which I had brought with me, in order to win their affection, and that they might be led to become Christians. They believe that all power, and indeed all good things, are in heaven; and they are firmly convinced that I, with my vessels and crews, came from heaven." His second expedition took out Father Buil and other Benedictines to La Navidad, the colony he had founded in Hispaniola or Hayti, that they might "bring the dwellers in the Indies to a knowledge of the holy Catholic faith lovingly." Alas! he found the colony broken up and its stragglers attacked by the Carib "cannibals." He founded another in a different part of the island, calling it Isabella, and sent home to the sovereigns of Spain a report, dated January 1494, of which we have the copy with the marginal orders of Ferdinand and Isabella. He declares that he has sent home some Indians from the Cannibal Islands *as slaves* to be taught Castillian, and so to become interpreters able to carry on the work of conversion. He proposes that, "for the advantage of their souls," such slaves be sent in payment of the cargoes required for the maintenance of the colony. "Los Reyes" reply that both the cannibals and the peaceful Indians of the colony should be brought to the holy Catholic faith "there" or on the spot, and disapprove of the despatch of slaves. We must not judge Columbus entirely by the standard of our own day. But that unfortunate despatch of 1494 was, historically, the beginning of what, under the colour of missionary motives, has ever since been the greatest crime against humanity. Soon Africans took the place of the weak Indians. To this day, unhappily, slave-buying and slave-owning is one of the missionary methods of the Latin Church in Africa, as it used to be in America and in the dark ages of Europe.

On the 20th May 1506, at the age of threescore and ten, Columbus entered into rest, after acts of penitence and faith, saying, in the Latin of the Vulgate, "Into thy hands, O Lord, I commend my spirit." From Valladolid, and Seville, and from San Domingo, his dust and that of his son, Don Diego, were successively conveyed to Cuba, where, in the cathedral of the Havana, they were last interred in solemn state in the year 1795. The wrongs suffered by the great admiral, culminating after his death in the giving of the name of a Florentine contractor, Vespucci Amerigo, to the New World, may be held to atone for the one blot on the purity, the nobility, and the everlasting memory of Christopher Columbus. He opened the widest of all doors to the gospel of Jesus Christ, so that we may well commemorate the great admiral on the missionary as on the geographical side of his unique achievement. This Italian, having vainly offered himself to England as well as Genoa, went forth from Spain to discover India by the west, and to Christianise Japan and China. By no accident, but in the almost fanatical faith which is fed by knowledge,[1] he revealed the New World,

[1] In the remarkable description he gave of himself to Ferdinand and Isabella in the year 1501, Columbus wrote: "At a very early age I became a sailor, and a sailor I have been ever since. . . . I have held traffic and converse with the wise and prudent, churchmen and laymen, Latins and Greeks, Jews and Moors, and many others of other persuasions. I found the Lord to be gracious to my desire, and received from Him the spirit of understanding. . . . During this time have I seen, and made it my study to see, all writings, cosmography, histories, chronicles, philosophies, and other arts, so that the hand of the Lord plainly opened my understanding to see that it was possible to sail from hence to the Indies, and set on fire my will for the execution thereof." To the last Columbus believed that it was the Indies he had found.

not only of still Romanist Mexiço and South America, but of what is now prevailingly Protestant Canada and the United States. The event of the 12th October 1492 meant the birth of the greatest evangelical and evangelising people of 1893 and the coming century.

Luther was a young monk of twenty-three when Columbus died. From his awakening, down to the work of Carey in Serampore, during three centuries the Reformed Churches were asleep as to missions, spending their strength in internal dissension. Like the German Lutherans, who had created the Unitas Fratrum, he went out of the Church to form his missionary organisation. Calmly surveying the fruits of the discoveries of Columbus and his successors when, as a shoemaker, he sat on his stall and made his map of the world and taught the village children, Carey resolved to translate the Word of God into the languages of the dark races, as John Eliot had begun to do for the Red Indians, whose ancestors Columbus had unwittingly enslaved. Well might Wilberforce, in the House of Commons, pronounce this a sublime conception. As Columbus had brooded over the idea of new lands in the west to be won for the Church of his day, and proved the idea a fact, so Carey's heart burned within him, even from boyhood, when he read the story of Captain Cook's completion of the exploring work of Columbus in that Pacific Ocean, where not only Japan but a thousand islands were waiting for the good news of God. Like the Genoese sailor, the English shoemaker organised his expedition for the conversion of India, and led it himself all through the years till he saw its early fruition. Columbus sought the East Indies and Cathay, and he found the West Indies and America that the great western people might become in our time one of the true evangelisers of India.[1] The Nestorians first, and then the

[1] The latest writer on the discovery of America, in the *Quarterly Review* for July 1893, remarks: "In that astonishing series of events which have broken the sword of Islam, subdued Asia under Christian influences, and made Europeans the conquering and civilising race among men, Columbus has proved himself a mighty leader. Enthusiasm like his works miracles of which science reaps the fruits."

Latin preaching friars, had failed to commend Christ to the Hindu, the Buddhist, and the Mohammedan of Southern Asia. A third attempt was to be made by Portugal through the Jesuit order, by Francis Xavier, Aleixo Menezes, and Robert de Nobilibus.

On the 20th May 1498 Vasco da Gama, having in a voyage of eleven months doubled the Cape of Good Hope and coasted along East Africa, landed at Calicut. It was a momentous event, second only to the action of Columbus six years before. The Pope, the worst of the whole line, Alexander Borgia, had distributed the undiscovered world outside of Christendom between Spain and Portugal by his famous Bull, thus asserting the most extensive practical missionary policy in all history up to that time. The King of Portugal was constituted by the supreme Christian authority of his day "Lord of the Navigation, Conquest, and Trade of Ethiopia, Arabia, Persia, and India." What in two voyages Vasco da Gama began, Albuquerque and Almeida, the first viceroy, gradually formed into an Eastern empire, which had one justification to set against its iniquities. It beat back the pressure of Solyman the Magnificent from Constantinople, and of the Sultan of Egypt from Alexandria, to keep sealed up the trade of India which, for the eighteen hundred years since Alexander the Great, had enriched both powers, and Venice and Genoa as their partners and middlemen. Portugal, all unwittingly, prevented the destruction of Christendom by "a colossal military empire on the Bosporus commanding the avenues of Asiatic trade,"[1] which might have postponed for centuries alike the Reformation of the Church and the spread of the English-speaking race propagating the Reformed faith. Portugal, happily, could not keep the trade which it was the first to divert to the natural channel of the ocean, because it did not prove worthy to be entrusted with the faith, which it used for selfish ends and degraded by unspiritual compromises. Absorbed for a time in Spain, its decadence

[1] Sir Alfred Lyall on *The Rise of the British Dominion in India.* London (Murray), 1893.

went on, step by step, as first the Dutch Republic and then the England of Queen Elizabeth opened wide the doors of the East and the West, which Philip II. vainly tried to shut again with an intolerance like that of the Turk before him.

Portugal had planted its trading forts on the shores of Western and Southern India for forty years before it became a proselytising power. Its first centre, at Calicut, was not far to the north of Cochin, in the ancient town of which, now known as Cranganor, first the Jews and then the Christians, both apostolic and Nestorian, had formed settlements. One of the many adventurers who followed Da Gama—Pedro Alvares Cabral—having seized the place became acquainted with the Syrian Christians. Two of them about to visit their Patriarch at Mosul, named Matthias and Joseph, were taken by Cabral to Lisbon, *en route* to Persia, and these were the first Christians of India seen in Europe. The elder died there, and the younger, when at Venice on his further journey, wrote an account of his co-religionists and of his travels in a Latin work entitled *Voyages of Joseph the Indian*,[1] and returned to India by Lisbon. Though no more a missionary Church in the aggressive sense than their fathers, the Malabar Christians in the first half of the sixteenth century were a prosperous and even powerful community. For military and political services to the rajas of Cochin they enjoyed all the privileges of a protected caste. They even aspired to sovereign nationality on their own account at an early period, having a tradition that Beliarte was the first of a line of Christian kings who governed from Udiampoor, a few miles south-east of Ernakolam, the Cochin capital, where, alas! the Portuguese archbishop, Menezes, was to destroy their spiritual independence by the decrees of his Latin Synod of Diamper in 1599.

We are thus introduced to the two men, the Spanish Francis Xavier and the Portuguese Aleixo de Menezes, who, in the sixteenth century, spread in South India Latin

[1] *Histoire Du Christianisme des Indes.* Par M. V. La Croze. À la Haye, 1758, 2 vols.

Christianity in its most debased form,—the Jesuit missionary, with a pure zeal which has placed him in the Romish Calendar beside the apostle St. Thomas, and the archbishop, with a fanatical intolerance which devised the tortures of the Inquisition and ended in the extinction of the Eastern empire of his country.

IV

FRANCIS XAVIER AND HIS SUCCESSORS—THE DUTCH ATTEMPT

"*If ye be dead with Christ from the rudiments of the world, why, as though living in the world, are ye subject to ordinances, after the commandments and doctrines of men?*"—COL. ii. 20, 22.

PERIODICALLY the city of Old Goa is filled by crowds of Roman Catholics, who present the sad spectacle in the midst of an idolatrous people of the worship of a mummy. A body, said to be that of the good and great Francis Xavier, is exhibited in the cathedral to deluded votaries, who for days defile before the repulsive object in solemn adoration. Pompous ceremonies and gay festivities add to the spectacle, and there are not a few who declare that the mummy has healed them of their diseases. Could Xavier himself address the deluded people, he would reprove them as he did those who eulogised him during his life. "What!" he replied to friends who asked him if it was true that he had raised a dead child to life, "I raise the dead! Can you really believe such a thing of a wretch like me?" Yet half a century after his death a solemn conclave of all the dignitaries of Romish Christendom, presided over by Pope Urban VIII., cited miracles such as this as a ground for canonising one who was a saint in a far truer sense than many in the Calendar. As time passed on the legends by which his Church obscured the real glories of Xavier were disbelieved, but even Protestant writers like Sir James Stephen showed, in dealing with his character, a singular carelessness as to historic truth. This writer in his *Essays in Ecclesiastical Biography*, which surpass Macaulay's in interest and equal them in ability, uses all his eloquence to justify the marvellous stories of Xavier's success in converting Asiatics, and of the facility with which he acquired in a few years languages so difficult and different as those of the western and eastern coasts of India, of Malacca, of the Spice Islands, of Japan, and of China, so that he was not only able to preach in them all, but to hold abstruse disquisitions on points of philosophy with the bonzes of Japan. It was high time that some writer, who really venerated the character of Francis Xavier, and had charity enough to remember who it was that reproved His disciples for repudiating the acts of those "who followed not with them," should apply to the records of the saint's life the simplest canons of historical criticism. This was done in 1862 by the late Henry Venn,[1] who, chiefly in the language of Xavier's own letters, manages to tell us the whole truth as it had never been told before, while our regard for the saint as a man and a missionary becomes at once more intelligent and intense. The Jesuits have preserved many of the letters of the greatest ornament of their order. In 1795 Father Menchacha carefully edited them in chronological order, in a Latin translation, and the Bologna edition, containing 146 letters, is in all respects the standard. Mr. Venn uses this

[1] *The Missionary Life and Labours of Francis Xavier, taken from his own Correspondence, with a Sketch of the General Results of Roman Catholic Missions among the Heathen.* By Henry Venn, B.D., Prebendary of St. Paul's, Honorary Secretary of the Church Missionary Society. London (Longman), 1862. With this work should be compared one published in 1872 (Burns and Oates), *The Life and Letters of St. Francis Xavier.* By Henry James Coleridge, of the Society of Jesus. 2 vols. 3rd ed., 1876. See also *The Life of St. Francis Xavier, Apostle of the Indies and Japan,* from the Italian of D. Bartoli and J. P. Maffei; especially the characteristic preface by the Very Rev. F. W. Faber of the Oratory, London, 1858. James Dryden, the poet's brother, translated the *Life of Francis Xavier* by Père Bonhours.

and the French translation published at Brussels in 1838. As these letters were written at different times from India, not only to friends such as Loyola and the Portuguese authorities at home, but to his brethren in India, they show us the whole man in his greatest and weakest points, while they describe his work and his aims in a manner which throws no little light on the character of Roman Catholic missions in the East.

Xavier narrowly escaped being a Protestant, and throughout the whole of his letters a conflict is visible between that higher piety which finds its satisfaction only in intelligent communion with God, and that which seeks it in mere ritualism. Born in 1506, in the kingdom of Navarre, his youth was surrounded by Protestant influences. The Court of Navarre, over which the sister of Francis I. presided, was filled with Reformers from Germany and Switzerland, who used not the weapons of theological lore, but the lighter artillery of satire and song. Pope Leo X. had, by the Concordat of 1517, struck a temporary blow at the liberties of the Gallican Church; but in the year 1533, so far had a spirit of toleration spread that Calvin and Cop, the Rector of the University of Paris, were so bold as to proclaim the new doctrines in the face of the whole Sorbonne. Xavier as a youth had entered into the gay and literary pursuits of the Protestant Court of Navarre, and distinguished himself at Paris by his ever-ready witticisms and martial spirit. It is singular that, at the very time he was expounding Aristotle to the students who flocked to his lectures, Calvin was writing his Institutes in the same city. Had that stern but large-minded man, at that time hardly out of boyhood, obtained an influence over young Xavier, early impressions might have been deepened, and there would have been one saint less in the Romish Calendar though not in the Church of Christ. But Ignatius Loyola obtained that influence, and in the first letter which has come down to us, dated from Paris, 24th March 1535, Xavier, writing to his brother in Spain, defends himself and Loyola from certain calumnies, and expresses his affectionate gratitude to his friend for assisting him with money when in distress, and for having rescued him from the influence of Protestant teachers. The expression is remarkable: "The benefit Ignatius Loyola has conferred of highest value is that of fortifying my youthful imprudence against the deplorable dangers arising from my familiarity with men breathing out heresy; such as are many of my contemporaries in Paris in these times, who would insidiously undermine faith and morality beneath the specious mask of liberality and superior intelligence." Calvin was not the least of these "men breathing out heresy."

But Loyola had done his work in securing Xavier as a coadjutor. A few months before, in 1534, a date to be remembered in the history of Eastern missions, he had, with six of his friends, including Xavier, formed an association for converting unbelievers. This was the precursor of that notorious Company of Jesus which has been suppressed and revived, and under the mask of religion has done untold injury to the spiritual and civil liberties of mankind. The first project of a mission to the Holy Land was given up on account of the war there. Xavier, as a mendicant friar, was attempting to revive the tone of religion at Bologna and other universities, when John III. of Portugal summoned him, Loyola, and their friend Lefevre, to head a Jesuit mission to the East Indies. The scheme did not commend itself to Loyola, who proposed to send the two most obscure of his order. But at last Xavier was permitted to set out, especially commissioned by the King, and accompanying the new Viceroy, to Goa. As a Papal nuncio he also bore letters to "David, King of Ethiopia," and to all the kings of the East from the Cape of Good Hope to the Ganges. He was accompanied by another Jesuit Father, Paul Camerte, and by a lay assistant, while a college was established at Coimbra for the support of two hundred Jesuit associates, who were to be trained for India missions. The Franciscans had for some time been labouring in the East, but John III. was not satisfied with their zeal.

At the age of thirty-six Xavier landed at Goa, in May

1542, and his labours till his death on a barren island on the coast of China were spread over ten years and a half. Goa he found more splendid and hardly more godless than Calcutta was last century. Small fleets at sea and small bodies of troops on land were engaged in incessant attacks on native governments, such as never rose to the dignity of political movements like those of the French and English at a later period. Hindoos were kept there by the Portuguese, as Africans are now in Mozambique, as slaves. A half-caste race sprang into existence not only from the vices of the godless settlers, but as a matter of policy, for Albuquerque had seized native women, and forcibly baptized them, that they might be married to his soldiers. In this mixed class the Portuguese sought to recruit their army and navy, seeing not that it is only in proportion as the conquering race maintains its moral and physical supremacy that its power to hold, to rule, and civilise the people will remain stable. There was a great work to be done in Goa, but if it had been this Xavier had wanted he might as well have remained in Europe. For a time he confined himself to the hospitals and asylums, but in a few months his career seems to have shaped itself.

Like the greatest of our Protestant missionaries, he resolved to establish in Goa a college for the training of native preachers, whom he would leave under the care of others, while he himself went forth to evangelise among the people. The Viceroy, who had been his fellow-voyager, persuaded him to visit a settlement of pearl-fishers near the modern Tuticorin. Already some of this poor community had professed to be Christians, while the Viceroy thought that by baptizing them all he would secure their loyalty to Goa, and consequently a monopoly of the lucrative fishery. Xavier had begun badly, as Commissioner of John III., as Papal Nuncio, as the friend and agent of the Viceroy, in advancing his political schemes. But, disapproving of missionaries taking part in political movements or depending on secular aid, we would not judge Xavier harshly. He lived at a time very different from the present, when the spirit of true toleration and the right of private judgment were hardly known even to the Reformers who battled so fiercely for the principles of both. Xavier, moreover, did little more than Bishop Mackenzie's Zambesi mission in their attacks on slave-hunting tribes long after. He held that the missionary is the pioneer of civilisation as well as of that Christianity on which it is based, and he reproved the godless among his countrymen in the East as its greatest obstacles. The following passage shows with what a pure spirit he entered on his work, and the zeal which burns in these words he showed to the last, even when sad experience taught him sometimes to doubt if an adult Hindoo could possibly be saved :—

"The miseries of a long voyage ; the dealing with the sins of other people, while you are oppressed by your own ; a permanent abode among the heathen, and this in a land which is scorched by the rays of the sun,—all these things are indeed trials. But if they be endured for the cause of God, they become great comforts and the sources of many heavenly pleasures. I am persuaded that those who truly love the cross of Christ esteem a life thus passed in affliction to be a happy one, and regard an avoidance of the cross, or an exemption from it, as a kind of death. For what death is more bitter than to live without Christ, when once we have tasted His preciousness ; or to desert Him, that we may follow our own desires? Believe me, no cross is to be compared with this cross. On the other hand, how happy it is to live in dying daily, and in mortifying our own will, and in seeking, not our own, but the things that are Jesus Christ's !"

"I trust that, through the merits and prayers of our holy mother the Church, in which is my chief confidence, and through the prayers of its living members, to which you belong, our Lord Jesus Christ will sow the gospel seed in this heathen land by my instrumentality, though a worthless servant. Especially, if He shall be pleased to use such a poor creature as I am for so great a work, it may shame the men who were born for great achievements ; and it may stir up the courage of the timid, when, forsooth, they see me, who am but dust and ashes, and the most abject of men, a visible witness of the great want of labourers. I will, indeed, cheerfully devote myself to be the constant servant of any who will come over here and devote themselves to work in the vineyard of our common Lord."

Xavier learned the lesson taught by events since his day, that "colonisation is the habitual, perhaps the indispensable, forerunner of the gospel among barbarians or half-civilised tribes." Sir James Stephen, who was well able from his position and daily duties to judge, years ago declared that we shall Christianise India only in proportion as we Anglicise her. He may be imaginative in thinking that if England had been, in Xavier's days, the sovereign of the East, that renovating process would even now have been complete, for it is only within this century that England has become really equal to the trust confided to her. Moreover the errors of twice a millennium do not die so quickly. But it is to Xavier's credit that he at least dimly apprehended this truth in a sense different from that of the conquering monarchs of Spain and Portugal, who would have spread the cross by the swords of men far worse in their lives than the idolaters they wanted to convert.

For three years beginning with May 1542, Xavier toiled as a missionary in South India. For two and a half he was occupied in a visit to the Chinese Archipelago. The subsequent four years he spent in superintending the Jesuit missions in India, and in a visit to Japan, where he resided two years, and then returned to Goa. The last year of his life he devoted to a disastrous attempt to enter China as he had done Japan.

Xavier's whole principles and modes of action as a missionary were based on the Romish and idolatrous sacramentarian theory. To put it theologically, he sought to secure in his so-called converts not an *opus operans*, a subjective change of nature working out into the life, but an *opus operatum*, an external work which required the consent of neither heart nor understanding, but only the recitation of a few prayers or the creed, and baptism. He never met the natural difficulty which is the stumbling-block of every Asiatic—that outward ceremonies cannot purge from sin. So far as a vague dread of Christianity was a cause of the Mutiny of 1857, the fear was based on ignorance of the fact that no loss of caste, no ceremonial defilement, no study of a mere book, can make a man a Christian. Roman Catholicism shares this error with all non-Christian religions, and hence, while we allow that its converts are better than they were as heathens, we cannot expect that, in the future any more than in the past, its missions will be successful. Xavier personally was much more free from this delusion as to the value of ritualism than many of his order and Church. That order had taken its rise from the severe spiritual struggles of accomplished men of the world like Xavier and Loyola. Not only so, but Xavier was familiar with that doctrine of "grace" which the Reformers preached in Navarre, in Paris, in Germany, and in Geneva, in his days. But the very difficulties presented by Hinduism and Buddhism to a change of heart in their votaries—obliterating the conscience as these systems do—led Xavier, in his desire for results, to be content with the outward show of belief, with baptism, and the unintelligent repetition of words denoting spiritual ideas far beyond the comprehension of the poor fishermen and peasants among whom chiefly he laboured.

Such being his principles, his modes of action corresponded. He did not make the mistake of his successors, in living as a Hindu and lowering the dignity of his soul to the degraded level of the idolater like Robert de Nobilibus and Abbé Dubois. But even when he despairs most of success, even when his moral sense and spiritual instincts are most shocked at the vices of his converts and of the unbaptized, he never loses his affection for them. Like his Master who wept over the city He had so often denounced, Xavier yearned for the people who were as sheep without a shepherd, and did not spare himself for their sake. But his letters clearly show that he never mastered one Oriental language, and that frequently he was without an interpreter. In some cases he bought his converts with money. Speaking of the villages of pearl-fishers at Tuticorin after he had been *two* years among them, he says he visits from village to village:—

"All being thus surveyed, my labour comes over again in the same order. In each village I leave one copy of the *Christian Instruction.* I appoint all to assemble on festival days, and to chant the rudiments of the Christian faith; and in each of the villages I appoint a fit person to preside. For their wages the Viceroy, at my request, has assigned 4000 gold fanams. Multitudes in these parts are only not Christians because none are found to make them Christians. Here I am, almost alone from the time that Anthony remained sick at Manapar, and I find it a most inconvenient position to be in the midst of a people of an unknown tongue, without the assistance of an interpreter. Roderick, indeed, who is now here, acts as an interpreter in the place of Anthony; but you know well how much they know of Portuguese. Conceive, therefore, what kind of life I live in this place, what kind of sermons I am able to address to the assemblies, when they who should repeat my address to the people do not understand me, nor I them. I ought to be an adept in dumb show. Yet I am not without work, for I want no interpreter to baptize infants just born, or those which their parents bring; nor to relieve the famished and the naked who come in my way. So I devote myself to these two kinds of good works, and do not regard my time as lost."

It is doubtful if the people understood the translations of the creed into their own language. After recounting a large number of baptisms, Xavier, in one of his letters, says they had mistranslated the very first word of the Creed, and that, instead of the word "I believe," (*credo*), they had been using the expression, "I will," (*volo*)! Xavier's phrase always is "*Feci* Christianos." At the same time he insisted, by a strict discipline, on at least outward conformity to the Decalogue, and when the only Brahman whom he had found to exhibit an intelligent and candid mind wanted to be secretly baptized, he refused to do it. Still the argument Xavier uses most frequently to stir up his brethren in Europe to send more missionaries, and to quicken the missionaries already in the field, is that they will thus be delivered from the pains of purgatory. To Mansilla, his colleague on the fishery coast, he writes — "God give you patience, which is the first requisite in dealing with this nation. Imagine to yourself that you are in purgatory, and that you are washing away the guilt of your evil deeds. Acknowledge the singular mercy of God in granting you the opportunity for expiating the sins of your youth while you live and breathe, which may now be accomplished by the merits of grace, and at a far less cost of suffering than in the world to come." Xavier's wondrous zeal was not incompatible with great fickleness as to the object to which it was directed, and with great impatience as to results. Hence his incessant journeys from place to place and country to country.

Two years were sufficient to convince him that to Christianise the poor pearl-divers was hopeless, even with the help of "gold fanams," and he resolved to direct his attention to the "kings" of India and the East. Hence his visit to the Spice Islands, in which he seems to have secured the nominal adhesion for a time of only two rajas, who expected political benefits from Goa. It is on his return to India for fifteen months, to organise all the Jesuit missions in the East, that the high elements of his nature appear. To this period of his life are due the rapid extension of Jesuit missions from the Cape of Good Hope to China and Japan, and the proportionate decline of the Franciscan and Augustinian missions. What Loyola was to the whole Jesuit order, Xavier was to all the Jesuit associates in the East. His instructions to these associates, his personal intercourse with them, and his directions as to their work, reveal in him the intelligent scholar, the zealous missionary, the wise ruler, and the courteous gentleman. By this time, disappointed both in poor and rich, he comes to the conclusion, which, in the different form of the superior importance of Bible schools to spasmodic preaching, Protestant missions are arriving at—"Believe me, trust my experience, all our ministry to this nation reduces itself to two capital points—the baptism of children, and their instruction as soon as they are capable of it." His remarks as to the treatment of native Christians are worthy of study now. He closes them by saying—

"In the presence of a Portuguese, take good care not to reprove or condemn the native Christians. On the contrary, defend them, praise them, apologise for them on every occasion. Point out to their detractors how short a time it is since they embraced the faith; that they are still in infancy; that if one considers how many helps to a Christian life are wanting to them, how many obstacles are opposed to their Christian advancement, by the penury of the priests, by the incursions of the barbarians, by their terror of the Badages—far from being surprised at the defects of so rude a nation, one can only wonder that they are not worse."

How well it would be if all modern preachers kept the following in mind:—

"Men will only listen attentively to that which responds to their internal consciousness. Sublime speculations, perplexed questions, and scholastic controversies, overshoot the capacity and the interest of men who grovel upon the earth: they make a vain sound, and pass away without effect. You must show men to themselves, if you wish to hold them enchained by your words. But before you can express what they feel in the depths of their heart, you must know it; and there is only one way of knowing it—to be much among them, to test them, to observe them. Take in hand these living books; hence derive your rules for teaching with effect; hence obtain your ability of dealing with sinners, of bearing with them, and, for the sake of saving their souls, of moving and bending their wills in the right direction." "There is but one key which will unlock those hearts, namely, the presentation to them, as I have said, of their interior convictions skilfully portrayed by a preacher well versed in human affairs, and brought home clearly to the apprehension of each individual."

Xavier throughout shows himself to be a man whom Protestantism would have made a Luther, or a later age a Cromwell. As time passed on and his work became less and less hopeful, in the bitterness of his spirit he proposes that India should be converted by the power of the secular arm. In Japan, where he was most successful, we find him writing to Ignatius Loyola, in words which show how little ritualism supported himself personally:—

"I can never describe in writing how much I owe to the Japanese, since God through their means penetrated my mind with a clear and intimate conviction of my innumerable sins. Hitherto my thoughts ever wandered beyond myself: I had not searched into that abyss of evil lying deep in my conscience, until, as midst the troubles and anguish of Japan, my eyes were a little opened, and the good Lord granted me to see clearly, and to have, as it were, a present and tangible experience of the necessity of having a friend to keep up an ever-attentive and sedulous care over me. Let your holy charity, therefore, suggest to you what you may do for me whilst subjecting to my government the souls of fathers and brethren of our Society. For, through the infinite mercy of God, I have lately discovered that I am so ill furnished with the necessary qualities for discharging this government, that I ought rather to hope to be myself commended by you to the care and supervision of my brethren, than that they should be committed to my guidance."

Xavier's end was like his life. Eager to introduce Christianity into China, and knowing that as a missionary he could not enter it, he planned an embassy from Goa to Peking, of which he was to be the head, but the Governor of Malacca arrested it on the way. Still, in a trader belonging to his friend, James Pereira, he left the Bay of Singapore and reached the island of Sancian, a low sandy spot off the coast, near Canton, where the Portuguese ships were accustomed to lie at anchor. Here he was stricken with fever, but his active spirit never ceased to be busy. Recovering after fifteen days, he wrote nine long letters regarding his missions, but still could not enter China. He succeeded in bribing a Chinese merchant for £300 to smuggle him in his junk, but his own interpreter refused to run the risk. In his last letter the words occur—"I shall not die before God wills my death. Long since, indeed, I have desired death, and life has been a weariness. But let not human curiosity indulge in useless disputes about the hour of my decease. It is fixed in the eternal decree, and vain thoughts can neither hasten nor delay it." In three weeks, on 2nd December 1552, Xavier died without friend or helper. In a mere shed on a barren island he drew his last breath, and there Portuguese merchants found him as he died. The first account we have as to the body is in a letter from a Jesuit in Goa, written to the Society in Europe just two years after the event. The writer's authority is a friend who heard the story from sailors. The merchants who were with him when he died buried his body in quicklime the sooner to consume it, that they might take his bones to India. After waiting long enough they found the corpse still perfect and were astonished at the miracle. It was taken in a coffin filled with quicklime to Malacca, and there buried with great pomp. A Jesuit brother, sent to investigate the circumstances of Xavier's death, found it there still perfect, placed it in a new coffin, and kept it in his own hermitage, till, about a year after Xavier's death, he and another took it to Goa. Dressed in splendid vestments, with hands crossed and sandals on the feet, it was deposited in the Jesuit chapel by a great procession headed by the Viceroy. Whether the body now periodically exhibited as a holy relic at Goa is indeed that of Francis Xavier, inquirers will decide according to the greater or less amount of their credulity.

Xavier certainly never underwent such actual dangers and hardships as modern missionaries of his own Church in China, or men like Henry Martyn, Williams, and Livingstone; but his visit to China shows that his spirit and energy were like those of Paul. In zeal approaching to fanaticism which would have used the sword; in self-denial not far removed from a sublime asceticism; in courage which reproved viceroys, advised kings, and faced all obstacles; in humility, sympathy with his brethren, and love for the erring convert like his Master's; in all that wins personal affection and devoted admiration, Francis Xavier is without a superior in the history of missions. If he left no abiding work behind him, let us at least be grateful that we have in his letters at once beacons to warn us from his mistakes, and the picture of a character which has such parallels in the history of the Church as the other Francis, of Assisi, and Raymund Lull.

Bishop Cotton, the most tolerant and impartial of all the Anglican metropolitans, next to Heber, wrote a remarkable letter to Dean Stanley, dated 4th January 1864, after a visit to Goa, in which this passage occurs—"The third church contains Xavier's tomb, and, therefore, all the remaining interest of Goa. The shrine is adorned by four fine bas-reliefs in bronze, representing Xavier preaching, baptizing, persecuted, and dying; and on the top of the shrine, which is very lofty, rests the coffin of solid silver containing his body. Just outside the chapel is a portrait of him, said to be perfectly authentic, and representing a face of marvellous pathos and devotion. I confess, however, that while he deserves the title of Apostle of India for his energy, self-sacrifice, and piety, I consider his whole method thoroughly wrong, its results in India and Ceylon most deplorable, and that the aspect of the native Christians at Goa and elsewhere shows that Romanism has had a fair trial at the conversion of India, and has entirely failed."

This is the criticism of his missionary work by the Abbé Dubois, writing after much experience of the descendants of his nominal converts a century ago—"At last Francis Xavier, entirely disheartened by the innumerable obstacles he everywhere met in his apostolic career, and by the apparent impossibility of making real converts, left the country in disgust."

Xavier's despair of converting adult Asiatics by substituting one ritualistic system for another, drove him, on his first departure from India, to ask John III. of Portugal, on 10th November 1545, the favour of introducing into Goa and his Indian dominions the Holy Office of the Inquisition. That accursed institution, which was devised at the end of the thirteenth century to extirpate the Albigenses, and had been for nearly a century used in Spain to burn recusant Jews and Mohammedans by the infamous Torquemada and like-minded priests, was thought of by Xavier as the only means of exterminating "the Jewish wickedness" which he asserted was daily spreading in Portuguese India.

In 1560 the Inquisition was established at Goa, and it continued its deeds of darkness down to the visit to Goa of Henry Martyn in 1811, when, he tells[1] Lydia Grenfell, "the priest in waiting acknowledged that they had some prisoners within the walls, and defended the practice of imprisoning and chastising offenders on the ground of its

[1] *Henry Martyn, Saint and Scholar.* London, New York, and Chicago, 1892, p. 323.

being conformed to the custom of the Primitive Church." Yes! the history of Christian missions, even of the Church in India, is stained by the use of the tortures of the Inquisition as a weapon. Under British influence it was abolished by the Prince Regent of Portugal in 1816.

Though thus intolerant to the venerable Jewish communities of Western and Southern India, Xavier refers to the Nestorian churches which he visited only in indifferent terms. His call was not to them, but to the non-Christians. Not so the Franciscans, to which order belonged the first Bishop of Goa, Don Juan d'Albuquerque, who in 1545 began those intrigues and persecutions which, followed up by the Jesuits, resulted in the despatch, by Philip II. of Spain, when he had seized the kingdom of Portugal, of Don Aleixo de Menezes as Archbishop of Goa. Twice had the Syrian bishop been shipped to Lisbon, and Mar Simeon, convicted by the Inquisition of the Nestorian heresy, had been declared no bishop and imprisoned. In 1595 Menezes sailed with full powers from Pope Clement VIII. to destroy the independence of the old and comparatively pure Nestorian Church of India. This Christian archbishop's mission was the destruction of Christianity. This much may be said for Portugal, that the time when alike its Church became accursed and its commerce ruined was during "the sixty years' captivity," when from 1580 to 1640 Spain was its master.

Antonio de Gouvea's Portuguese history of the *Mission of Aleixo de Menezes to the Christians of S. Thomas* and the abridgment of the narrative by our own Geddes and Hough, as well as by La Croze[1] in his *Histoire du Christianisme des Indes*, tell a tale of iniquity which we may most fairly characterise in the language of the national historian, the learned and literary Manuel de Faria e Sousa, who, in his *Asia Portuguesa*, ascribes the ruin of all the

[1] La Croze, who was in charge of the Royal Library at Berlin in the first half of the eighteenth century, seems to have been the first to hazard the guess that the various alphabets of India arose from the "Hanscrit" or Sanskrit. The Danish-Halle missionary, Schultze was one of his correspondents.

persons who went to the Indies to their rapacity and wrong-doing: "Whereas God permitted the discovery of this country only for the propagation of His name and the true worship (but not by such barbarous methods as the fore-mentioned, I venture to say), these travellers have for the most part pursued the ends of a sacrilegious covetousness, committing many acts of injustice to fill their coffers, instead of having any regard to religion."

The parallel narrative to this we find in a Mohammedan description of the coast of Malabar by Zeir-ed-deen Mukhdom,[1] translated from the Arabic by Jonathan Duncan, who afterwards died Governor of Bombay. The work brings down the Portuguese history in Malabar to 1579-80. Literally translated, the writer says—

> "The Mussulmans sinned so that God turned from them, and did therefore command the Europeans of Portugal, who oppressed and distressed the Mohammedan community by the commission of unlimited enormities. . . . They also endeavoured to make converts to their own religion, and enjoined churches of their own faith to be consecrated, tempting people for these objects with offers of money; and they dressed out their own women in the finest ornaments and apparel in order thereby to deceive and allure the women of the believers. They did also put Hajjis and other Mussulmans to a variety of cruel deaths . . . and confined the Mohammedans, and loaded them with heavy irons, carrying them about for sale, from shop to shop, as slaves. . . . They confined them also in dark, noisome, and hideous dungeons."

Such were the impressions produced by the missionary work of the Archbishop Menezes, backed by the Inquisition, which ended in the private subscription by the archdeacon who represented the Syrian Church, of ten articles, the meeting of the Synod of Diamper in 1599, and the decadence of Portugal for ever in the East on the capture of Cochin by the Dutch in 1663. Then the old Malabar Christian Church, which had not faith enough to produce martyrs, but had bent for the hour to the Hispano-Papal storm, rose again from the persecution, weakened in spirituality, in numbers, and in prestige, and without

[1] *Asiatic Researches*, vol. v. London Reprint, 1807.

their own prelates from Mosul. Indeed, the Nestorian Church in India ceased in 1599, and when it recovered liberty in 1665 it became, what it has ever since been, Jacobite in creed, under Mar Gregory consecrated and sent by the Patriarch of Antioch. But, by a historical irony, those of the original Church who adhered to the Latin rite, have ever since been known as the Old Church or Catholics of the Syrian rite, while the really independent majority who accepted Mar Gregory and his Jacobite creed are the New Church.

All Francis Xavier's zeal and self-sacrifice, followed up by the intolerance of the Inquisition and the secular power of Portugal, failed, by his own confession, to found a self-propagating Christian Church in India. Condemning his at least honest attempts, his successors devised the policy which resulted in the greatest scandal of all Romanist missions, greater even than the curse of the Inquisition—what was known as the Malabar Rites in South India and the Chinese Rites in North China. If the corrupt Christian system of the Council of Trent had proved too pure, on even Xavier's methods, to win over the people of Portuguese India and make them better, then perhaps an altogether paganised teaching, in which Christianity was disguised as a form of Brahmanism in India and of Buddhism in China, might delude the natives into accepting the faith. By the unconscious or magical sacramentarian influence of the Jesuit Brahmans and Bonzes, the natives might become Christians in spite of themselves. The policy was one of devilish despair, and it ended in rapid defeat. There is, unhappily, no doubt as to the facts. They are to be found, not in the attacks of Protestant controversialists or historians, but in the confessions of the Jesuits themselves, in the careful reports of cardinals, and in the judicial Bulls of Popes. The three Jesuit Fathers, one of whom devised, the second died for, and the third executed the scheme, were by birth and culture the noblest of them all. These were Robert de Nobilibus, John de Britto, and Father Beschi.

When Madura was still the splendid capital of

Tirumala and the Nayak kings of South India, Robert de Nobilibus, grandnephew of a pope and nephew of Cardinal Bellarmine, resolved to win it over to Rome. Fifty years after Xavier's death the profession of Christianity had not spread beyond the poor fishermen (Paravas) around Cape Comorin. The Hindus proper hated the Portuguese, or Parangis, because they lived with such pariah outcasts, because they ate the flesh of the cow, and used intoxicating drinks. But Robert, transmuting the saying of the Apostle who became all things to all men that he might win them to Christ, into the Jesuit doctrine that the end sanctifies the means, determined to appear literally a Hindu that he might save Hindus.[1] Having obtained the sanction of his own Archbishop of Cranganor to the propagation of the living lie that he was a Brahman-prince from Rome and a Saniyasi or Hindu devotee of the strictest profession, he disappeared one day in the Brahman quarter of Madura, where he was waited on by Brahman servants alone. In due time the rumour spread that a holy ascetic from a distant region was hidden in the city, invisible to all because rapt in meditation on God. He had mastered the Hindu ritual and the Tamil language. Gradually the few who were seekers after some new theory, and then the many impelled by curiosity, were admitted to his presence, when they beheld the new Brahman clad and surrounded like the idol Shiva.

The imposture was successful for a time. Converts to the new order were made with a facility common enough in every century under the elastic eclecticism of Brahmanism. The great king Tirumala himself favoured the sage so much as to cease building temples, with the result that the Brahmans awoke to the danger, got rid of their king, and began the persecution of 1693. The most famous victim of this national reaction was John Hector de Britto, a noble of Lisbon, drawn to the missionary's career by the

[1] See the sympathetic and most valuable District Manual, *The Madura Country*, compiled by J. H. Nelson, M.A., of the Madras Civil Service, and late Fellow of King's College, Cambridge, and published by Government, 1868.

example of Francis Xavier. His letters are left to tell us at once of his evil methods and his gentleness under suffering. Retiring to Ceylon from the storm after forty-two years spent in deception so gross, that he made oath upon a forged scroll[1] before the suspicious Brahmans that he had in very truth sprung from the god Brahma, he died finally in a mud hut near the church of St. Thomas, not far from Madras, attended by four Brahmans. He has left several works in the Tamil language, which are praised by experts for the purity of their style and idiom, especially *The Kandam*, a diffuse manual of Jesuit theology, adapted to the taste of the Hindus.

After renewed persecution in 1714, the Madura mission revived under the last and most scholarly of its Jesuit superiors, R. C. J. Beschi, whose Tamil works, and especially his *Tembavani* poem or the *Gospel Mysteries* (1726), is considered a masterpiece of pure style. After him the Society of Jesus was suppressed. The discovery of the lie on which the Madura mission rested resulted in the apostasy of thousands. Christianity became more than ever discredited because its only representatives were the Jesuits of Portugal. The pure Churches of the Reformation were still asleep, or represented abroad only by the early traders of the Dutch and English East India Companies.

The scandals[2] of the Jesuit rites in India, first practised in China by Matteo Ricci, were eagerly reported at Goa and then to Rome by the rival Franciscan and Dominican missionaries. Even Menezes condemned them. Put upon their defence, the Jesuits protested that the rites

[1] The most audacious and skilful of his literary forgeries was the Fifth Veda, best known by its French title *L'Ezour Védam*. Sent from Pondicherry in 1761, it was published in 1778, and so far deceived the learned of Europe, that Voltaire cited its mixture of theistic Brahmanism and Biblical truth as a proof of the superiority of Hinduism to Christianity.

[2] See for the most restrained and judicial account of the Malabar and Chinese Jesuit scandals, the elaborate article in the *Calcutta Review*, vol. ii. (1846) by Dr. Duff's colleague, Dr. W. S. Mackay, a most accomplished scholar and saintly Scottish gentleman.

were only civil observances, contrary neither to faith nor morals, and required for the successful propagation of the Church in India. In 1623 Gregory XV. issued, but only to the accused privately, a "constitution," allowing certain of the objectionable customs on this civil plea, but beseeching them to give up every practice that savoured of heathenism, and to allow of no caste distinction in worship. Till the end of the seventeenth century the Jesuits concealed the document and went on as before. By 1782 the evil had become again so notorious, that Clement XI. sent out the ablest and most honest Italian ecclesiastic of his day, Cardinal de Tournon of Savoy, as legate *a latere* to report, and meanwhile to enforce obedience. He did his work so thoroughly that the Jesuits caused him to perish in a Macao dungeon. This decree of 8th July 1704 exposed and rebuked the semi-paganism of the Madura and afterwards of the Peking missions, but confessed that much had been left still unreformed. It was confirmed in 1706 by the Pope, but Brief after Brief was necessary up to 1745, when the Bull *Omnium Sollicitudinum* of Benedict XIV., following one on the Chinese rites, ended the iniquity, and the Society of Jesus was soon after put down for a time.

Under Portuguese influence chiefly, travellers like Mandelslo and Pietro della Valle, and Romish missionaries of the three chief orders, found their way north and east to Mysore and Agra, conciliating the native rulers. The great Emperor Akbar turned to such for information regarding Christianity, partly to please his Christian wife, and partly to help him in the elaboration of his new religion. Francis Xavier's nephew, Jerome, wrote for him the *Persian Histories of Christ and of the Apostle Peter*, which appeared at Leyden, from the Elzevir press, with a Latin translation and many warning notes by Ludovicus de Dieu. There is a striking passage in the *Ain i Akbari*, the greatest of the Mohammedan histories of India, which Akbar's minister Abulfazl compiled to record the *Ain* or "mode of governing" followed by the mighty Emperor:—

"Learned monks also came from Europe, who go by the name of *Pádre.*[1] They have an infallible head called *Pápá.* He can change any religious ordinances as he may think advisable, and kings have to submit to his authority. These monks brought the gospel and mentioned to the Emperor their proofs for the Trinity. His Majesty firmly believed in the truth of the Christian religion, and wishing to spread the doctrines of Jesus, ordered Prince Murád[2] to take a few lessons in Christianity by way of auspiciousness, and charged Abulfazl to translate the Gospel. Instead of the usual *Bismillah-irrahmán-irrahím,*[3] the following lines were used—

Ai nám i tu Jesus o Kiristo

(O Thou whose names are Jesus and Christ),

which means, 'O thou whose name is gracious and blessed'; and Shaikh Faizi added another half in order to complete the verse—

Subhánaka lá siwáka Yá hú

(We praise Thee, there is no one besides Thee, O God!)

"These accursed monks applied the description of cursed Satan and of his qualities to Mohammed, the best of all prophets—God's blessings rest on him and his whole house!—a thing which even devils would not do." Again Akbar, we are told, in his eclectic worship, while following some Hindu customs to please "the numerous Hindu princesses of the hareem," ordered the ringing of bells as in use with Christians, and the showing of the figure of the cross "and other childish playthings of theirs" daily.

The Jesuit Fathers went as far as Nepal, which they first entered in 1661. The fine library of the Propaganda College at Rome contains several translations into Nepali.

[1] Page 182 of the lamented Professor Blochmann's Translation, vol. i., which he did not live to complete (Calcutta, 1873).

[2] Then about eight years of age.

[3] Formula used by every schoolboy before he begins to read from his text-book.

Southern Asia might have received Christianity under Akbar, as in the tolerant and inquiring days of Chinghiz Khan and his successors Central Asia was open to it, had the Christian Church been alive to the duty and privilege. But its Romanist like its Nestorian representatives again failed. The former did not give the people the Word of God in their own language; they rather travestied its doctrines, obscured its teaching, withheld its self-evidencing revelation.

We need not trace the progress of Papal missions in India, in detail, to the present time. When at Vizagapatam, in North Madras, in 1869, the writer personally studied the working of the Roman Catholic mission there with the aid of the courteous Belgian bishop. He did not guarantee the statistics published in the *Madras Catholic Directory* annually, nor did he say that there was any earnest proselytism or pastoral and educational work among the natives. The truth is, that the Roman Catholic authorities do not collect statistics of the native peoples of India professing the Latin rite with the same accuracy or in the same detail as we find in the decennial returns of the Reformed missionary organisations. But their figures in the gross approach so closely to the results of the Government census that they may be accepted. In British India and its native States in 1891 there were 1,277,926 of a Roman Catholic population. In Portuguese India the number was 281,248, chiefly in Goa. In the little French settlements, principally Pondicheri and Karikal, there were 35,727. The total was thus 1,594,901. Deducting the British soldiers and Eurasians, we may say that there are in India one and a quarter million of Roman Catholic native Christians, dating chiefly from the time of Xavier—though a quarter of a million of these are descendants of the forcibly converted Nestorians—against three quarters of a million of natives belonging to the Reformed Churches. The former do not increase, as the latter do, by active proselytism.

The Papal Church in India is now rent into two divisions—one administered under the old Portuguese right of "padroado," or patronage of all benefices granted by the Popes from 1534 to 1606, and the other under the Propaganda at Rome since 1838, when Gregory XVI. confined the Portuguese jurisdiction to Goa and Daman. His successors vacillated between the conflicting claims, intensifying the schism, till 1886, when the King of Portugal surrendered his undoubted right over the whole of India for a compromise. The matter was the more urgent that the Romanist military chaplains whom we pay were frequently unable to speak a word of English, and even yet, though no longer Portuguese, they are too often Belgians or French-speaking. Still, the relics of power and interference left to the Archbishop of Goa in British territory are so annoying to the British Roman Catholics there that they are perpetually complaining. The Jesuits, once expelled from India, have now large colleges in Bombay and Calcutta and elsewhere affiliated to the Universities. The most interesting communities are those of Agra, Bettia, Gwalior and Sirdhana, which, in origin, go back to the tolerant days of Akbar and his Christian wife.[1]

[1] The latest authoritative figures showing the contributions of the whole Church of Rome for missions to non-Christians are those for 1891, when 6,694,458 francs, or £267,778, was acknowledged, being 378,354 less than in 1890. The official *Illustrated Catholic Missions Magazine* remarks it as noteworthy that more than four millions of the above sum came from France. "Alsace-Lorraine sent 315,000 francs, while all united Germany contributed but 6000 more. Algiers and Tunis and the French population of Mauritius bring the contributions of the Dark Continent to almost five times the amount sent from Asia. In other countries there are found surprising variations. Thus, while Austro-Hungary gives only 80,000 francs, Holland gives nearly 100,000; and while Belgium gives 379,000 francs, Spain contributes less than half that amount. Of the total of 155,380 contributed by the United Kingdom, the largest sum sent by any diocese is that of 24,900 sent by Dublin, the second and third places being taken by Westminster with 17,000 and Cashel with 12,000. But far the largest diocesan subscription is that of Lyons, which amounts to 480,000 francs. Italy subscribed 330,000 francs, and North America 580,000, the larger proportion of which came from Mexico." Although

The whole subject of Romanist missions in India, their principles, methods, and results, was pretty well exhausted in two works, by Abbé Dubois and Cardinal Wiseman, which appeared in 1823 and 1836, and in the answers to these by the Rev. James Hough, whose evidence, also, as given before the Committee of the House of Commons on the 19th July 1832, deserves study. The Abbé Dubois, after thirty years' experience in Mysore as a missionary, published his *Letters on the State of Christianity in India, in which the Conversion of the Hindoos is considered impracticable.* He declares that "the disappointment and want of success of Xavier ought to have been sufficient to damp the most fervent zeal of the persons disposed to enter the same career"; that he himself had toiled in vain; that his brethren had met with no better success than himself, and that the few Protestant missionaries in India up to that time (including Schwartz and Carey, be it remembered,) had altogether failed. He accordingly came to what has been well called the astounding conclusion, that the time of the conversion of India had passed away; that Christianity had done its work in the world; that the six hundred millions of souls, as then estimated, in India and China, Africa and Oceania, in pagan darkness, were to be abandoned to the Almighty's irrevocable decree, which doomed them to perdition. Writing of his own experience, he admitted, "I have made in all two or three hundred

Roman Catholic priests receive State grants for their necessary services as chaplains to the Irish troops, it is Africa, not India, which has of late called forth the missionary zeal of this Church under men with political aims like the late Cardinal Lavigerie, and those who were guilty of the Uganda scandal. "During the year 1891, 309 new missionaries left Europe for the purpose of taking part in the evangelisation of heathen countries. Of these no fewer than 147 were of French nationality, no other country forwarding an equally large contingent. They belonged, moreover, to various religious congregations, that which supplied the most of them being the recently founded congregation of Don Bosco, which sent 72 missionaries to Africa and Patagonia. In the year 1891, 195 nuns of various religious congregations likewise left Europe; while 139 missionaries are reported as having died whilst engaged in missionary labour."

converts of both sexes," but, "I will declare it, with shame and confusion, that I do not remember any one who may be said to have embraced Christianity from conviction and through quite disinterested motives. Among these new converts many apostatised." Cardinal Wiseman, though quoting the Abbé when it suits his object, adopts the opposite opinion, that the whole world is to be converted to Christianity, and that the Romanists alone have been generally successful in their efforts, desiring thus to support the first of the assaults, which continue to the present time with unceasing force, against the Protestantism of Great Britain and America.

Speaking before the House of Commons Committee more than sixty years ago, with modesty, with gravity, and with charity to all, James Hough uttered this prophecy,[1] which, as we shall see hereafter, the Holy Spirit of God, in whose strength he spake, has largely fulfilled and is daily completing:—

"How could we expect a body of people to place their confidence in religious teachers who set out with an imposture? On the other hand, I would account for the success of the Protestant missionaries by reverting to the simplicity of the means which they have used . . . precisely the means that were employed by the primitive teachers of the Christian religion,—I mean, the dissemination of the Word of God, the diligent preaching of that Word, and the education of youth." Then follows the unconscious prophecy now being realised: "*If the missionaries persevered in the course which they have hitherto taken, nothing, with the Divine blessing on their labours, can prevent them from ultimately succeeding in diffusing the Christian religion throughout the vast continent of India.*"

Persecuting intolerance like that embodied in the Inquisition, audacious deceit like that of the Jesuits, were not the only antichristian methods by which the Church of Rome sought the conversion of India. It was the first

[1] Page 131 in Appendix I. to *The Protestant Missions Vindicated against the Aspersions of the Rev. N. Wiseman, D.D., involving the Protestant Religion*, 1837. London.

to apply deliberately, on a great scale, the motive of worldly interest. Writing in 1546 to the Viceroy of Goa, John III. of Portugal laid down this principle: "Pagans may be brought over to our religion not only by the hopes of salvation, but also by temporal interest and preferment." The order accordingly went forth that professing converts were to be provided with places in the Customs, to be exempted from impressment for the navy, and to be maintained by the distribution of rice from the public revenue. In peninsular India it was not easy to carry this into effect. But in Ceylon the Buddhist character, so obsequious to power and indifferent to conscience, was at once caught by the material bribes, while the Tamil immigrants from the opposite coast and the fishermen of the Gulf of Manaar accepted the teaching of Xavier, and have ever since clung to it as raising them in the social scale. Sir Emerson Tennent is satisfied with the evidence that, within a very few years of its occupation by the Portuguese in 1548, almost the entire population of the Jaffna province of Ceylon, including even the Brahmans, had submitted to be baptized.[1]

In 1658 the Dutch ejected the Portuguese from the fortress of Jaffna, but developed on a still greater scale the policy of securing the nominal profession of Christianity as the price of office and worldly advantage. There is no nobler page in history than that which records the heroic and successful struggles of the United Provinces against Philip II. of Spain, nor can the services of the house of Orange to the spiritual and political liberties of Great Britain and Ireland be ever forgotten. It was Queen Elizabeth's recognition of the Dutch Republic as against Spain that led to the founding of the London East India Company, and started the commercial and political movement which has given us our Indian Empire. The first of the Protestant peoples to trade with the East, the Dutch, determined that the Presbyterian Church should become a missionary propaganda to the races of India. For this purpose Hugo Grotius wrote his great work,

[1] *Christianity in Ceylon.* London (John Murray), 1850.

De Veritate Religionis Christianæ, which was translated into the principal European languages as well as Arabic.[1] Ten years before the Propaganda College at Rome was established, or in 1612, Walæus founded in the University of Leyden, itself the first fruit of freedom, a college for the training of missionaries. In the two centuries from Grotius and Walæus to Vanderkemp, the friend of Henry Martyn, little Holland sent forth remarkable missionaries. But what the treatises of the eighteenth century described as "their High Mightinesses the illustrious States-General of the Free United Netherlands and mighty Dutch East India Company,"[2] or their administrators and merchants in the Indies, were always more careful as to their commercial advantages than their spiritual calling.

The Dutch, as they destroyed the power of Spain and Portugal in India, found the spice trade so enormously valuable that they sought to monopolise it in the islands of the Eastern Archipelago, and so both directly and indirectly led the English to confine their principal settlements to the peninsula of India proper. In Formosa, where, till their expulsion by Chinese pirates in 1661, their missionaries began a spiritual work;[3] in Amboyna, stained by their massacre of the English; in Java, Celebes, and Sumatra, which was given up to them after Lord Minto's expedition and the hopeful administration of Sir Stamford Raffles, the Netherlands East Indian Company exploited the populations under the famous culture system

[1] From Lipstadt prison Grotius sent forth his book, in which he writes: "My design was to undertake something which might be useful to my countrymen, especially seamen, who in their long voyages will everywhere meet either with Pagans, as in China or Guinea; or Mohammedans, as in the Turkish and Persian Empires, and in the kingdoms of Fez and Morocco; and also with Jews, who are the professed enemies of Christianity, and are dispersed over the greatest part of the world." See Dean Clarke's translation (1805) of Le Clerc's edition.

[2] See Aitchison's *Collection*, vol. v. page 501, for the last treaty made with the King of Kandy or Ceylon in 1766.

[3] See *Missionary Success in Formosa*. London, 1889.

denounced by some of the more patriotic Hollanders at home. The Netherlands and the Rhenish societies conducted missions there with varying success since the English withdrawal under the treaty of 1824. But it is true of South-Eastern as of Western Asia, that Islam has spread its baneful half-civilisation because of the failure of the Christian Churches.

In India proper the Dutch settlements were isolated and few, on or near the coast at Cochin,[1] Negapatam, Palakollu, and Sadras, and at Chinsurah on the Hoogli River above Calcutta, where Clive brought their influence to an end in 1759. It was to their Governor of Palakollu, opposite Ceylon, in 1636, that the King of Kandy sent an invitation to help him to expel the Portuguese. In 1642, six years after, the Reformed Church of Holland was established as the religion of the new colony. The State, and that a foreign power seeking commercial profit through a monopoly company, established its own Church, with the inevitable results of intolerance rising to persecution, especially of its Roman Catholic predecessor, and a widespread hypocrisy with an equally extensive apostasy on the removal of the State pressure. In the veracious pages of Baldæus, one of the first Dutch missionaries, we can trace the wholesale unspiritual process, by which, with only two colleagues to help him where there had been forty priests, in the northern province of Jaffna, the number of native "converts" from Hinduism was reported as "exceeding 180,000," though the candid admission was made that "they still retained many of the superstitions of paganism." In the southern provinces the Buddhists were told by *plakaat*, or proclamation, that baptism, communion in the State Church, and subscription to the Helvetic Confession, were essential preliminaries not only to appointment to office, but even to farming land.

In every village the schoolhouse became the church,

[1] *The Land of the Permauls; or, Cochin its Past and its Present*, by the distinguished naturalist, Francis Day, F.L.S., of the Madras Medical Service (Madras, 1863), contains the best account of the Dutch in India proper, based on the official records.

and the schoolmaster the registrar of documents involving the rights and succession to property. The number of children under instruction and baptized rose to 85,000. Nowhere was there any evidence of genuine conversion, nor were there missionaries sufficient to give simple instruction in Christian truth. In despair some resorted to attempts to forcibly suppress Buddhism, and others appealed to the Church at home. In 1700 the Classis of Amsterdam remonstrated with the Consistory of Colombo, reminding it that compulsion can never generate conviction, nor penalties inculcate belief. At a later date the Classis declared the converts to be *sine Christo Christiani*, so few were communicants, so many were idolaters. Not one had been a Moorman or Mohammedan, all were Tamils or Singhalese. When the English conquest of the Dutch settlements in India in 1782 was followed in 1796 by the permanent occupation of Ceylon, the articles of capitulation stipulated that "the clergy and other ecclesiastical servants shall continue in their functions and receive the same pay and emoluments as they had from the (Dutch) Company."

The Dutch Reformed Church left nearly half a million [1] professing converts in Ceylon, or a fourth of the population at that time, and only fourteen clergy. As soon as these Asiatics realised the fact that the British Government, under the benevolent administration of the Hon. Mr. North, afterwards Earl of Guilford, disowned intolerance in religion while enthusiastic as to education, and abolished the Dutch penal laws against Roman Catholics, the half-million disappeared. Till 1816 the Article of Capitulation was observed so far that the Dutch ministers were reinforced by young divines from Edinburgh, while episcopal congregations were placed under the see of Calcutta, and ultimately under a bishop of their own, now no longer a state functionary. In 1806 Claudius Buchanan on his visit pronounced the Reformed Christianity to be extinct in Ceylon. Writing in 1850 Sir Emerson Tennent

[1] At the same time the "converts" in Java were reported to be 100,000.

declared that of the many planted by Baldæus and Valentyn, and even by the great Schwartz during a year's visit, not a single congregation existed.

Portugal, Holland, and France in India, like France in America, made the mistake of seeking to extend their limits without securing a foothold before taking further steps, and so their outlying settlements were cut off and they lost India.

The first attempt of the Reformed Church towards the conversion of India was as lamentable a failure as that of the preceding Romanists and Nestorians, because it proceeded on similarly false and unchristian methods. "Such things are not of Christ, nor calculated to advance His kingdom," as the Amsterdam Classis sadly bewailed, but in vain. Not so are idolatry and caste, the Buddhist nihilism, the Mohammedan fanaticism, the Parsee dualism, and the Jewish blindness to be overcome, and self-propagating Churches and spiritual communities called out and built up into Christian nations. Like Francis Xavier, Baldæus and his fellows preached through interpreters. The watchwords of the missionary must be these—the vernacular Bible, vernacular preaching, daily teaching, the conversion of the individual, that he may in turn aggressively propagate the faith which he has received. Where these have been so long and persistently applied under the continual sense of the influence and aid of the Spirit sent by Christ to enable His disciples to do greater works than even those of His public ministry, Christianity necessarily triumphs, is consolidated and becomes the life of nations and of races all down the centuries, for it is the assured hope and stimulus of every true believer.

So apostolic Christianity swept away the paganism of Greece and of Rome. So post-apostolic Christianity won over the northern nations. So the teaching of John the divine and Paul the apostle of the nations, in particular, early seized all the powers of the Scots of Ireland and Iona, through them transformed the Saxons and the Germans, and sent forth the swarms of the English-speaking peoples west and south and east. It was possible for whole tribes to follow their chief down into the waters of baptism, for they at once joined an organisation which absorbed them and their children in a generation. But where, as in the far East, in Cathay and India proper, and Farther India, heathenism was, and is still apparently, a compact mass bound together by caste and ritual, and Islam is a brotherhood fanatical in its conceit, nothing short of the transformation by the Spirit of God of each separate convert will suffice for the first story of the living temple which is to grow upward and outward from the Rock, till all nations flow into it. The same spiritual influence, the same sweet persuasion which swept away paganism in four centuries will alone, but most certainly, destroy the lie of Mohammedanism and the idolatry of the East.

V

THE BRITISH EAST INDIA COMPANY'S WORK OF PREPARATION

"*The law was our schoolmaster to bring us unto Christ.*"—GAL. iii. 24.

THREE hundred years ago, at the close of the sixteenth century, the conversion of India seemed more distant than in the third, when the post-apostolic missionary Pantænus left his college at Alexandria for the primitive Christian settlements in Malabar. At times, in the intervening centuries, all Asia had been open to the European with the divine message intrusted to him for its proclamation, as inner Asia is not open even now. Yet Buddhism on the one side and Mohammedanism on the other had proved to be the successful missionary religions from Peking to Ceylon, and from Constantinople right across the continent to Malaysia. The Greek and the Latin Churches had added two small sects to the multitude whom Brahmanism tolerated and disarmed, since the elder Aryans first crossed the Indus on their southward march. That was all. The Reformation of the Latin Church had, meanwhile, been doctrinally completed in Europe, and the Dutch Protestants had begun their attempt to Christianise the natives of the farther East on lines almost as contrary to those of Jesus Christ as their predecessors. Each of the three organised missions had come short of that which went before it. The Nestorian departed from the orthodox teaching of Alexandria, and, by adopting a compromise as to the person of Christ, ceased to be aggressive, yet was itself always tolerant, and remained true to its Persian faith. The Roman began by deceiving and persecuting first the Nestorian, then the Mohammedan, and then the Hindu, till the Papal supremacy which was thus propagated led to the disappearance of the political power of Portugal in the East almost altogether. The Dutch experiment, especially in Ceylon, exhausted the evil methods of spreading any faith or any truth. So far as the millions of Asia were concerned, Christians had discredited the name and the claims of Jesus Christ on every man whose nature He, in His love and in His pity, had taken to redeem him.

The English were now, in God's providence, led all unconsciously to take the first step in the extension of the kingdom described by its Founder as "not of this world." The Scottish patriots and reformers had taught England and the world the true principles of civil and religious liberty.[1] Elizabeth, forced into the position of the defender of these liberties against the Papal League, had broken the power of Spain, and had helped to independence the Dutch, a little nation of sailors and traders who speedily made their way to the East. Then in 1599 they raised the price of pepper against the English from three shillings to eight shillings a pound. This was too much for the Lord Mayor and merchants of London, who resolved to form an association of their own for direct trade with India, and induced the Queen to send Sir John Mildenhall by Constantinople to the Great Mogul to secure privileges for the new company.[2] On the last day of the year 1600, in the forty-third year of her reign, Queen Elizabeth signed the first charter creating "one Body Corporate and Politick, in Deed and in Name, by the name of the *Governor and Company of Merchants of London trading into the East Indies,*" and nominating Alderman Thomas Smith as

[1] See Hill Burton's *History*.

[2] See Sir George Birdwood's *Report on Old Records in the India Office*.

first Governor with twenty-four "committees" or directors, all to be elected annually thenceforth by the shareholders, then a hundred and twenty-five in number, with a capital of £70,000. Out of the vindication of spiritual liberty by Scots, Hollanders, and English, and because of the monopoly price of pepper, there sprang *the* East India Company. So out of the American vindication of liberty and the cargo of the Company's tea in Boston harbour there leapt into independence the United States. Thus, "by a way that they knew not," by a strange irony, were the two English-speaking peoples first prepared for the conversion of India.

The England of Elizabeth's day did not think of its duty to the peoples of the East any more than the Reformed Churches of Europe at that time, although the charters granted to the proprietary colonies in America did recognise the call to give the gospel to the Indians. The new East India Company's charter provided only "that they at their own Adventures, Costs, and Charges, as well for the Honour of this our Realm of *England* as for the Increase of our Navigation and Advancement of Trade of Merchandise with our said Realms and the Dominions of the same, might adventure to set forth one or more Voyages . . . . in the Countries and Parts of *Asia* and *Africa* . . . . to the benefit of our Commonwealth." We search the twenty-four printed quarto pages of that first charter [1] in vain for any allusion to the natives of these regions, among which Africa is specially mentioned, or to any other object than commerce. But none the less did that document start all who use the speech and read the literature of Queen Elizabeth's days on the missionary enterprise. The East India Company lasted 257 years, during one-half of which it was a trading, and during the other half a political and administrative organisation, while all through its history, when it departed from the principles of toleration, it was hostile to Christian missions

[1] *Charters granted to the East India Company from* 1601, *also the Treaties and Grants made with and obtained from the Princes and Powers in India from the year* 1756 to 1772.

from a blinded selfishness. Yet it was used by the Sovereign Ruler of the human race to prepare the way and open wide the door for the first hopeful and ultimately assuredly successful attempt, since the apostolic Church swept away paganism, to destroy the idolatrous and Musalman cults of Asia.

The greatest legal intellect of this generation, Sir Henry Sumner Maine, who has recently passed away, recognised this when, in December 1857,[1] writing on the extinction of the East India Company, then under discussion and effected on the 1st November 1858, he exclaimed: "That Board of Administrators, which traces its pedigree to a company of merchants, just as the most famous and durable polity of the Middle Ages was born among the traffickers of the Venetian lagunes! The East India Company, it would be impossible to reflect without emotion on the extinction of so mighty a name! That wonderful succession of events which has brought the youngest civilisation of the world to instruct and correct the oldest, which has reunited those wings of the Indo-European race which separated in the far infancy of time to work out their strangely different missions, which has avenged the miscarriage of the Crusades by placing the foot of the most fervently believing of Christian nations on the neck of the mightiest of Mahometan dynasties, will inevitably be read by posterity as the work not of England, but of the English East India Company."

Queen Elizabeth's charter of 1600 was renewed, amplified, modified by charters and letters patent by James I., Charles I., Cromwell, Charles II.—who sought to obliterate all trace of the great Protector's action—William III., under whom, in 1709, it became "The United Company of Merchants of England trading to the East Indies," in return for heavy loans to the State for its monopoly, and thereafter by Parliament every twenty years till 1853, the last. These charters mark the successive victories of free trade and toleration, through which Christianity for the first time in the history of

[1] *The Saturday Review.*

India took its place as the one divine religion, and because divine, to be commended to every man's conscience by its own self-evidencing authority, and sweet persuasiveness alone. No sovereignty with physical force, no Church with inquisition tortures, no republic with equally intolerant enforcement by self-interest, but a company royally chartered to bring an empire to the birth, and create for the Christian Church, as for all cults, an environment of law and order, of peace and liberty, of fair play and neutrality, such as even the Roman Empire never secured! The "Pax Britannica" and all that it involves for India began with the charter of Queen Elizabeth. We may more accurately describe what Christian Britain and America have done and are doing for the peoples of the East, as the "Pax Evangelica."

The royal prerogative of granting by charter powers and privileges not inconsistent with the law of the land, and generally in later times confirmed by Parliament, has never been exercised with such beneficent results, not even in our own days when British Borneo and British Africa have similarly received the protecting and civilising influence of the empire. In India three centuries ago the chartered company preceded the evangelical missionary, at a time when vital, aggressive Christianity was under eclipse, and consequently was long in asserting its inherent right to go everywhere subject to the powers that be, but in defiance of them if their orders conflicted with those of the Kingdom that is universal and everlasting. In Africa, in the last half of the nineteenth century, the missionary has, happily, gone before traders and administrators, taking his life in his hand and opening up regions the white man never knew, for which the politicians have scrambled. This we owe to one man, David Livingstone, and to that foresight of his which was misunderstood by his own missionary society. It is inevitable that settled government should follow the missionary among barbarian peoples as they begin to receive Christianity. The late Sir William Mackinnon's British East Africa Company has saved Uganda, and given hope to that continent from the

Indian Ocean to the Nile. The Niger and South African Companies and the Borneo Company are blessings to the native peoples under their influence. But none of them, even with all the advantages of the present day, approach in value and importance the East India Company, of which they are in a sense the offspring.

In the two and a half centuries from the great Queen Elizabeth to the greater Queen-Empress Victoria the Chartered Company was a happy device, and was on the whole happily worked, to prepare both the varied millions of India and their ultimate rulers in the West to come face to face with each other at the set time of God's providence. In the Mutiny of 1857, the last remaining elements of disorder and crime—in removing which the East India Company had spent a period equal to that of the Roman Empire between the fall of Jerusalem and the elevation of Constantine, while it consolidated a progressive empire—burst forth and were swiftly extinguished. Sir Alfred Lyall, the latest and the ablest writer on India, represents the Chartered Company as invented to suit the conditions of existence at the close of the sixteenth century in Europe and the East, "for extending commerce, and for securing it by territorial appropriations, without directly pledging a government to answer for the acts of its subjects."[1] John Stuart Mill, the greatest political thinker of the last generation, whose father, the historian, drafted many of the East India Company's despatches in Leadenhall Street, where Charles Lamb also was a clerk, devotes the last chapter of his *Representative Government*[2] to a discussion of the Government of Dependencies by a Free State. Even that cultured Radical lamented the extinction of the East India Company, and the substitution for it of uninformed party government in distant London. It has been the destiny of the Company, he writes, "to suggest the true theory of the government of a semi-barbarous dependency by a civilised country, and, after having done this, to perish."

[1] See *The Rise of the British Dominion in India.* London, John Murray, 1893.

[2] London, 1861.

In its relation to the propagation of Christianity the East India Company reflected the opinion and the action of England itself. So long as it was a purely trading organisation, it was careful to give instructions for the moral good of its own officials and was indifferent to that of the natives. It was tolerant of, it even helped missionaries like Schwartz and Kiernander up to the time of Clive. But as it grew to be a territorial and political power its servants practically encouraged the native faiths, and kept out Christian missionaries under the rules passed to protect the monopoly of trade against interlopers. Schwartz, indeed, was honoured, and the Company erected his marble tomb in Madras, but at the very same time Carey was smuggled into Bengal in a Danish ship, and was suffered to remain only as an indigo planter with a license. Up to the charter of 1833 passports were necessary for a missionary like Alexander Duff. The Company's opposition to missions, indeed, became virulent so late as 1807, and after the Vellore Mutiny, when some were deported, with the providential result that Judson took the gospel to Burma, and others to Ceylon and the Indian Archipelago. "They that preached the word were scattered abroad."

Let us look at the process. From the first the Directors of the East India Company recognised and enforced their duty to their own servants by sending them many good counsels and a few chaplains.[1] The commanders of the little ships used in the first five voyages to the East, measuring from 130 to 600 tons,—men like Lancaster, Middleton, and Keeling, who in 1607 carried King James's first ambassador, Hawkins, to Jahangir at Agra,—were exhorted "first to depend confidentlie upon Godes providence," to see to the due execution of religious worship, setting apart "certeine hours and tymes in every day for publique prayer and calling on the name of God, and to put down blasphemy, idle and filthy communications and dice-playing." When on the defeat of the Portuguese fleet by Captain Best, leader of the tenth voyage in 1612, the first

[1] Sir George Birdwood has done service by editing *The Register of Letters of the Company from 1600 to 1619.* (Quaritch) 1893.

English factory was founded at Surat, and afterwards at Madras, Hoogli, and Calcutta, a chaplain was settled at each. The first with whose name we meet was Henry Lord, so early as 1616. A good as well as an able man, he was induced to leave one of the English ships for the Surat Factory, where he found another chaplain, named Lescke. Lord was the first of all Orientalists in point of time, for he carefully studied the literature and mythology of the Hindu, Mohammedan, and Parsee communities;[1] and Sir Thomas Herbert and Bernier acknowledge their indebtedness to him.

He is described as "preacher to the Honourable Company of Merchants"; and in Kerridge, the governor, he found a man of like mind. At the same time one Joseph Salbank was sent to Agra as Company's factor there. A shrewd and honest but illiterate person, he showed himself a true missionary when he wrote home, urging the Company to send out "not only solid and sufficient divines that may be able to encounter with the arch-enemies of our religion, but also godly, zealous, and devout persons, such as may, by their piety and purity of life, give good example to those with whom they live." The next vacancy at Surat that occurred was caused by the death of the Rev. John Hall, Fellow of Corpus Christi, Oxford, and he was succeeded by Mr. Terry, who was chaplain of the embassy of Sir Thomas Roe. His narrative is most honourable to his character. He is the author of the too true report, that the natives said of the English, whom alone they knew, "Christian religion, devil religion; Christian much drunk; Christian much do wrong; much beat; much abuse others." Sir Thomas Roe wrote in the same strain, often protesting against the despatch of hopeless young men and the arrival of runaway adventurers for whom he had to provide. It is sad to read of a

[1] *A Display of Two Foraigne Sects in the East Indies, vizt. the Sect of the Banians, the Ancient Natives of India, and the Sect of the Persees, the Ancient Inhabitants of Persia, together with the Religion and Manners of each Sect, Collected into two Bookes.* By Henry Lord. Imprinted at London for Francis Constable, 1630.

Herbert, one of the Earl of Pembroke's and the saintly George Herbert's blood, thus shipped out to India. All that can be said in apology for the lives of the first English traders in the East is, that they were no worse than the class to which they belonged at home under the Stewarts.

When Cromwell guided affairs devout men were no longer afraid to show their religion, even in India, and the despatches savoured of Puritanism. The letters to the Court of Directors at this period always end with some such formula as "commending you to God's merciful guidance." The report of the death of a factor is followed by the words, "God of His mercy so direct our hearts, who must follow him, that we may be always ready for the like sudden summons." When governors of good family and high character were in power, like Oxenden, Aungier, and Streynsham Masters, the chaplain was next in precedence to members of council, and his pay was in proportion. Prayers were offered morning and evening in the factory, and thrice on Sunday, when at least one sermon was preached. But the practice of the English was still after the approved fashion of the *Book of Sports*. The sermon was followed by shooting and gambling in the suburbs. The Dutch were the only foreign power who took care to provide wives for their servants. The Portuguese allied themselves with the natives, and the result is seen now in the degradation of the race.

Not till 1681 was the first English church begun in India. The good Oxenden had raised money, and had also appealed to the Directors for a building in which the English should worship, and the natives "observe the purity and gravity of our devotions." He passed away, but his successor Aungier did not let the project drop. He looked forward to the time when "the merciful pleasure of God should touch the natives with a sense of the eternal welfare of their souls." But Sir John Child is said to have made away with the £5000 collected for the purpose, and it was not till three-quarters of a century later that, in 1718, St. Thomas's Cathedral was erected at Bombay. Aungier's friend, Streynsham Masters, however, was promoted to be chief at Madras, and there he built a church at his own cost, unconsecrated, and described by a visitor in 1703 as a large pile of arched buildings. It is to the administration of that good man that we owe such orders as these in the *Madras Records* of 1678, although the Second Charles was reigning: "Forasmuch as, by persons of all professions, the name of God ought to be hallowed, His service attended upon, and His blessing upon men's endeavours sought by daily prayers, as the quality therefore of our place and imployment requires, and in discharge of our duty both to God and man—First, we doe Christianly admonish every one imployed in the service of the Honorable English East India Company to abandon lying, swearing, curseing, drunkenness, uncleanness, prophanation of the Lord's day, and all other sinfull practices, and not to sleep, be drunk, or abusive upon or absent from their watch, or from their houses or quarters late at night, nor absent from or neglect morning and evening Prayers, nor committ any offence to the dishonor of Almighty God, the corruption of good manners, or against the peace of the government." Again, this entry occurs: "Nine boys that repeated the Catechism by heart in the Chapel on the Lord's day, to have 2 rupees each for their encouragement, according to the Honorable Company's order."

When the "English Company" was established in opposition to the East India Company's monopoly, and each appealed against the other to the King and to Parliament, the new corporation finally prevailed, and in 1698 obtained a charter, which applied to both when in 1708 they united. The document is of great value from its provisions for an educational and a missionary as well as a religious establishment. A schoolmaster and minister were to be maintained in every garrison and superior factory, a decent place was to be set aside for divine worship, and every ship of 500 tons burden was to carry a chaplain. The clergy were to be approved by the Archbishop of Canterbury or Bishop of London, and were to be treated with respect. All were to learn Portuguese within a year after their arrival, and were to study the vernacular language, "the better to enable them to instruct the Gentoos, that shall be the servants or slaves of the same Company, or of their agents, in the Protestant religion." In the first century of the Company's settlements in India the whole number of chaplains did not exceed nineteen—a small number, if we reflect on the terrible mortality of European life in the East in these early times. On the accession of William the factors in Western India had not one chaplain, and begged their masters to send them "two good orthodox ministers," along with "a little good English beer, as they call stout, and a little wine from your honours."

A few years before the charter of King William, the East India Company's agent at the Bengal Factory of Hoogli, having quarrelled with the local authorities, moved down the river of that name some thirty miles to the village of Kalkatta, so called from the adjoining temple of the devouring Kali, which is still the most famous Hindu shrine in the country. It was on the 20th December 1686, and under the last of the great emperors of Delhi, Aurangzeb, that the English took possession of the spot destined to form a century after the metropolis, not merely of British India, but of Southern Asia, with a present population of a million of souls. In due time Fort William was built, and named in honour of the king. By 1710, when there were 1200 English, consisting of the troops, the civilians, the sailors, and some private merchants residing there, and when in one year 460 burials had been registered in the clerk's book of mortality, the residents subscribed for the erection of a handsome church. A visitor of those days represents the chief persons in the Fort as regular in their observance of the public worship of God. But the lives led by the majority of the residents may be imagined from the orders of the Court of Directors, who sent out strict rules for the conduct of their subordinates, and also directed the use of a form of prayer, beseeching God "that these Indian nations, amongst whom we dwell, seeing our sober and righteous conversation, may be induced to have a great esteem for our most holy profession of the gospel."

The new Protestant church did not prosper. The cyclone of 1737, accompanied by an earthquake, levelled its spire, and the chaplains died so rapidly, that young merchants were allowed an addition of £50 a year to their salary to read prayers and a sermon every Sunday. Captain Alexander Hamilton, who spent the period from 1688 to 1723 in travelling by sea and land between the Cape and Japan, draws this picture of the ecclesiastical affairs of the place—"In Calcutta all religions are tolerated but the Presbyterians, and they are browbeat. The pagans carry their idols in procession through the town. The Roman Catholics have their church to lodge their images in, and the Mohammedans are not discountenanced; but there are no polemics except what are between our High Churchmen and our Low." In 1756 old Calcutta was swept away by Sooraj-ood-Dowlah. St. John's Church, to which the governor, the civilians, and the troops had walked in procession, was destroyed. Of its two chaplains, one, the Rev. Jervis Bellamy, was found lying dead among the victims of the Black Hole tragedy, hand-in-hand with his son, a young lieutenant. The other, the Rev. R. Mapletoft, had escaped down the river, but there only to die with many more of malarious fever.

The next thirty years proved as sad a time for religion in Bengal as they were remarkable for the conquests of Clive and Warren Hastings. The compensation exacted for the loss of the church was applied to the foundation of the free school for the illegitimate children of the residents. The Protestants, the Portuguese Catholics, and the Armenians worshipped all that time in thatched chapels. There were chaplains, but few cared to attend the services. The population, of whom some 2000 were Europeans, grew to half a million, for whose instruction nothing was done. Even our own soldiers were neglected, for it happened more than once that profane commanding officers refused to allow a sermon to be preached to them. Tennant, a military chaplain, wrote: "It must happen that many persons have left England at an early age, and resided in India for twenty or thirty years, without once having heard divine service till their return." Even later than this, Dr. Claudius Buchanan was not allowed to preach, save in his own house, during the three years that he was chaplain to the troops at Barrackpore, within twelve miles of Calcutta. But few were like Claudius Buchanan.

Lord Teignmouth, when Governor-General, reported to the Court of Directors thus in 1795:—"Our clergy in Bengal, with some exceptions, are not respectable characters. Their situation is arduous, considering the general relaxation of morals from which a black coat is no security." The truth is, the chaplains had been as badly paid as the rest of the Company's servants, so that they were driven to private trade, and even gambling, to live. Gradually their salary had been raised from £50 to £230 a year. and in 1764 an addition of £120 was made because of the great increase of expenses in Calcutta. They had shares in Clive's monopolies of salt, betel-nut, and tobacco, which enabled some of them to retire with fortunes rising to £50,000. An undoubtedly able and evangelical minister, the Rev. John Owen, who was a friend of Cecil, came home with £25,000 after ten years' service. And if such were the ministers and the laity in and around the capital, where the Governor-General himself, Warren Hastings, and his malicious colleague, Sir Philip Francis, lived openly in adultery, what shall we say then of the lives of officers, civil and military, in the far-out stations? Many had zananas, where, as one described it, they allowed their numerous black wives to run about picking up a little rice, while they pleased them by worshipping their favourite idol.

All this time and up to the close of the eighteenth century, when Wellesley became Governor-General, the East India Company had been laying the foundations of an empire amid the chaotic ruins of Aurangzeb's. It was no blind chance that led its administrators in India, from the time when Calcutta, Madras, and Bombay stood forth as the independent centres of a power that enlisted its own sepoys and white soldiers, that collected revenue from land and customs, and coined money in its own name. Clive and Warren Hastings, at least, were deliberate conquerors, and by no means stumbled into empire. From Mohammedan intolerance, from Maratha savagery, and from French Catholicism of the type that had failed in Portugal's hands, and has failed elsewhere up to our own day as in Algeria, Central Africa, and Anam, they saved the peoples of India. It was not for such men to do more; and they did that with a pure patriotism and a stern courage which place them higher in the history of the evolution of Christian empire than any of those who attacked them—than any contemporary statesmen up to George Washington. He indeed did a similar, and in one sense a parallel work in the West under very different conditions, both as to the white and the dark races, and his personal character made him nobler than they.

Meanwhile, as the outward fabric of imperial order and law was being painfully founded and slowly built up by the Company's servants all through the eighteenth century, the good seed of the kingdom of Christ, free from tares, and destined to grow into the great harvest of the conversion of India, was silently sown under Danish protection from Tranquebar on the Madras coast, and afterwards from Serampore in the Gangetic valley. On 9th July 1706, after the territory had been in the possession of the Danish East India Company for eighty-five years, the Pietists Ziegenbalg and Plütschau landed in India. They at first found the Danish officials as hostile to evangelical religion as the British and the Lutherans continued to be. On "Lord's day, October 13th, 1799," Marshman and Ward, soon after joined by William Carey, landed at Danish Serampore. All through that century "the coast mission," as it was called, in South India had made Christ known in His fulness alike by the Tamil Bible, the Christian school, incessant preaching in the towns and villages, and public services amid English, French, and native wars, till the name of Schwartz the missionary, who died in 1798, was the most honoured in the East. Ward, editor and printer, when Carey took up the mantle of Schwartz, declared God's revelation of Jesus Christ, printed, preached and taught, so as to work a supernatural change in the faith and life of each honest receiver under the influence of the Spirit of God, to be the only effectual means of the conversion of India. "With a Bible and a press," were his first words, "posterity will see that a missionary will not labour in vain even in India." Hannah Marshman for the first time began to make the revelation known to its women. There remained to be supplied only the other missionary method, that of healing, to realise amid the dumb millions of the peoples of India the fulness of the love and the purity of the teaching and the example of the Son of Man.

Twice in the East India Company's history had the skilful services of its surgeons, Boughton and Hamilton, to the Mohammedan emperors or their families, secured additions to the British territory and influence. Now there appeared the first medical missionary. We read in the *Indian Gazette* of 1st November 1783, an advertisement for a Christian. The advertiser was John Thomas, surgeon on board of the "Earl of Oxford" East Indian, who afterwards induced Carey to accompany him to Bengal, and died at Serampore. Good John Newton saw that advertisement in England, and accepted it as a proof that there were religious stirrings in the country. There were two answers, one from the chaplain of the day, the Rev. W. Johnson, who soon after left India with £35,000. He had so preached that Thomas said, "the sermon as well as the text was 'The Unknown God,'" and did not reply to him. The second response advised the opening of a subscription for a translation of the New Testament into Persian and the vernacular. There were, however, at least three godly men among the officials of that day, Charles Grant, George Udny, who succeeded him as Company's agent at Malda where he gave Carey an asylum, and William Chambers, Master in Chancery in the Supreme Court, who used to call the English Calcutta and the Dutch Batavia, Sodom and Gomorrah.

Charles Grant was born in 1746, and went out to Bengal, first as a merchant, and then as a civil servant. When living in Calcutta as we have already described it, and about thirty years of age, he says, "I was brought under deep concern about the state of my soul. There was no person then living there from whom I could obtain any information as to the way of a sinner's salvation." He went to Kiernander, a missionary whom Clive had invited from Cuddalor to Calcutta. "I found him lying on a couch. My anxious inquiries as to what I should do to be saved appeared to embarrass and confuse him exceedingly; and when I left him, the perspiration was running from his face in consequence, as it appeared to me, of his mental distress. He could not answer my questions, but he gave me some good instructive books." Grant had suffered domestic affliction, being one of the few civilians who had brought out with him his wife, her mother, and sister. Mr. William Chambers, who had been influenced by the great Schwartz, married the sister, and a Mr. O'Beck, a pupil of Schwartz, became Mr. Grant's steward. Not only Mr. Udny's mother, but the mother of Sir Robert and William Chambers, joined them in India at this time. A Christian society was thus formed, and Christian family life was thus exhibited, probably for the first time in India, with the happiest results. The Serampore missionaries found a home and congenial spirits ready for them. The Rev. David Brown too, of Magdalen College, Cambridge, was sent out to superintend the Military Orphan Society's Schools, and he became an evangelical chaplain. Even before Thomas had laid hold of Carey, Mr. Grant had projected a mission of gospel ministers from England to India, and Brown had named eight students at home as fit persons. Before the immortal three of Serampore had landed in the country, Mr. Chambers, being officially Persian interpreter, had begun a translation of the Scriptures. Mr. Grant was himself to support two of the eight missionaries on £240 a-year each, with books and teachers besides. Simeon of Cambridge was formally asked to become their agent, and it seemed as if the Church of England would be the first to do its duty. The application bore good fruit, though at a later time, in the birth of the Church Missionary Society and the arrival of such chaplains as Martyn and Corrie. Meanwhile Carey was on his way to Danish protection at Serampore, where the two sets of ardent evangelical men met often in after days for prayer and loving conference, now in the deserted pagoda which still bears Martyn's name, and now in Brown's cool retreat of Aldeen, between that and the Serampore mission-house.

While thus working through Simeon at home, Charles Grant, now a member of his Council, approached Lord Cornwallis on the subject. That Governor-General had introduced into English society a reign of apparent morality at least. Would he support a mission to the natives? All that could be got from him was the assurance that he would not oppose it. He had no belief in the conversion of the people of India, they were too bad for that! But his neutrality, which in some of his successors, down even to Lord Canning's days after the Mutiny, became cold and occasionally active opposition, encouraged Grant to send for the two missionaries whom he was ready to support. They were to study the languages and literature of the natives for three years at Benares, "after which they may begin their glorious work of giving light to the heathens with every probability of success." Significant words, well applied in Carey's case at Serampore, and in Duff's in another direction at Calcutta, and afterwards carried out at Benares itself by the Church missionaries, in a college endowed by Jeynarain, a Hindu who died almost a Christian. Grant soon after went home to one of the "Chairs" of the East India Company's Directors, and in due time became chairman. There, and in the House of Commons, where he long represented the county of Inverness, he did more for the Christianising of India than any other man of his day. In India he saw Carey begin his work, in England he became not the least of the cultured "Clapham Sect," whose good deeds find a biographer in Sir James Stephen. No man ever wielded such influence, or used it for higher ends, alike by his despatches from Leadenhall Street, his private correspondence with successive Governors-General and members of Council, his speeches in Parliament, and his action as an evangelical leader of the Church of England.[1] His eldest son became principal Secretary of State for the Colonial Department, and was raised to the peerage as Baron Glenelg in 1836. His second son, Sir Robert, became Governor of Bombay, the friend of the Scottish missionary, Dr. John Wilson, and left a memory dear to the Church for the hymns of his which it sings.

Greater than all Charles Grant's efforts for the good of the people of India, or any other Christian statesman's, we reckon his *Observations on the State of Society among the Asiatic Subjects of Great Britain*, addressed in 1797, when he was fresh from a thirty years' study of the people, to his brother Directors, and on "a subject pressed by repeated proposals on your attention, namely, the communication of Christianity to the natives of our possessions in the East." What he modestly called a tract was kept back by his colleagues, till Mr. Dundas laid it before the House of Commons during the critical charter discussions of 1813. There it found men like Wilberforce prepared to compel the House to adopt it by the intrinsic fairness of its principles, as well as by the eloquence of the orator, and so it has become the real charter of liberty and light to the East. The otherwise majestic Company that blindly resisted its appeals has passed away, the victim of its own shortsightedness, while Charles Grant's counsels have prevailed to build up an empire stronger than that which the Mutiny purged of its clay. In this light how significant these words of the preface of 1797:—

"In earlier periods the Company manifested a laudable zeal for extending as far as its means then went the knowledge of the gospel

---

[1] His papers have yet to see the light. The MSS. we have seen are rich in their value; without them the history of India and of missions cannot be adequately written. See the fullest account of him published, with a portrait, in *Good Words* for September 1891.

to the pagan tribes among whom its factories were placed. It has since prospered to become great in a way to which the commercial history of the world affords no parallel; and for this it is indebted to the fostering and protecting care of divine Providence. It owes therefore the warmest gratitude for the past, and it equally needs the support of the same beneficent Power in time to come, for the 'chances and changes' to which human affairs are always liable, and especially the emphatic lessons of vicissitude which the present day has supplied, may assure us that neither elevation nor safety can be maintained by any of the nations or rulers of the earth, but through Him who governs the whole. The duty therefore of the Company, as part of a Christian community, its peculiar superadded obligations, its enlarged means, and its continual dependence on the divine favour, all call upon it to honour God by diffusing the knowledge of that revelation which He has vouchsafed to mankind."

At the time Charles Grant was writing his folio of 116 pages, the aged Schwartz addressed these words to the Society for Promoting Christian Knowledge, as quoted on the last page:—

"I am now at the brink of eternity, but to this moment I declare that I do not repent of having spent forty-three years in the service of my divine Master. Who knows but God may remove some of the great obstacles to the propagation of the gospel? Should a reformation take place amongst the Europeans, it would no doubt be the greatest blessing to the country."

Mr. Grant treats his great theme in five chapters. The first reviews the British territorial administration in the East, from Plassey to the Cornwallis reforms in 1786, in twenty of the wisest pages ever written by an Indian ruler. In this occurs the famous description of the great famine of 1769-70. The second describes the state of society among the Hindu subjects of Great Britain, particularly with respect to morals. The third traces the causes which have produced that state. And the fourth, most important of all in its far-reaching and beneficial consequences, inquires into the measures which might be adopted by Great Britain for the improvement of the condition of her Asiatic subjects, and answers objections. How much is implied and anticipated in the following passage, "written chiefly in the year 1792," on the removal of the ignorance and consequent error of the Hindus by the English language!—

"It is perfectly in the power of this country, by degrees, to impart to the Hindus our language: afterwards through that medium, to make them acquainted with our easy literary compositions, upon a variety of subjects; and, let not the idea hastily excite derision, *progressively* with the simple elements of our arts, our philosophy, and religion. These acquisitions would silently undermine, and at length subvert, the fabric of error; and all the objections that may be apprehended against such a change, are, it is confidently believed, capable of a solid answer.

"The first communication, and the instrument of introducing the rest, must be the English language; this is a key which will open to them a world of new ideas, and policy alone might have impelled us, long since, to put it into their hands. To introduce the language of the conquerors seems to be an obvious mean of assimilating the conquered people to them. The Mohammedans, from the beginning of their power, employed the Persian language in the affairs of government, and in the public departments. This practice aided them in maintaining their superiority, and enabled them, instead of depending blindly on native agents, to look into the conduct and details of public business, as well as to keep intelligible registers of the income and expenditure of the State. Natives readily learnt the language of government, finding that it was necessary in every concern of revenue and of justice; they next became teachers of it; and in all the provinces over which the Mogul Empire extended, it is still understood, and taught by numbers of Hindus. It would have been our interest to have followed their example; and had we done so on the assumption of the Dewannee,[1] or some years afterwards, the English language would now have been spoken and studied by multitudes of Hindus throughout our provinces. The details of the revenue would, from the beginning, have been open to our inspection; and by facility of examination on our part, and difficulty of fabrication on that of the natives, manifold impositions of a gross nature, which have been practised upon us, would have been precluded. An easy channel of communication also would always have been open between the rulers

---

[1] The revenue and civil administration personally granted to Clive, as representative of the East India Company, by the Emperor of Delhi on the 12th of August 1765. That "memorable day in the political and constitutional history of British India," is described by Marshman, at p. 310 of vol. i. of his *History of India*, which is still the best.

and the subjects; and numberless grievances would have been represented, redressed, or prevented, which the ignorance of the former in the country languages, and the hindrances experienced by the latter in making their approaches, have sometimes suffered to pass with impunity, to the encouragement of new abuses. We were long held in the dark, both in India and in Europe, by the use of a technical revenue language; and a man of considerable judgment, who was a member of the Bengal administration near twenty years since, publicly animadverted on the absurdity of our submitting to employ the unknown jargon of a conquered people. It is certain that the Hindus would easily have conformed to the use of English; and they would still be glad to possess the language of their masters, the language which always gives weight and consequence to the natives who have any acquaintance with it, and which would enable every native to make his own representations directly to the Governor-General himself, who, it may be presumed, will not commonly, henceforth, be chosen from the line of the Company's servants, and therefore may not speak the dialects of the country. Of what importance it might be to the public interest that a man in that station should not be obliged to depend on a medium with which he is unacquainted, may readily be conceived.

"It would be extremely easy for Government to establish, at a moderate expense, in various parts of the provinces, places of gratuitous instruction in reading and writing English; multitudes, especially of the young, would flock to them; and the easy books used in teaching, might at the same time convey obvious truths on different subjects. The teachers should be persons of knowledge, morals, and discretion; and men of this character could impart to their pupils much useful information in discourse; and to facilitate the attainment of that object, they might at first make some use of the Bengalese tongue. The Hindus would, in time, become teachers of English themselves; and the employment of our language in public business, for which every political reason remains in full force, would, in the course of another generation, make it very general throughout the country. There is nothing wanting to the success of this plan, but the hearty patronage of Government. If they wish it to succeed, it can and must succeed. The introduction of English in the administration of the revenue, in judicial proceedings, and in other business of government, wherein Persian is now used, and the establishment of free schools for instruction in this language, would insure its diffusion over the country, for the reason already suggested, that the interest of the natives would induce them to acquire it. . . .

"With our language much of our useful literature might, and would, in time be communicated. The art of printing would enable us to disseminate our writings in a way the Persians never could have done, though their compositions had been as numerous as ours. Hence the Hindus would see the great use we make of reason on all subjects, and in all affairs; they also would learn to reason, they would become acquainted with the history of their own species, the past and present state of the world; their affections would gradually become interested by various engaging works, composed to recommend virtue and to deter from vice; the general mass of their opinions would be rectified; and above all, they would see a better system of principles and morals. New views of duty as rational creatures would open upon them; and that mental bondage in which they have long been holden would gradually dissolve.

"To this change the true knowledge of nature would contribute; and some of our easy explanations of natural philosophy might undoubtedly, by proper means, be made intelligible to them. Except a few Brahmans, who consider the concealment of their learning as part of their religion, the people are totally misled as to the system and phenomena of nature; and their errors in this branch of science, upon which divers important conclusions rest, may be more easily demonstrated to them than the absurdity and falsehood of their mythological legends. From the demonstration of the true cause of eclipses, the story of *Ragoo* and *Ketoo*, the dragons who, when the sun and the moon are obscured, are supposed to be assaulting them,—a story which has hitherto been an article of religious faith, productive of religious services among the Hindus,—would fall to the ground; the removal of one pillar would weaken the fabric of falsehood; the discovery of one palpable error would open the mind to farther conviction; and the progressive discovery of truths, hitherto unknown, would dissipate as many superstitious chimeras, the parents of false fears and false hopes. Every branch of natural philosophy might in time be introduced and diffused among the Hindus. Their understandings would thence be strengthened, as well as their minds informed, and error be dispelled in proportion.

"But perhaps no acquisition in natural philosophy would so effectually enlighten the mass of the people as the introduction of the principles of mechanics, and their application to agriculture and the useful arts. . . . The scope for improvement in this respect is prodigious. What great accessions of wealth would Bengal derive from a people intelligent in the principles of agriculture, skilled to make the most of soils and seasons, to improve the existing modes of culture, of pasturage, of rearing cattle, of defence against excesses of drought and of rain, and thus to meliorate the quality of all the produce of the country! All these arts are still in infancy. The husbandman of Bengal just turns up the soil with a diminutive plough, drawn by a couple of miserable cattle; and if drought parches, or the rain inundate the crop, he has no resource; he thinks he is destined to this suffering, and is far more likely to die from want than to relieve himself by any new or extraordinary effort. Horticulture is also in its first stage: the various fruits and esculent herbs, with which Hindustan abounds, are nearly in a state of nature; though they are planted in enclosed gardens, little skill is employed to reclaim them. In this respect, likewise, we might communicate information of material use to the comfort of life and to the prevention of famine. In silk, indigo, sugar, and in many other articles, what vast improvements might be effected by the introduction of machinery! The skilful application of fire, of water, and of steam, improvements which would thus immediately concern the interests of the common people, would awaken them from their torpor, and give activity to their minds.

"But undoubtedly the most important communication which the Hindus could receive through the medium of our language, would be the knowledge of our religion, the principles of which are explained in a clear, easy way, in various tracts circulating among us, and are completely contained in the inestimable volume of Scripture. Thence they would be instructed in the nature and perfections of the one true God, and in the real history of man; his creation, lapsed state, and the means of his recovery, on all which points they hold false and extravagant opinions; they would see a pure, complete, and perfect system of morals and of duty, enforced by the most awful sanctions, and recommended by the most interesting motives; they would learn the accountableness of man, the final judgment he is to undergo, and the eternal state which is to follow. Wherever this knowledge should be received, idolatry, with all the rabble of its impure deities, its monsters of wood and stone, its false principles and corrupt practices, its delusive hopes and vain fears, its ridiculous ceremonies and degrading superstitions, its lying legends and fraudulent impositions, would fall. The reasonable service of the only and the infinitely perfect God would be established; love to Him, peace and good-will towards men, would be felt as obligatory principles.

"It is not asserted that such effects would be immediate or universal; but admitting them to be progressive, and partial only, yet how great would the change be, and how happy at length for the outward prosperity and internal peace of society among the Hindus! Men would be restored to the use of their reason; all the advantages of happy soil, climate, and situation would be observed and improved; the comforts and conveniences of life would be increased; the cultivation of the mind and rational intercourse valued; the people would rise in the scale of human beings, and as they found their character, their state, and their comforts improved, they would prize more highly the security and the happiness of a well-ordered society. Such a change would correct those sad disorders which have been described, and for which no other remedy has been proposed, nor is in the nature of things to be found."

"Prediction" is the word we might apply to such far-seeing wisdom and benevolence directed to the twofold work of converting India—the creation of a Christian Church and of self-governing Christian nations.

This was written in the prospect of the debates in Parliament on a new charter for the East India Company. The philanthropists and evangelicals of Clapham were led by Grant to work for the Christianisation of India, from this time forward, as heartily as for the emancipation of the slave. Wilberforce was the moving spirit in Parliament, and he gained over to the cause, from the secular point of view, his friends Pitt and Dundas. Hannah More, Scott, Cecil, and afterwards Charles Simeon, worked, in their own way, towards the same end. The boy Macaulay was nursed amid conversations and debates on India missions and education, which he himself was to bring to a consummation after 1833. Wilberforce carried the first point through Parliament in 1793, with results thus described in his journal of that year:—

"*May* 15*th*.—East India Resolutions in hand and slave business. Lord Carhampton abusing me as a madman. 17*th*.—Through God's help got the East India Resolutions in quietly. *Sunday* 19*th*.—Scott morning; Cecil afternoon. Called at Grant's—Miss More there. The hand of Providence was never more visible than in this East India affair. What cause have I for gratitude, and trust, and humiliation!"

The Resolution, as it finally passed, was to the effect—

"That it is the peculiar and bounden duty of the British Legislature to promote, by all just and prudent means, the interest and happiness of the inhabitants of the British dominions in India; and that for these ends such measures ought to be adopted as may gradually tend to their advancement in useful knowledge, and to their religious and moral improvement."

Alas! the Resolution stood there on the records of the House of Commons as a declaration of the national duty, but the India House raised such an alarm at the prospect of the deluge of missionaries and schoolmasters which was to sweep away the Company's rule in the East, that even Pitt and Dundas had to forgo their pledge to Wilberforce. "My clauses thrown out," he writes, "Dundas most false and double; but, poor fellow, much to be pitied." India, he wrote to a friend, "is left in the undisturbed and peaceable possession and committed to the providential protection of Brahma." His last appeal has a curious interest in the present day. He declared that the rejection of his Resolutions would be

"to declare to the world that we are friends to Christianity, not because it is a revelation from Heaven, not even because it is conducive to the happiness of man, but only because it is the established religion of this country. . . . Beware how this opinion goes abroad. Think not that the people of this land will long maintain a great Church establishment from motives of mere political expediency."

Spoken a century ago on the floor of the House of Commons, are these words another prophecy? By refusing to insert a clause so vague and moral in the charter of 1793, the Government and Parliament, at the dictation of the East India Company, went back from the far more pronounced and Christian clause, which makes the charter of 1698 for ever memorable.

When 1813, the time for a renewal of the charter, came round, Charles Grant had more power, Wilberforce more influence, and the country more wisdom. The progress was due also to another Scotsman, of whom his country has reason to be proud. When Whitefield preached at Cumbuslang, one Alexander Buchanan was parish schoolmaster there, and he married the daughter of Claudius Somers, who was an elder of the kirk. The new life which they found in the excitement of the revival showed itself in the son, Claudius Buchanan. Tutor at Dunstaffnage, and student of Glasgow University, he was early destined for the Scottish ministry, but determined first to see the world, avowedly like Goldsmith. After strange adventures and stranger experience of heart, he came under the influence of a man of similar antecedents, John Newton, of Olney. Mr. Henry Thornton, first of the Clapham men, sent him to Cambridge, where Isaac Milner completed Newton's good work. In 1796 Claudius Buchanan went out to Calcutta as a chaplain to the Honourable Company, for godly directors like Grant looked out for evangelical chaplains like Brown and Buchanan, Martyn, Corrie, and Thomason. Lord Wellesley, following the good example of his predecessors Lords Teignmouth and Cornwallis, encouraged church-going, and had made it more attractive by "punkahs" and "tatties," the cooling apparatus in the hot season. His Excellency had also added a chapel to that famous college of Fort-William which he created for the civilian students. So many as fifty octavo Bibles were sold in three months in Calcutta, wrote Buchanan in 1805. All Christian sects of east and west were represented at the services; but he says, "a name or sect is never mentioned from the pulpit, and thus the word preached becomes profitable to all."

The time had come, he thought, for a regular episcopal establishment of the Church in India, and in that year he published his *Memorial* on the subject. The persistent representations of good men of all sects on behalf of what had been called the "pious clauses," rejected from the charter of 1793, led to inquiry by a parliamentary committee. Very valuable, for historical and biographical reasons, is the evidence given before that committee. When Warren Hastings, in his eightieth year, entered the House, the body which had once impeached him rose and uncovered as before majesty. The old man represented, but in a vastly modified form, the conservative fears of the Company of his early days. His successor twice removed, Lord Teignmouth, with more force spoke the opinions of a wiser and later time. Great military statesmen, like Sir Thomas Munro and Sir John Malcolm, found their political expediency confronted by the bolder principles of the retired Lord Wellesley, fortunately Wilberforce's friend, as he had been Carey's. It fell to Lord Castlereagh, of all men, to apologise for making the "pious clauses" law. On the ground, "that while British subjects in India were governed by British laws, they should be permitted to exercise their national religion," he said the ecclesiastical establishment would "only amount to one bishop and three archdeacons to superintend the chaplains of the different settlements." The bishop and three archdeacons passed after a long conversation, and without a division, but not so the missionary clause. On the 22nd June, Wilberforce's most elaborate address carried it by a majority of 53 in a House of 125. On the 1st July, a Madras barrister of scoffing ability, Mr. Charles Marsh, reduced the majority to 22 in a House of 86. At last, however, the good cause triumphed on the 1st July, when, in a House of only 72, a majority of 24 carried that which twenty years before, Parliament had allowed the East India Company to neutralise when Wilberforce brought it forward. Even his renewed Resolution would probably have proved a dead letter for many a year, had not provision been made in the charter to compel the Company to grant the funds wherewith to carry out the educational portion of it. The retired Advocate-General of Calcutta, Mr. Robert Percy Smith, who was almost as witty as his better-known brother Sydney, procured the insertion of this addition, that it shall be lawful for the Governor-General in Council to direct that "A sum of not less than one lakh of rupees (then above £10,000) in each year shall be set apart and applied to the revival and improvement of literature and the encouragement of the learned natives of India, and for the introduction and promotion of a knowledge of the sciences among the inhabitants of the British territories of India."

The charter of 1813 was thus the foundation, not only

of the ecclesiastical establishment,[1] but, what is of far more importance for the civilisation and the Christianisation of its people, of the educational system of India, and all that that system as subsequently developed by Dr. Duff involves. The two will be seen to work themselves out in parallel lines in the Anglicising of native education in 1835, the Education Despatch of 1854, the University Charters of 1857, the despatch on vernacular education and school cess for that end in 1859, and the adoption of the principle that Western truth may be communicated to learned Orientals through their classical languages as in the Punjab University.

As, on the whole, throughout the two and a half centuries of its history, it had reflected the public opinion and morals of England, the East India Company's administration of India gradually advanced in toleration and a just neutrality. In London the Court of Directors was checked by the Board of Control and stimulated by Parliament. In India the successive Governors-General, especially Wellesley, Lord Hastings, Bentinck, and the Marquis of Dalhousie—last and perhaps greatest of all—were influenced by such remarkable men as the missionaries Carey and Duff in succession, whose services they utilised and whose educational methods they copied for the public good. In the subordinate provinces the same liberalising process went on. Madras will never forget the influence of the Marquis of Tweeddale and the missionary John Anderson. Bombay will ever be grateful for statesmen and judges like the two Elphinstones, Sir James Mackintosh and Bartle Frere, and for John Wilson and his missionary associates. At Agra Thomason and his school, notably Sir William Muir, and his brother John, the greatest of Christian Sanskritists—*par nobile fratrum*—did a memorable work for the ignorant millions of the North-Western Provinces in their land assessment and educational measures. In the new province of the Punjab, after the first and second Sikh wars, there flourished towards the close of the Company's rule the

[1] Act 53 George III. c. 155.

band of Christian officials who, from Delhi, saved the Empire in 1857. John Lawrence, Montgomery, Edwardes, Lake, Cust, Inglis, and many more, carried over into the new period of the direct rule of the Crown the same everlasting principles of truth and justice by which they had welded warring Sikhs and Mohammedans into a peaceful and prosperous people, while Christianity had from the first been allowed the same fair field.

At no period in the history of the Christian Church, not even in the brilliant century of legislation from Constantine's edict of toleration to the Theodosian code, has Christianity been the means of abolishing so many inhuman customs and crimes as were suppressed in India by the Company's Regulations and Acts in the first half of the nineteenth century. The Christlike work kept rapid step with the progress of Christian opinion and beneficent reforms in Great Britain, but it was due in the first instance to the missionaries in India. In the teeth of the supporters of Hinduism, European as well as Brahmanical, and contrary to the custom of centuries, it ceased to be lawful, it became penal, even in the name of religion (1) to murder parents by suttee, by exposure on the banks of rivers, or by burial alive; (2) to murder children by dedication to the Ganges, to be devoured by crocodiles, or daughters by the Rajpoot modes of infanticide; (3) to offer up human sacrifices in a temple or to propitiate the earth-goddess; (4) to encourage suicide under the wheels of idol cars, or wells, or otherwise; (5) to promote voluntary torment by hook-swinging, thigh-piercing, tongue-extraction, etc., or (6) involuntary torment by mutilation, trampling to death, ordeals and barbarous executions. Slavery and the slave-trade were made illegal. Caste was no longer supported by law, nor recognised in appointments to office. The long compromise with idolatry during the previous two centuries ceased, so that the Government no more called its Christian soldiers to salute idols, or its civil officers to recognise gods in official documents, or manage the affairs of idol temples and extort a revenue from idol pilgrimages. A long step was taken by legislative Acts to protect the civil rights of converts to Christianity as to any other religion, and to leave Hindu widows free to marry.

Religious intolerance ceased, almost for the first time in the history of Christianity, with the one temporary exception, that Christian officials of the ruling class were not, in their private character, allowed the same liberty to do their conscientious duty to Christ which Mohammedans enjoyed and used in commending their prophet. But that too was soon conceded in the spirit of the royal proclamation which extinguished the Court of Directors. The last fifty years of the almost imperial sway of the East India Company, in trust for the British people, mark a greater advance towards the conversion of India than we are yet able impartially to estimate. When Claudius Buchanan invited the youth of the universities, at the beginning of the century, to study the conversion of Asia, and was the means of calling Adoniram Judson to the work, the young Charles Grant of Magdalen College, and Francis Wrangham, F.R.S., of Trinity College, Cambridge, published prize poems on the subject. The vision indulged by the latter even the East India Company saw partially realised, before it ceased to exercise its high trust:—

> ". . . Even now I see them move,
> The mild evangelists of peace and love.
> Unstained with Afric's blood, they bend their prows
> Where in his fiery belt Dahomey glows;
> Hoist round the stormy Cape, then straining sail
> From Yemen's mountains woo the fragrant gale,
> And bear, strange merchandise, to Asia's shore
> The gospel's bright imperishable ore.
> Unsold to deal its unbought wealth,[1] their plan;
> Their traffic to redeem the soul of man.
> To check their eager march Tibetan snows
> And Caggar's sands their trackless wilds oppose:
> Onward they press at duty's sacred call,
> O'er Deccan's ghauts and China's northern wall;

[1] St. Matt. x. 8, "*Freely ye have received, freely give.*"

Stretch uncontrolled their Saviour's gentle reign,
And art and nature bar their way in vain,
On mosques where late the lurid crescent shone
On pagods reared to shrine an idol-stone—
Seringham's walls, spread many an acre o'er,
And the proud domes of gorgeous Ghazipore—
Her bannered cross victorious Albion waves
Beneath that symbol strikes, beneath that symbol saves.

. . . .

O haste your tardy coming, days of gold
Long by prophetic minstrelsy foretold!
Where yon bright purple streaks the Orient skies.
Rise Science, Freedom, Peace, Religion, rise!
Till from Tanjor to farthest Samarkand
In one wide lustre bask the glowing land,
And, Brahma from his guilty greatness hurled
With Mecca's lord, MESSIAH rule the world."

VI

GREAT BRITAIN'S ATTEMPT

"Through Him we both have access by one Spirit unto the Father. Now therefore ye are no more strangers and foreigners, but fellow-citizens with the saints, and of the household of God."—EPH. ii. 18, 19.

ON Monday, the 1st day of November 1858, as the tropical sun neared its setting, from the steps of Government House, Calcutta, there was read to the fifth of the human race, who from that hour formed her direct subjects, the Proclamation of "Victoria, by the grace of God, of the United Kingdom of Great Britain and Ireland, and of the Colonies and Dependencies thereof in Europe, Asia, Africa, America, and Australasia, Queen, Defender of the Faith." The Act of Parliament had become law on the 2nd day of August, the fourteenth Earl of Derby being Prime Minister. His son Lord Stanley, who had been President of the Board of Control, and from that date became the first Secretary of State for India, had at once drafted a proclamation setting forth the principles on which the peoples of India were thenceforth to be governed. But when the document reached the Queen, then with the Prince Consort and their eldest daughter, the Princess of Prussia, at Potsdam, Her Majesty returned it, desiring[1] the Premier to rewrite it, "bearing in mind that it is a female sovereign who speaks to more than a hundred

[1] *The Life of His Royal Highness the Prince Consort*, by Theodore Martin, vol. iv. pp. 284 and 335 (1879).

millions of Eastern peoples on assuming the direct government over them, and after a bloody civil war, giving them pledges which her future reign is to redeem, and explaining the principles of her government. Such a document should breathe feelings of generosity, benevolence, and religious toleration, and point out the privileges which the Indians will receive on being placed on an equality with the subjects of the British Crown, and the prosperity following in the train of civilisation."

To the new draft the Queen added, with her own hand, on the suggestion of the Prince Consort, the words which we print in italics, in the central paragraphs and the closing prayer of the Proclamation:—

> "We hold Ourselves bound to the natives of Our Indian Territories by the same obligations of duty which bind Us to all Our other subjects, and those obligations, by the Blessing of Almighty God, We shall faithfully and conscientiously fulfil. . . . .
>
> "*Firmly relying Ourselves on the truth of Christianity, and acknowledging with gratitude the solace of religion*, We disclaim alike the Right and the Desire to impose Our convictions on any of Our subjects. We declare it to be Our Royal Will and Pleasure that none be in any wise favoured, none molested or disquieted, by reason of their religious faith or observances; but that all shall alike enjoy the equal and impartial protection of the law: and We do strictly charge and enjoin all those who may be in authority under Us, that they abstain from all interference with the religious belief or worship of any of Our subjects, on pain of Our highest displeasure. . . . .
>
> "When, by the Blessing of Providence, internal tranquillity shall be restored, it is Our earnest desire to stimulate the peaceful industry of India, to promote works of public utility and improvement, and to administer its government for the benefit of all Our subjects resident therein. In their prosperity will be Our strength; in their contentment Our security; and in their gratitude Our best reward. *And may the God of all Power grant to Us and to those in authority under Us, strength to carry out these Our wishes for the good of Our people.*"

Lord Canning, the Governor-General, who now became the first Viceroy of India, having reported that the Proclamation had been received throughout India with cordial and unqualified approval, her Majesty replied, "The Queen rejoices to hear that the Viceroy approves the passage about religion. She strongly insisted on it." To Lord Stanley, on the same day that he addressed the Queen, Lord Canning had written, "I cannot tell you with what pleasure I have read the passages relating to religion. They are in every way admirable, and I almost envy you being *persecuted* for them, as you infallibly will be." It was not so. The comment of the *Friend of India* [1] on the Proclamation was more just: "The official recognition of Christianity as the religion of the ruler will terminate many discussions, while the act of mercy is a graceful commencement of a new *régime*. . . . The revolution is one the vastness of which only the next generation will appreciate. It is the principle of our Government, not its external form, which has been changed, and to the mass of men a new principle is as imperceptible as the soul. . . . A century hence men will date the history of progress from the Proclamation of the Queen." [2]

No constitution, not even that of the United States of America until its thirteenth amendment in 1865, had ever before so completely recognised the principle of toleration in matters of faith and worship involving the conscience and the right of private judgment, or had so generously conceded to multitudinous aliens equality before the law and in the administration. At its highest and widest the citizenship of Imperial Rome, in which the apostle Paul rejoiced, was a small thing compared with the gift made to peoples of almost every race, creed, and colour, now numbering nearly three hundred millions, and that after mutiny and partial rebellion. From the hour of that concession the history of the British Empire of India really began. From the day which put Christianity, though the avowed faith of the ruling race, on the same equal platform as Hinduism, Parseeism, Buddhism, Mohammedanism, Animism, and all other purely human modes of propitiating God, as Christ Himself put it before

[1] Then edited by Meredith Townsend, Esq., now of *The Spectator*.

[2] Under Act of Parliament the Queen was proclaimed Empress of India on 1st January 1878.

His Roman judge, the conversion of India to the one true and living God became an assured certainty. Not a metaphysical distinction as to the incarnation, not a lie or a deception backed by the fear of torture and persecution, not a theological system or rite attracting by the hope of office and the favour of the ruler, but Christ Himself commending the truth to every man's conscience, His redeeming love to every sinner's heart, has since 1858 been the message of Christendom in the East.

One generation has passed since that Proclamation, and the new principle has been seen working itself out in the two regions of State legislation and administration and of evangelical persuasion and absorption. For the first time in the long three thousand years' history of the elder Aryans in Southern Asia, the revelation of the one and universal personal God of love has been made to them; and the truth that God is in Christ reconciling the world unto Himself, not imputing to men their trespasses, has been declared to India's conflicting, groping, despairing, caste-bound, or indifferent peoples, under conditions of more absolute freedom to accept or reject it than exist in Christendom itself outside of the United States of America. The imperial Sovereign, her Viceroy, and the whole ruling class, claim for themselves only what they concede to the Hindu and Mohammedan, and every religionist. The conversion of India since the middle of the nineteenth century proceeds on the principle of Jesus Christ in the middle of the first. The constitutional position and administrative action of the British Government of India cannot be too carefully studied or too strongly insisted on in the history of the religious development of its peoples.

Heartily accepting the principle of the perfect equality of all creeds and religions before the law, the Christian power entrusted with the Government of India after so historically unique a fashion had two duties: First, the State must secure perfect liberty to its own Christian servants to discharge their personal service to God in their non-official character. Second, the State must, by legislation, on the one hand remove every obstacle to the unfettered freedom of worship of all religionists, while on the other it guards against the danger of indirectly sanctioning and, as it were, fossilising quasi-religious customs and beliefs which are contrary to humanity, to good morals, or to liberty.

The course of the history of British India during the last thirty-five years, illustrates these points. Even Lord Canning, a year after he had expressed such keen satisfaction with the provision of the Queen's Proclamation as to religion, censured a high civil officer in the Punjab for attending in his private capacity and his leisure hours the baptism of a native convert.[1] Inferior officers at the head of the provincial departments of public instruction, themselves sceptics, attempted to prevent Christian professors in the State colleges[2] from privately, in their own houses and out of college hours, instructing inquirers. Lord Canning had even objected to the distribution of anonymous tracts among the natives near Benares, so sensitive was he as to what came to be called the "neutrality" promulgated in 1858. The worst, and we may say the last instance of this violation of neutrality by the Viceroy himself, was an order cautioning officers to guard against compromising themselves in matters of religion in native regiments. Up to this time, except among the Romanist sepoys of the Madras army, the profession of conversion to Christ by any sepoy whatever had involved persecution and dismissal. Prabhu Deen, sepoy, was so expelled in the year 1819. The compulsion to salute idols had driven from the high office of commander-in-chief Sir Peregrine Maitland, and that iniquity was brought to an end. But the 170,000 sepoys of the East India Company's army had been always carefully guarded from the free and natural influence of Christian truth, and the result was the delusion which used the greased cartridges as an occasion of mutiny.

[1] Mr. R. N. Cust, LL.D., at Amritsar, afterwards Lord Lawrence's Home Secretary in Calcutta.

[2] Notably in Bengal and Bombay.

The 24th Punjab Regiment, consisting of Muzabi or low-caste Sikhs whose fathers had been Thugs, when fighting for the British Empire at the siege of Delhi, found among its spoils some Christian books which led them to ask instruction from their officers. These referred the inquirers to the Church missionaries at Amritsar, and afterwards at Peshawur. The Viceroy's action was taken by all parties as "a ban upon the Christian religion," and the bishop, then happily Dr. Cotton, did his duty.[1] The result was a despatch, described by him in a letter to the Viceroy as "very fair and very conciliatory. . . . It certainly should help to disabuse people of the notion that Government wish to impede the quiet and peaceful progress of Christianity." That particular movement was checked by the action of Government, which has since enrolled the Christian Karens in a battalion during the last Burmese war, and it is well understood that military no less than civil officers may use their private influence and leisure time, as enjoined by their Master, without question, but with discretion. It is well recognised that the profession of Christianity by the natives of India means a loyalty to the Empress which nothing can buy, and the only safeguard for satisfactory self-government when the time is full.

Nowhere shall we find the principle of religious equality applied to the many peculiar difficulties that arise out of the government of the non-Christian millions of India by a Christian state, with such wisdom as by John, afterwards the first Lord Lawrence, when at the head of the fifty-six choice civil and military officials, through whom he recovered North-Western India from the chaos of the Mutiny. While still Chief Commissioner, Lawrence wrote his great Minute of 21st April 1858. Sir Herbert Edwardes[2]

[1] The whole case is very fairly stated in the *Memoir of George Edward Lynch Cotton, D.D.*, edited by Mrs. Cotton, p. 156 (1871).

[2] Ruskin's hero. See *A Knight's Faith: Passages in the Life of Sir Herbert Edwardes*, collected by John Ruskin, 1885; also Edwardes' Lecture on *Our Indian Empire: its Beginning and End*, to young men in Exeter Hall, 1860.

had officially sent him a somewhat extreme memorandum on "the elimination of all unchristian principle from the Government of India." Sir Donald M'Leod passed on the communication with a letter which he pronounced "more moderate in its tone and marked by an enlightened and excellent spirit." Lawrence was willing to teach the Bible in State schools, and in voluntary classes wherever there were Christian teachers, "in order that our views of Christian duty might be patent to the native public." Edwardes would have resumed idol endowments, Lawrence declared that "the judgments of Providence would become manifest in the political disaffection which might ensue," and such a step would retard the progress of Christianity while it is condemned by the whole tenor of its teachings. On the subject of caste John Lawrence pointed out that Government had not recognised it except in the sepoy army, urged the raising of sweeper regiments as he himself had done, and of corps from the non-Aryan tribes, and anticipated the "happy time" when regiments of native Christians could be raised. But while encouraging sepoys to consult missionaries, he condemned preaching to the native soldiers in a body, unless they were of the aboriginal tribes destitute of a faith. He refused to disallow native holidays; earnestly desired to see the law altered in reference to polygamy and early betrothals; would prohibit religious processions in public as he did in the case of the Mohurrum at Delhi, and would interdict obscenities in temples; would restrict prostitutes to their houses; would increase the number of married soldiers and improve the condition of their wives and widows; condemned the opium monopoly, but did not agree as to the evil tendency of the liquor excise in the Punjab, where it has diminished the drunkenness encouraged in the Sikh *régime*. The despatch concludes with this noble passage:—

"Sir J. Lawrence has been led, in common with others since the occurrence of the awful events of 1857, to ponder deeply on what may be the faults and shortcomings of the British as a Christian nation in India. In considering topics such as those treated of in this despatch, he would solely endeavour to ascertain what is our Christian duty.

Having ascertained that according to our erring lights and conscience, he would follow it out to the uttermost, undeterred by any consideration. If we address ourselves to this task, it may, with the blessing of Providence, not prove too difficult for us. Measures have, indeed, been proposed as essential to be adopted by a Christian Government which would be truly difficult or impossible of execution. But on closer consideration it will be found that such measures are not enjoined by Christianity, but are contrary to its spirit. Sir John Lawrence does entertain the earnest belief that all those measures which are really and truly Christian can be carried out in India, not only without danger to British rule, but on the contrary, with every advantage to its stability. Christian things done in a Christian way will never, the Chief Commissioner is convinced, alienate the heathen. About such things there are qualities which do not provoke nor excite distrust, nor harden to resistance. It is when unchristian things are done in the name of Christianity, or when Christian things are done in an unchristian way, that mischief and danger are occasioned. The difficulty is, amid the political complications, the conflicting social considerations, the fears and hopes of self-interest which are so apt to mislead human judgment, to discern clearly what is imposed upon us by Christian duty and what is not. Having discerned this, we have but to put it into practice. Sir John Lawrence is satisfied that, within the territories committed to his charge, he can carry out all those measures which are really matters of Christian duty on the part of the Government. And, further, he believes that such measures will arouse no danger; will conciliate instead of provoking, and will subserve to the ultimate diffusion of the truth among the people.

"Finally, the Chief Commissioner would recommend, that such measures and policy, having been deliberately determined on by the Supreme Government, be openly avowed and universally acted upon throughout the empire; so that there may be no diversities of practice, no isolated tentative or conflicting efforts, which are, indeed, the surest means of exciting distrust; so that the people may see that we have no sudden or sinister designs; and so that we may exhibit that harmony and uniformity of conduct which befits a Christian nation striving to do its duty."

So he gave back to the Mohammedans of Delhi, in due time, their great mosque, and when Viceroy he restored the Pearl Mosque of Agra and the Grand Mosque of Lahore, which in Ranjit Singh's time the Sikhs had desecrated. When the petty chief of Rajgarh, in Central India, a Rajpoot, became a Mohammedan, and the outcry of his Hindu nobles against him was such that he proposed to abdicate, Lord Lawrence ascertained that his people were satisfied with his rule, and decided that so long as their chief was just they must be loyal without reference to his creed. When the man took a Mohammedan name, after circumcision, the paramount Government gave him a Mohammedan title. Even in the Feudatory States of India there was at last that religious toleration which the missionary John Wilson [1] had claimed when he settled the Irish Presbyterians in Kathiawar, and Stephen Hislop [2] when he secured the liberty of Pandurang, the Brahman convert, in Nagpoor State. Rajgarh is the leading case which establishes in Native States the principle accepted by the Legislature in civil affairs, that "no rights shall be forfeited or impaired merely by change of religion or loss of caste." [3] There is now no great Native State in India, Hindu or Mohammedan, in which there are not Christian missionaries and churches. There only, in all the world of Islam, are Mohammedans constrained to be tolerant. From the first, such Hindu governments as those which still exist in Cochin and Travankor, received Jewish, Christian, and Parsee refugees all along the Western Coast of India. But such communities were not aggressive in the high spiritual sense of the present missionaries of the evangel sent by the Reformed Churches.

In the department of Public Instruction, which in each of the twelve Provincial Governments of India benevolently undertakes the education of the millions not in the Feudatory States, it has been difficult even up to the present time to observe strictly the principle of the Proclamation of 1858. Theoretically the State should keep aloof from direct teaching, confining its administration to inspection and grants-in-aid for secular efficiency. After the evidence before the Committee on the Charter of 1853 given by two remarkable men of missionary antecedents, Dr. Alexander Duff and John Clark Marshman, C.S.I., the

[1] *Life of John Wilson, D.D., F.R.S.*, 1st ed., p. 294 (1878).

[2] *Stephen Hislop*, 2nd ed., p. 106 (1889).

[3] *Lord Lawrence.* By Sir Charles Aitchison. Oxford (1892).

despatch of 1854 laid down this principle, and added, with respect to religious instruction in the Government Institutions: "These Institutions were founded for the benefit of the whole population of India; and in order to effect their object it was, and is, indispensable that the education conveyed in them should be exclusively secular. The Bible is, we understand, placed in the libraries of the colleges and schools, and the pupils are free to consult it. This is as it should be, and, moreover, we have no desire to prevent or to discourage any explanations which the pupils may of their own free will ask from their masters on the subject, provided such information is given out of school hours." The same despatch established on a catholic basis the Universities of India, now five in number. But its provisions were long so applied that the State colleges became virtual monopolies which destroyed Hinduism and discouraged Christianity, while putting nothing in the place of their moral sanctions. Under the influence of the missionary representatives in their Syndicates the Universities were at first practically fair to all needs; but the native majorities have of late eliminated the legitimate Christian element from their administration. Ten years ago a commission appointed by Lord Ripon led to a return to neutrality; but so long as State colleges exist, however few, that is incomplete. On the other hand, it is the independent Christian colleges and schools which, by the superior efficiency of their teaching of literature and science, secure greater popularity and a larger proportion of the grants than the non-Christian independent colleges.

The legislative even more than the administrative action of the Government of India, since the East India Company gave place to the Crown, is calculated to allow a fair field to the evangelisation of India. In 1860 the Penal Code became law, and at one stroke gave the varied cults of Southern Asia, in common with the Christians, the most humanising and indirectly Christianising piece of jurisprudence that the world has seen. Aided by Sir J. M. Macleod, Lord Macaulay, sixty years ago, drafted this body of criminal enactments on the basis of Livingston's Code of Louisiana and the Code Pénal of France, just at the time Austin published his great work. The draft was distrusted by a whole generation of Indian experts till one of Macaulay's successors, Sir Barnes Peacock, took it in hand and passed it through the Legislative Council as Act XLV. of 1860. The Code owes to Macaulay its good English and its remarkable illustrative cases under each section. The experience of the Code during the past generation has falsified the fears of the local judges, and has more than justified Macleod and Macaulay. So acute an expert as Sir Fitz-James Stephen has declared it to be "triumphantly successful." His successor as law member of the Governor-General's Council, Mr. Whitley Stokes, the great scholar, describes its study in English by Hindus and Mohammedans as "self-education." It has been translated into all the languages of India, with results in teaching humanity and justice which place our fellow-subjects there at the head of all the peoples of the East. Since it was drafted, this Indian Code has found imitators in those of the State of New York and the German Empire. These have improved on it only in the methodical arrangement, and they have had few of its difficulties to contend with, arising from crimes peculiar to India or Asia, and from the political position.

The Code, embodying and applying the principles of religious toleration, is in one sense the charter of that liberty which Christianity alone teaches, and, when true to itself, enforces and secures. Jurists like Macaulay and Barnes Peacock were succeeded by one greater than either in this region, Sir Henry Sumner Maine. Alike as law member of the Governor-General's Council for seven years, and as Vice-Chancellor of the Calcutta University for four, that statesman applied to India, to its native Christians as to its Parsees, to its European and American Christians as to its Hindus and Mohammedans, the best fruits of Christian legislation in the West, in all those matters of inheritance, marriage, and civil rights which lie at the foundation of society, as they are the finest practical fruit of the Christianised intellect and conscience. Except in the two questions of Hindu child-marriages, and minors and the age of discretion—the latter still left to the equity of judges in Christendom—Maine completed, substantially, the State's duty in the conversion of India. In the Rede Lecture which, after his return to England, he delivered before the University of Cambridge in 1875, he used this language, which the Christian apologist will interpret as true of the Hellenic fulness of the time:—

"The difficulty of the experiment of governing India, if conscientiously examined, will be regarded with more consideration. There is a double current of influences playing upon this remarkable dominion. One of these currents has its origin in this country, beginning in the strong moral and political convictions of a free people. The other arises in India itself, engendered among a dense and dark vegetation of primitive opinion, of prejudice if you please, stubbornly rooted in the *débris* of the past. As has been truly enough said, the British rulers of India are like men bound to make their watches keep true time in two longitudes at once. Nevertheless, the paradoxical position must be accepted. If they are too slow, there will be no improvement; if they are too fast, there will be no security. Those who, guided solely by Western social experience, are too eager for innovations which seem to them undistinguishable from improvements, will, perhaps, be overtaken by a wholesome distrust when they see in institutions and customs which would otherwise appear to them ripe for destruction the materials of knowledge by which the past, and to some extent the present, of the West may be interpreted. On the other hand, though it be virtually impossible to reconcile the great majority of the natives of India to the triumph of Western ideas, manners, and practices, which is, nevertheless, inevitable, we may, at all events, say to the best and most intelligent of them that we do not renovate or destroy in mere arrogance. Whatever be the nature and value of that bundle of influences which we call 'Progress,' nothing can be more certain than that, when a society is once touched by it, it spreads like a contagion. Yet, so far as our knowledge extends, there was only one society in which it was endemic, and, putting that aside, no race or nationality left entirely to itself appears to have developed any very great intellectual result, except perhaps poetry. Not one of those intellectual excellences which we regard as characteristic of the great progressive races of the world—not the law of the Romans, not the philosophy and sagacity of the Germans, not the luminous order of the French, not the political aptitude of the English, not that insight into physical nature to which all races have contributed--would, apparently, have come into existence if these races had been left to themselves. To one small people, covering in the original seat no more than a handful of territory, it was given to create the principle of progress, of movement upwards and not backwards or downwards—of destruction tending to construction. That people was the Greek. Except the blind forces of Nature, nothing moves in this world which is not Greek in its origin. A ferment spreading from that source has vitalised all the great progressive races of mankind, penetrating from one to another, and producing results accordant with its hidden and latent genius, and results, of course, often far greater than exhibited in Greece itself. It is this principle of progress which we Englishmen are communicating to India. We did not create it. We deserve no special credit for it. It came to us filtered through many different media. But we have received it, and, as we have received it, so we pass it on. There is no reason why, if it has time to work, it should not develop in India effects as wonderful as in others of the societies of mankind."

In 1850 the last of the East India Company's Governors-General, the Marquis of Dalhousie, had caused Act XXI. to be passed for securing, in his own language,[1] "liberty of conscience, and for the protection of converts, and especially of Christian converts, against injury in respect of property or inheritance by reason of a change in their religious belief." What was thus done for inheritance Maine elaborated and applied to marriage and divorce in Act XXI. of 1866. On the day on which, under the administration of Lord Lawrence as Viceroy, the Act was passed, the great lawyer happened to preside in Council, and from the Viceroy's seat he closed his exposition of the law of conversion, especially in an empire like British India, with these memorable words: "We will not force any man to be a Christian; we will not even tempt any man to be a Christian; but if he chooses to become a Christian, it would be shameful if we did not protect him and his in those rights of conscience which we have been the first to introduce into the country, and if we did not apply to him and his those principles of equal dealing between

[1] *Minute by the Most Noble the Governor-General of India, dated the 28th of February* 1856 (Calcutta).

man and man of which we are in India the sole depositaries." What a contrast to the Greek and the Roman, the Portuguese and the Dutch principles and precedents!

But the good work is not yet accomplished. In the development of society, and the growth of the Christian Church in India, questions, generally of detail rather than of principle, are always demanding settlement. The Legislature cannot in these go ahead of Hindu and Mohammedan opinion too fast, while the Church must beware of asking the State to attempt by prohibitive enactment what should be the natural, if slow, outcome of ethical and spiritual progress. Hence the reply[1] of the Government of India in 1881 to a memorial from the American Marathi missionaries in Western India: "It would scarcely be possible for the Government of India to embark on legislation in connection with infant-marriages except at the wish and with the co-operation of the classes most closely interested. . . . It may be hoped that the growing enlightenment of the Hindus may lead them before long to seek an alteration of the Hindu law regarding infant-marriages, in order that the injustice and unhappiness which are so often occasioned by it may be averted from all, whether they are received into the Christian community or remain Hindus."

In 1853, when, as Lieutenant-Governor, he opened the Government college at Benares, James Thomason, the most wisely benevolent of all the East India Company's administrators since Charles Grant, spoke to the Brahmans of that central stronghold of Hinduism of the coming conversion of the races of India. With assured faith he described it as "a new state of things when a higher philosophy and a purer faith will pervade this land, not enforced by the arbitrary decrees of a persecuting government, not hypocritically professed to meet the wishes of a proselytising government, but cordially adopted by a willing people yielding to the irresistible arguments placed before them." This sure because supernatural process of

[1] See *Report of the Third Decennial Missionary Conference held at Bombay* 1892-93, p. 61.

evangelical persuasion and absorption is slow on account of the human factor. The faith and obedience of every Christian comes far short of the promises and the command of the great God our Saviour. For centuries these were invisible even in the Reformed Churches, which, in their standards, ritual, and theological systems, almost ignore the doctrine of the Kingdom of Christ. England had been put in trust of India for two hundred years before an English missionary as such gave the message of Christ to its millions, and then he dared not leave the protection of the Danish flag.

When, at the end of the eighteenth century, individual Christians as distinct from Church organisations introduced what was then called the new era of Benevolence, it seemed as if India would continue to be abandoned by Christendom to commercial monopolists and antichristian intolerance. The awaking enthusiasm sought the negro slaves of America, just as the temporarily-aroused conscience of Puritan Britain had attempted to save its Red Indians. Next in interest to the negroes were the allied islanders of the Pacific Ocean when first revealed by Captain Cook. Then came, as the objects of compassion, the negroes of West Africa. Charles Grant had written from India to Charles Simeon, offering to support English missionaries in Bengal, but not an Englishman could be found to preach the gospel there.

The Moravian Brethren,[1] the Wesleys, the Edinburgh, the Glasgow, and the London[2] Missionary Societies, even the Church Missionary Society, passed India by through the first thirteen years of the nineteenth century. By small collections or grants of money and books only, and by a message from King George I., through the two Anglican Societies for the Promotion of Christian Knowledge and for the Propagation of the Gospel,[3] was the faint attempt made to discharge the responsibility of English-

[1] The brief and abortive mission of Dr. Heyne and another to Calcutta, Serampore, and Patna in 1777.

[2] Mr. Forsyth was sent out to Calcutta and Chinsurah in 1798.

[3] *Classified Digest of the Records of the S.P.G.*, 1701-1892.

speaking Christians. The United States of America did not send missionaries to India, Congregationalist or Baptist, till the year 1813, when the Church Missionary Society also ordained its first Englishman. The Wesleyans followed in 1817. Southey, himself an Anglican, taunted his Church with its failure to supply missionaries for India: "The first step towards winning the natives to our religion is to show them that we have one. . . . There is ability and there is learning in the Church of England, but its age of fermentation has long been over.[1]

The Englishman who was chosen by God to change all that was the Baptist shoemaker and schoolmaster, William Carey. Yet as Paul when sent to Macedonia essayed to penetrate Asia, Carey himself sought Tahiti. In him were found the necessary faith and humility, the burning fire which Christ came to send on the earth, and the gift of tongues or scholarship conferred by the Wisdom of God. He was as really called by Christ and trained by the Holy Spirit and the Providence of God to be the English apostle of India as the young Pharisee, Saul, was to be the apostle of Europe. All that went before him in the Coast Mission of the south was preparatory, save only the translation of the Word of God into the Tamil tongue, first published in 1725. Ziegenbalg, Schultze, and even Schwartz, were Germans, and all that Denmark could do for them, as for Carey, was to give them the protection of its flag in Tranquebar and Serampore. While for forty-one years Carey did his own work in Northern India, and he and his brotherhood influenced all Asia from the Persian Gulf to the China Sea, this apparently obscure Calvinist was used by God to summon Great Britain to the conversion of India. Society after society started into life at his simple call. Scottish gentlemen, like Robert and James Haldane, caught the impulse; the former sold Airthrey and endowed with its price, £35,500, the mission to Benares, for which Charles Grant had vainly pled with the

[1] See the first number of *The Quarterly Review* for April 1809, where Southey answers Sydney Smith's attack on missions to India in *The Edinburgh Review*.

Church of England, only to have their offering and themselves driven back by William Pitt and Henry Dundas, to the gain of Home Missions for the time. Englishmen like the Cambridge Senior Wrangler, Henry Martyn, learned from him to do the work of an evangelist to the Mohammedans of India, Arabia, and Persia, protected by the chaplain's office, as the missionary had been first by the indigo-planter's calling and then by the Danish Government. Americans, like Adoniram Judson and his wife, sailed from New England to be sent by Carey to Burma, and to found the great Maratha mission of Western India. In 1830, four years before his death, Carey wrote, "But a few years have passed away since the Protestant world was awakened to missionary effort. Since that time the annual revenues collected for this object have grown to the then unthought-of sum of £400,000," or one-seventh of what, sixty-three years after, is given for the evangelisation of the whole non-Christian world.

The Churches which had kept out, and even cast out, the evangelical missionaries, foreign and home, up till 1830, then atoned, in Scotland at least, for their treachery to their Head. The old historic Church of Scotland, as a Church, became a missionary organisation. Thomas Chalmers and Dr. Inglis chose India as its field, the capital Calcutta as the centre of its operations, and Brahmanism as the special object of its aggressive action. Its first missionary, Alexander Duff, landed in Bengal in time to receive the apostolic succession, in the highest sense, from the venerable Carey. No longer compelled by the East India Company's intolerant system to hide his mission in the interior, Duff opened his Christian school in Calcutta, in the chief native thoroughfare of Chitpore Road. He planted his mission-house and lecture-room, and finally his college, in the great educational centre of the city, beside which there has since risen the Catholic Calcutta University.

From the day that Carey's earliest "Periodical Accounts" reached Edinburgh and the Ochils, Scotland has been true to the duty of the British Empire to the people of India.

The opposition of Pitt drove the agents of the Edinburgh Missionary Society, founded in 1796, to the Foulahs of West Africa and the Mohammedan Tartars on the Caspian Sea. But after the more tolerant charter of 1813, when the Scottish as well as the English Established Church, led by Claudius Buchanan, first sent out chaplains, that missionary society transferred its men to India, sending out in 1823 Donald Mitchell, who, when a lieutenant in the Company's army, had found Christ for himself, and burned to preach the good news to the people. In the district south of Bombay where he lies, he was followed by university men of equal devotedness and culture, like Robert Nesbit and John Wilson, who in 1835 formally represented the Church of which they had been ordained ministers. Duff's early successes, like those of Carey, set in motion a second tide of missionary enthusiasm, on which John Anderson and others were wafted to the city of Madras and South India in 1837. The disruption and historical cessation of the old Church of Scotland in 1843 resulted in the two organisations of the Church of Scotland Free and Established. The former, retaining all the missionaries and converts, has ever since extended its operations in India and elsewhere. The latter, after a time, has in the old building and with the old endowments in Calcutta and Madras, and in the new fields of the Punjab and Darjeeling, conducted vigorous missions.

In South India the Danish and the German missionaries repeated, on a smaller scale but still with similarly disastrous results, the mistake of the Dutch there and in Ceylon. They made a compromise with Hinduism, which from the first poisoned their native Church and, after the death of Schwartz in 1798, brought it almost to an end. Receiving the pure message of the evangel, having in their hands the Word of God in their mother tongue, with schools for their children, and foreigners of apostolic life and doctrine as their pastors, the Tamil Christians, who individually professed conversion to Christ to the number of at least fifty thousand last century, proved to be no more a self-propagating and spiritually aggressive Church than that of the Syrians of Malabar, or that of Rome by their side. Caste faced the missionaries through the eighteenth century, from Ziegenbalg to Schwartz, with a power that seemed as if it could never be shaken or broken. The Lutherans followed the Roman Catholics in recognising it as a social distinction, and in perpetuating it even at the Lord's Table. Brotherhood in the Christian communities became impossible, the graces of the Holy Spirit were choked from the first; distrust and dissension, pride and malice, made havoc of the infant evangelical Church. The thousands of the Tranquebar, the Tanjor, the Trichinopoly, the Cuddalor, and the Madras caste converts, instead of spreading after Schwartz's death like the leaven, died out, leaving as successors a few score who dotted the desolation of the coast when in 1849 Duff[1] visited it. For the second time in India the Reformed Churches of the Continent of Europe made a fatal mistake.

As the nineteenth century went on, three great Missionary Societies of England, besides the first, that of the Baptists in North India, practically mapped out South India among them. The Society for the Propagation of the Gospel, in 1829 becoming directly missionary towards non-Christians, took over the native congregations and schools under six German missionaries in the British districts, relieving the Christian Knowledge Society which had been supporting them, and extended the work begun by Schwartz and by Satiyanādan, the first native ordained by the Tranquebar missionaries in Tinnevelli. Before that, in 1820, when Mr. Hough was chaplain at Palamkotta, he brought about the Church Missionary Society's entrance into that since fruitful field. The London Missionary Society at a still earlier period, 1804, began to divide with the Church Missionary Society the equally hopeful region of Travankor and Cochin, the scene of the failures of the Syrians, the Romanists, and the Lutherans. In Madura

[1] See Dr. Duff's Diary, at pp. 133-144, vol. ii. of his *Life* (1879), for the effect of caste on the Lutheran and Roman Catholic converts; also *Bishop Wilson's Life* by Bateman, and Sherring's *History of Protestant Missions in India*, 1875.

also the Propagation Society inherited the Lutheran work at Ramnad, while the American Board, in 1834, began their network of missions there, which, after a struggle[1] with caste among the Danish converts and their descendants, has spread over the district where the great Jesuits failed so lamentably. In 1850 Henry M. Scudder, M.D., of the Reformed (Dutch) of America, began among the million and a half of the Hindus of North Arcot the medical mission which has since made that Church and the Scudder family illustrious. Taught by the experience of the Danish-Halle Lutherans, and by the early failure of an attempt at Mangalor to meet illegitimately the pressure of the Home Churches for baptisms, the Basel Evangelical Missionary Society, representing the warm piety of Wurtemberg, has since 1834 covered the western districts of the province of Madras with industrial missions identified with the names of Hebich, Moegling, and Gundert. The Wesleyan Missionary Society, true to the spirit of Samuel Wesley, Rector of Epworth, who with his wife desired to go out to India where Ziegenbalg and Schultze were doing so much, sent missionaries under Dr. Coke to Ceylon in 1813, and began soon after the remarkable mission in the hill country of Mysore, now a self-governing Hindu state of five millions of people, in the council of which one of its missionaries is a representative.

With hardly an exception the British and American Christian missions to India have from the first—that is from the year 1793, when William Carey began his mission work in the indigo swamps of the Dinajpore district of North Bengal—vigilantly avoided every appearance of compromise with Hinduism in life, doctrine, and ritual, and have consistently taught (Matt. xxviii. 18-20) the people all things whatsoever Christ commanded.

[1] In July 1847, the American missionaries passed this resolution—"That the mission regards caste as an essential part of heathenism, and its full and practical renunciation, after instruction, as essential to satisfactory evidence of piety; and that renunciation of caste implies at least a readiness to eat, under proper circumstances, with any Christians of any caste."

The methods followed by all were first laid down by Carey, and most persistently applied to the middle and educated classes of the Hindus, especially the Brahmans, by Duff.

The first and greatest is the Word of God translated into the mother tongue of the people, and printed, circulated, and taught so as to be in every hand and in many memories. To secure this was Carey's first and chief duty, not only for his own densely peopled provinces of Bengal, Bahar, Orissa, and Assam, but for all Southern Asia. In the eighteen hours of every day of the forty-one years during which he lived in India, he did every kind of missionary work short of the medical, but all he did was meant to result in the production and printing of the vernacular Bible [1] for every race in the southern half of Asia, except the Tamils, who already had received the treasure. When he and Marshman and Ward had fairly started this enterprise, enlisting the chaplains Henry Martyn and Thomason, and even a Roman Catholic scholarly priest, with a fine catholicity, in the enterprise, the Serampore brotherhood added to this and their daily vernacular preaching the foundation and endowment of a Christian

[1] Sir Charles U. Aitchison, K.C.S.I., now a Vice-President of the C.M. Soc., in his address at the Centenary of the Baptist Missionary Society, thus spoke of the Bible in India :—"The Bible is the best of all missionaries. Missionaries die, the printed Bible remains for ever. It finds access through doors that are closed to the human foot, and into countries where missionaries have not yet ventured to go ; and, above all, it speaks to the consciences of men with a power that no human voice can carry. It is the living seed of God, and soon it springs up, men know not how, and bears fruit unto everlasting life. I can tell you, from my own personal knowledge, that no book is more studied in India now by the native population of all parties than the Christian Bible. There is a fascination about it that, somehow or other, draws seekers after God to read it. To thousands who are not Christians, but who are seeking after God, the Bible in the vernaculars of India is an exceedingly precious book. The leader of the Brahmo Somaj, which represents the highest phase of educated Hindu thought, in a recent lecture to the students of the Punjab University, exhorted them seriously to study the Scriptures as the best guide to purity of heart and life."

college. Carey and Marshman were the first educational missionaries, not only because they were men of culture and foresight, missionary statesmen who must adapt their means so as to make all subservient to their divine end, but because they sought at once the conversion to Christ of the born leaders of the people, and the creation of an educated indigenous ministry.

So early as the first year of this century Carey saw the need of English education as a weapon in the warfare with Brahmanism, when he wrote to his Society: "There appears to be a favourable change in the general temper of the people. Commerce has roused new thoughts and awakened new energies; so that hundreds, if we could skilfully teach them gratis, would crowd to learn the English language. We hope this may be in our power some time, and may be a happy means of diffusing the gospel. Is not the universal inclination of the Bengalees to learn English a favourable circumstance which may be improved to valuable ends?"

In 1816 he thus wrote to the American Baptist General Convention of Burma, to which he had sent Judson, following his eldest son:—

"We know not what your immediate expectations are relative to the Burman empire, but we hope your views are not confined to the immediate conversion of the natives by the preaching of the Word. Could a church of converted natives be obtained at Rangoon, it might exist for a while, and be scattered, or perish for want of additions. From all we have seen hitherto, we are ready to think that the dispensations of Providence point to labours that may operate, indeed, more slowly on the population, but more effectually in the end: as knowledge, once put into fermentation, will not only influence the part where it is first deposited, but leaven the whole lump. The slow progress of conversion in such a mode of teaching the natives may not be so encouraging, and may require, in all, more faith and patience; but it appears to have been the process of things, in the progress of the Reformation, during the reigns of Henry, Edward, Elizabeth, James, and Charles. And should the work of evangelising India be thus slow and silently progressive, which, however, considering the age of the world, is not perhaps very likely, still the grand result will amply recompense us, and you, for all our toils. We are sure to take the fortress, if we can but persuade ourselves to sit down long enough before it. 'We shall reap if we faint not.'

"And then, very dear brethren, when it shall be said of the seat of our labours, The infamous swinging-post is no longer erected; the widow burns no more on the funeral pile; the obscene dances and songs are seen and heard no more; the gods are thrown to the moles and to the bats, and Jesus is known as the God of the whole land; the poor Hindu goes no more to the Ganges to be washed from his filthiness, but to the fountain opened for sin and uncleanness; the temples are forsaken; the crowds say, 'Let us go up to the house of the Lord, and He shall teach us of His ways, and we will walk in His statutes'; the anxious Hindus no more consume their property, their strength, and their lives in vain pilgrimages, but they come at once to Him who can save to 'the uttermost'; the sick and the dying are no more dragged to the Ganges, but look to the Lamb of God, and commit their souls into His faithful hands; the children, no more sacrificed to idols, are become 'the seed of the Lord, that He may be glorified'; the public morals are improved; the language of Canaan is learnt; benevolent societies are formed; civilisation and salvation walk arm in arm together; the desert blossoms; the earth yields her increase; angels and glorified spirits hover with joy over India, and carry ten thousand messages of love from the Lamb in the midst of the throne; and redeemed souls from the different villages, towns, and cities of this immense country constantly add to the number, and swell the chorus of the redeemed, 'Unto Him that loved us, and washed us from our sins in His own blood, unto HIM be the glory';—when this grand result of the labours of God's servants in India shall be realised, shall we then think that we have laboured in vain, and spent our strength for nought? Surely not. Well, the decree is gone forth! 'My word shall prosper in the thing whereunto I sent it.'"

Two years after Carey applied this to India in his Serampore "College for the Instruction of Asiatic, Christian, and Other Youth in Eastern Literature and European Science."

By the time, in 1830, that Duff began his career in India, all things were ready for such an evangelical movement in British India, under Lord William Bentinck, then not only tolerant but ready to applaud and imitate the missionary. The first Metropolitan, Dr. Middleton, had meanwhile avowedly followed Carey's example by building Bishop's College, but that was neither catholic nor in the centre of affairs, and has now ceased, like Serampore itself, to influence the educated natives. Not so the institution which bears the name of the Duff College in Calcutta. What Henry Martyn had pronounced to be so difficult as to amount to a miracle, what long after Bishop Caldwell,[1] a missionary worthy of Carey and Duff, lamented as non-existent outside of Christian colleges, Christendom saw and thanked God for the sight—Brahman after Brahman putting on the yoke of Christ by baptism, and in turn becoming, like Paul, the ordained preachers of the faith which once they had persecuted or contemned, and that in Anglican and American, as well as Scots Presbyterian Churches. The native historian of the Church of India, while he records the fact of the first five of his countrymen baptized by Ziegenbalg on the 12th May 1807—"five adult heathen slaves of Danish masters"—and the names of Satiyanādan, first ordained minister in 1799, and of Krishna Pal, the carpenter whom, in 1800, Carey led down into the waters of the Ganges, will not forget the Koolin Brahman, the Rev. Professor Krishna Mohun Bannerjea, afterwards honorary LL.D. of the Calcutta University, and the Rev. Gopinath Nundy, who witnessed a good confession before the Mohammedan rebels of Allahabad in the darkest time of the Mutiny of 1857. Mr. Sherring records that of the forty-eight educated converts of Duff's mission in 1871, nine were ministers, ten catechists, seventeen professors and higher grade teachers, eight were Government servants of the higher grade, and

[1] After forty-two years' experience in the Presidency of Madras, that able missionary wrote thus in his protest against *Reserve in Communicating Religious Instruction to Non-Christians in Mission Schools*, in 1879—"I have had some experience in the work of conversion myself, and have tried in succession every variety of method. Let me mention then the remarkable fact, that during the whole of this long period not one educated high-caste Hindu, so far as I am aware, has been converted to Christianity in connection with any mission or Church, except through the Christian education received in mission schools. Such converts may not be very numerous, and I regret that they are not, BUT THEY ARE ALL THAT ARE."

four were assistant-surgeons and doctors. On the other side of India Dr. John Wilson was doing a similar work; in 1839 he baptized two Parsee students, "the first proselytes from the religion of Zoroaster in modern times"; of these the Rev. Dhanjibhai Naoroji still survives.

Up to 1830, when Dr. Duff developed in Calcutta the system of evangelising by teaching, and by training an educated Asiatic ministry, the number of native members of the various reformed communities in all India and the adjoining lands of Burma and Ceylon did not exceed 27,000.[1] The caste-compromise of the Lutherans and the restricted methods of the new and then inexperienced English societies account for this. Ten years after Duff, Wilson, and Anderson had, in the three great Presidency centres, linked evangelical Christianity to truth and progress of every kind in the future history of India, the number was 57,000. Twenty years after it was 127,000. The whole number in May 1857, a hundred years after the battle of Plassey had given Clive virtual supremacy in Bengal and all India, may be taken at 130,000; in 1861 a careful census shows that it was 138,731. The Mutiny was provoked and used by discontented Hindu and Mohammedan leaders, like Nana Dhoondopant, the ex-king of Oudh, and their followers, to substitute their own rule for that of the British, under the restored suzerainty of Bahadoor Shah as emperor. So far, in the few districts of North and Central India which they influenced, the movement may be viewed as rebellion. But there is no evidence that it was favoured by the mass of the people, or that it was occasioned by any of the timid and partial reforms which culminated in 1850 in Lord Dalhousie's legislative grant of toleration to converts from one faith to another. The mutineers, and still more the rabble of the cities who revelled in the chaos, treated native Christians as identified with the governing class.

In the first century's history of the evangelical conver-

[1] According to those cautious statists, the late Joseph Mullens, D.D., and M. A. Sherring, LL.B.

sion of India, the Sepoy Mutiny of 1857 opened a new period. It tested, by persecution, the reality and the character of the faith of the converts. It proved to be a call to the conscience of Christendom.

The number of white Christians known or believed to have been butchered by the mutineers and their brutal agents was fifteen hundred, of whom thirty-seven were missionaries, chaplains, and their families at Delhi, Sialkot, Shahjahanpoor, Futtehghur, Futtehpoor, Muttra, Goruk-poor, Gwalior, and Cawnpore above all. With them were catechists like Wilayat Ali, Thakoor, Dhokul Parshad, Paramanand, Solomon, Ramchunder Mitter, Jiwan Masih, Raphael, Dr. Chaman Lal, and others all done to death, all martyrs of Christ. The Mohammedans always and the Hindus occasionally offered such their lives at the price of denying their Lord. Not one instance can be cited of failure to confess Him by men and women, very often of weak physique, and but yesterday of the same faith as their murderers.[1] The only known cases in which life was purchased by denial were those of one officer of mixed blood and some band-boys of Portuguese descent and religious profession. Happily the records of the infant Church of India contain the narrative of a confessor who survived the torture of that time. Gopinath Nundy, third of Duff's Brahmanical converts in 1832, had been given to the American Presbyterian Mission and ordained over the station of Futtehpoor. Sent off by Robert Tudor Tucker, the Company's judge, who soon after fell himself a martyr for Christ,[2] Gopinath was on his way in charge of all the Christian women of the station to Allahabad Fort, when he and his family were seized by the Moulavi Lyakut Ali after the massacre of the European officers of the Sixth

[1] See Sherring's *The Indian Church during the Rebellion*, 2nd ed. 1859, and Duff's *The Indian Rebellion: its Causes and Results*, 2nd ed. 1858.

[2] See Sir John Kaye's *History of the Sepoy War in India*, vol. ii. p. 363. R. T. Tucker was brother of the well-known Commissioner of Benares and uncle of A. L. O. E., still the devoted Christian missionary lady and writer in the Punjab.

Native Infantry. The Moulavi had set up the green standard of the titular Emperor of Delhi in the garden known as Khusroo Bagh, while the Christian refugees were shut up in the fort and the city raged with sedition. The Bengali missionary and his wife thus confessed Christ before the bloodthirsty Mohammedan:—

"When we were brought before him, we found him seated on a chair, surrounded by men with drawn swords. We made our salaams; upon which he ordered us to sit down, and put to us the following questions: 'Who are you?' 'Christians.' 'What place do you come from?' 'Futtehpore.' 'What was your occupation?' 'Preaching and teaching the Christian religion.' 'Are you a padre?' 'Yes, sir.' 'Was it not you who used to go about reading and distributing tracts in the streets and villages?' 'Yes, sir; it was I and my catechists.' 'How many Christians have you made?' 'I did not make any Christians, for no human being can change the heart of another; but God, through my instrumentality, brought to the belief of His true religion about a couple of dozens.' On this the man exclaimed, in a great rage, and said, 'Tauba! tauba! (repent). What downright blasphemy! God never makes any one a Christian; but you Kafirs pervert the people. He always makes people Musalmans; for the religion which we follow is the only true one. How many Mohammedans have you perverted to your religion?' 'I have not perverted any one, but, by the grace of God, ten were turned from darkness to the glorious light of the gospel.' Hearing this, the man's countenance became as red as fire; and he exclaimed, 'You are a great "haramzadah" (traitor to your salt)! you have renounced your forefathers' faith, and become a child of Satan, and now use your every effort to bring others into the same road of destruction. You deserve a cruel death. Your nose, ears, and hands should be cut off at different times, so as to make your sufferings continue for some time; and your children ought to be taken into slavery.' Upon this, Mrs. Nundy, folding her hands, said to the Moulavi, 'You will confer a very great favour by ordering us all to be killed at once, and not to be tortured by a lingering death.' After keeping silent for a while, he exclaimed, 'Subhan Allah, you appear to be a respectable man. I pity you and your family; and, as a friend, I advise you to become Mohammedans: by doing so, you will not only save your lives, but will be raised to a high rank.' My answer was, 'We prefer death to any inducement you can hold out.' The man then appealed to my wife, and asked her what she would do. Her answer was, thank God, as firm as mine. She said she was ready to submit to any punishment he could inflict, but she would not renounce her faith. The Moulavi then asked if I had read the Koran. My answer was, 'Yes, sir.' He then said, 'You could not have read it with a view to be profited, but simply to pick out passages in order to argue with Mohammedans.' Moreover he said, 'I will allow you three days to consider, and then I will send for you and read a portion of the Koran to you. If you believe, and become Mohammedans, well and good; but if not, your noses shall be cut off.' We again begged and said to him, that what he intended to do had better be done at once, for as long as God continued His grace we would never change our faith. He then ordered his men to take us into custody.

"While on the way to the prison I raised my heart in praise and adoration to the Lord Jesus, for giving us grace to stand firm and to acknowledge Him before the world. When we reached the place of our imprisonment, which was a part of the Serai, where travellers put up for the night and where his soldiers were quartered, we found there a European family and some native Christians. We felt extremely sorry at seeing them in the same difficulty with ourselves. After conversing together, and relating each other's distress, I asked them to join us in prayer, to which they readily consented. While we knelt down and prayed, one of the guards came, and, giving me a kick on the back, ordered me either to pray after the Mohammedan form or to hold my tongue.

"The next day, Ensign Cheek, an officer of the late 6th N. I., was brought in as a prisoner. He was so severely wounded that he was scarcely able to stand on his legs, but was on the point of fainting. I made some gruel of the suttoo (flour) and goor (sugar) which we brought with us, and some of which was still left, and gave him to drink; also a potful of water. Drinking this, he felt refreshed, and opened his eyes. Seeing me, a fellow-prisoner and minister of the gospel, he related the history of his sufferings, and asked me, if I escaped in safety, to write to his mother in England, and to his aunt at Bancoorah; which I have since done. As the poor man was unable to lie down on the bare hard ground, for that was all that was allotted to us, I begged the darogah (constable) to give him a charpoy (truckle-bed). With great difficulty he consented to supply one; and that was a broken one. Finding me so kindly disposed to poor Cheek, the darogah fastened my feet in the stocks, and thus caused a separation, not only from him, but also from my poor family. While this was going on, a large body of armed men fell upon me, holding forth the promise of immediate release if I became a Mohammedan. At that time Ensign Cheek cried with a loud voice, and said, 'Padre, padre, be firm; do not give way.' My poor wife, not willing to be separated, was dragged away by her hair, and received a severe wound in her forehead. The third day, the day appointed for our final execution, now came, and we expected every moment to be sent for to finish our earthly course; but the Moulavi did not do so. Every ten or fifteen minutes some one of his people would come and try to convert us, threatening, in case of refusal, to cut off our noses. It appeared that the cutting off of noses was a favourite pastime with them.

"On the sixth day the Moulavi himself came over into the prison, and inquired where the padre prisoner was. When I was pointed out, he asked me if I was comfortable. My answer was, 'How can I be comfortable, whilst my feet are fastened in the stocks? however, I am not sorry, because such has been the will of my heavenly Father.' I then asked him, 'How he could be so cruel as not to allow a drop of milk to a poor innocent baby?' for our little one lived principally upon water those six days. The same day, the European and Sikh soldiers came out under Lieutenant Brasyer, and after a desperate fight, completely routed the enemy. Several dead and wounded were brought where we were, as that was his headquarters. The sight of these convinced us that the enemies would take to their heels. They gradually began to disperse, and by the following morning not one remained. We then broke the stocks, liberated ourselves, and came into the fort to our friends, who were rejoiced to see us once more in the land of the living. Ensign Cheek died the same day after reaching the fort. His wounds were so severe and so numerous, that it was a wonder how he lived so many days, without any food or even a sufficient quantity of water to quench his burning thirst. It must be a great consolation to his friends to hear that he died in the Fort and received Christian burial. I had not sufficient conversation with him to know the real state of his mind; but the few words he expressed, at the time when the villains fastened my feet in the stocks, led me to believe that he died a Christian, and is now in the enjoyment of everlasting rest in heaven.

"Other dear English and native Christians were in similar dangers and trials, but many if not all were massacred; yet we are still in the land of the living. The manifestation of God's grace to us at the time we needed it most was infinite. It was nothing but His grace alone that kept us firm. The enemy tried his utmost to throw us down. He put forth, on the one hand, all the worldly inducements a person can conceive, if we renounced our faith; on the other hand, he brought before us a sure death, with all the cruelties a barbarous man could think of, if we did not become Mohammedans. But thank God, we chose the latter. The sweet words of our blessed Saviour, which are recorded in the 18th, 19th, and 20th verses of the 10th chapter of St. Matthew, were strikingly fulfilled in our case: 'And ye shall be brought before governors and kings for My sake, for a testimony against them and the Gentiles. But when they deliver you up, take no thought how or what ye shall speak: for it shall be given you in that same hour what ye shall speak. For it is not ye that speak, but the Spirit of your Father which speaketh in you.' When the Moulavi failed by arguments, threats, etc., in bringing me to renounce my faith, he appealed to my wife; but she too, thank God, was ready to give up her life rather than become a follower of the false prophet. When she saw the Moulavi was in a great rage, and was ready to order us to be tortured, by taking off our noses or ears, she began to instruct the twin boys—'You, my children, will be taken and kept as slaves, while we shall be killed; but remember my last words, do not forget to say your prayers both morning and evening, and as soon as you see the English power re-established, which will be before long, fly over to them, and relate to them everything that has befallen us.' 'For He said, Surely they are My people, children that will not lie: so He was their Saviour. In all their affliction He was afflicted, and the angel of His presence saved them: in His love and in His pity He redeemed them' (Isa. lxiii. 8, 9)."

When by 1858 the campaigns and sieges of Havelock and Outram, Nicholson and Baird Smith, Colin Campbell and Hugh Rose had restored order in the valleys of the Jumna and the Upper Ganges and in Central India, the Christians of Great Britain and America were touched with their Lord's Spirit when He said of His murderers, "Father, forgive them, they know not what they do." The contemporary literature of those years, letters, journals, and biographies, from the Prince Consort's Life to the columns of the daily newspapers, remind the reader of "the great cry . . . for there was not a house where there was not one dead," as mail after mail carried the news of cruel massacre and bloody conflict. The East India Company's government of India was passing—passing away—through the fire. The British Empire of India thus brought to the birth, was being baptized in blood. Had not the time begun to come to the millions of India, of which the Jewish seer spoke while yet in 732 B.C.

their Aryan fathers were descending on its Punjab plains, and ours were savages in the woods of the melancholy West?—"*The people that walked in darkness have seen a great light. . . . For all the armour of the armed man in the tumult, and the garments rolled in blood, shall even be for burning, for fuel of fire. For unto us a child is born, unto us a son is given; and the government shall be upon His shoulder. . . . Of the increase of His government and of peace there shall be no end.*"[1] The history of Christian India began in the year 1858; all before was for that a preparation. India, too, is to receive the Messiah, not in name only—as its early converts rejoice to do, so proclaiming themselves His slaves and no longer Mohammed's or Shiva's—but in power and with righteousness for ever. *The zeal of the Lord of hosts shall perform this.*

The Churches and Societies of England and Wales, of Scotland and Ireland, of the United States of America and Canada, even of Germany, Denmark, and Sweden, confessed with shame how little they had done for the only part of the continent of Asia where every door was open, where toleration was complete, where even the convert from Islam was protected. While the older organisations showed fresh life, new and catholic agencies were established, notably that which is now termed the Christian Literature Society for India, founded as a loving memorial of forgiveness, to propagate Christian literature and train native Christian teachers. Duff directed the Methodist Episcopal Church of America to the vast districts of Oudh and Rohilkhund, until the Mutiny uncared for. Wilson, who had sent the Irish Presbyterian Church to the native states of Kathiawar and North Bombay, now despatched Dr. Shoolbred and the missionaries of the United Presbyterian Church of Scotland—till that time confined to the negroes—to the vast group of native states, Mohammedan and Hindu, with aboriginal tribes, which form Rajpootana. The Moravian Unity of the Brethren, the Society of Friends, the Original Secession

[1] Isaiah ix. 2, 5, 6, 7 (revised version). See "The Book of Isaiah" in *The Expositor's Bible*, vol. i. chapter vii.

Church of Scotland, the Presbyterian Church of Canada, many an isolated or independent mission seeking to do simply on a smaller scale the will of God towards the people of India, settled in British districts and native states before neglected. As the Eastern Empire of Great Britain extended, through the second Afghan and Burmese Wars, the evangelical missionary followed the British flag which, in some cases on the Punjab frontier, only military force had kept him from preceding in his zeal to proclaim the gospel of peace to the regions beyond. The medical missionary, Dr. Downes, was brought back from Kafristan; the pilgrim missionary of the Punjab, Maxwell Gordon, died as a volunteer chaplain outside the gates of Kandahar.

We shall see how the missionaries of Reformed Christendom to the three hundred millions of Southern Asia under British protection have increased fourfold in the last forty years. Yet how miserably small is their number—seventeen hundred—at the opening of the second century of India's evangelisation! But from Buddhist Mandalay on the far north-east, where Britain marches with China, right west for two thousand miles to Mohammedan Quetta between Afghanistan and Persia, and from that lofty base-line down on either side of the great Hindu Peninsula to Cape Comorin, the land has been for the first time taken possession of for Jesus Christ, and only the little faith of every Christian delays the coming conversion of India.

VII

THE UNITED STATES OF AMERICA'S CO-OPERATION

"*Whether any do enquire of Titus, he is my partner and fellow-helper concerning you; or our brethren, they are the messengers of the churches, and the glory of Christ.*"—2 COR. viii. 23.

THE foreign politics of the United States of America are Foreign Missions. Starting into national life, free alike from the ecclesiastical bonds, the feudal institutions, and the political interests of Europe, but possessing the full heritage of British history, literature, and character, the Americans were from the first prepared to become the chief messengers of Christ to the human race. In four hundred years they have, by Christian colonisation and home missions, evangelised their own continent from the Atlantic to the Pacific Ocean, bringing into the Church the remnant of the Red Indian tribes, and giving to Christendom its "richest acquisition" in sixty-five millions of Christian citizens, whom every year increases in number and influence. In the whole development of mankind during six thousand years there has been only one people and one land ready made, as it were, to be itself free, and to all beside the apostle of liberty in its highest form—the freedom which is in Christ Jesus.

The first duty of the Christians who sought liberty of conscience and the profits of commerce at Manhattan Island, Plymouth Rock, and the various colonies, was to the natives. The Dutch West India Company, attracted by the furs of the New World, as their East India Company had been a quarter of a century before by the pepper of Malabar and the spices of Malaysia, received its charter in 1621.[1] Eight years after Jonas Michaelius organised the first reformed congregation on the continent of North America. In his letter "from the island of Manhatas, in New Netherland, this eleventh August, Anno 1628," he pictures the "entirely savage and wild" character and customs of the Red Indians, and arrives at this conclusion, "Let us, then, . . . begin with the children who are still young." He would instruct them "not only to speak, read, and write in our language, but also especially in the fundamentals of our Christian religion. . . . But they must speak their native tongue . . . as being evidently a principal means of spreading the knowledge of religion through the whole nation. In the meantime it must not be forgotten to pray to the end with ardent and continual prayers for His blessing. . . . May God have mercy upon them finally that the fulness of the heathen may be gradually accomplished."

In the fifty-five years during which the Dutch Company held the territory which they named New Netherlands, from the Connecticut River to the Delaware, many pastors preached the gospel to the red man. But the only name beside that of the good Michaelius, who returned to Holland in 1633, is that of Van Mekelenburg, better known in its Hellenized form, Megapolensis. In 1643 he began near the present city of Albany his mission to the Mohawks, whose language he spoke with eloquence, and he received many of them into the fellowship of the Church. He used his influence with the red tribes to save more than one Jesuit from torture and death. He was the counsellor who advised the surrender to the English in 1664 to prevent effusion of blood—that decisive act which proved a turning-point in history.[2]

[1] See Bryce's *American Commonwealth*, vol. iii. p. 497, for a view of the religious superiority of America, which, however, does not mention the foreign missionary aspect, but generalises "works of active beneficence."

[2] Joannes Megapolensis thereafter returned to Holland, with his

John Robinson, from his refuge at Leyden, had offered to take four hundred Puritan families to the New Netherlands, but the Pilgrim Fathers landed at New England in 1620. If trade, rather than freedom to worship God which they had secured for themselves and others, was the first object of the Dutch settlements, the Puritans who found a home at Leyden around the cultured and devoted Robinson, were missionaries. They took back with them Squanto, the only survivor of the twenty Indians whom Hunt had six years before perfidiously carried to Spain, whence he found his way to London. Then it was that our forefathers used to sing a missionary hymn with these words,

Dark America convert,
And every pagan land.

In 1631 the great missionary of the Puritans, John Eliot, landed at Boston, a year after the foundation of the city, and became minister of its Roxbury suburb. He learned the Mohican language; in 1660 he formed his converts into a Church at Natick on the Charles River, and the year after began to print at Cambridge his translation of the Bible and other works. The illustrious Harvard University there really originated in his college to train native pastors and teachers.

What Holland began and England continued was followec up by Scotland till the United States started on their

medical missionary son, Samuel. His account of the Mohawk Indians, written in 1644, is translated in Hazard's State Papers. His Dutch epitaph is thus translated in Dr. E. T. Corwin's *Manual of the Reformed Church in America*:—

"New Netherlander, weep,
Check not the gushing tear,
In perfect shape doth sleep
Megapolensis here.
New Netherland's great treasure,
His never-tiring work
Was day and night to pray,
And zeal in the Church exert.
Now let him rest where may,
He scorn all worldly pleasure."

separate career. In 1641 the John Knox of his day, Alexander Henderson, and five other Scots ministers, signed the petition of William Castell, "parson of Courteenhall," in Northamptonshire, which, with the "Eliot Tracts," led Cromwell and the Long Parliament to create the still-existing Corporation for the Propagation of the Gospel in New England. In 1645 "The Directory for the Publick Worship of God," adopted by the General Assembly, instructs ministers and people "to pray for the propagation of the gospel and kingdom of Christ to all nations." Yet, like all other Confessions of Faith and Catechisms, those of the Westminster Assembly do not allude to the Church's duty to heathen, Mohammedans, and Jews. But in 1672 there appeared one of the least known, though most excellent, works of Dr. John Owen, his "Discourse concerning Evangelical Love, Church Peace and Unity,"[1] in which he more fully states and enforces the duty of Christendom "towards the infidel, pagan, and Mohammedan world, Jews and Gentiles."

The first attempt of Scotland, as such, to send missionaries to the heathen was in 1699 and 1700, when two successive General Assemblies enjoined the ministers who formed part of the unhappy Darien expedition to labour among the natives of America. "The Lord, we hope, will yet honour you, and this Church from which you are sent, to carry his name among the heathen." Michael Shields, friend of Renwick, the last Scottish martyr, was one of these ministers, and may be called the first foreign missionary from Scotland, after the Scoto-Irish. "Whether he died in the wilds of Caledonia, on the sea, in Jamaica, or at Charleston bar in Carolina, we know not, but he never returned," is the record of the editor of his *Faithful Contendings Displayed.* With this the action of the Church of Scotland, as a Church, ceased till 1825, and its godly members joined with others in missionary societies.

In 1701, some private gentlemen who used to meet in Edinburgh "for reformation of manners, reflecting on the

[1] See pp. 71-73 of vol. xv. of his Works, edited by Rev. Dr. W. H. Goold, 1851.

ignorance, atheism, popery, and impiety that did so much abound in the Highlands and Isles of Scotland, did justly reckon that they flowed in a great measure from want of suitable means of instruction," whence the foundation of the Society in Scotland for Propagating Christian Knowledge. In 1706 they applied to the General Assembly for aid, and received a national collection. In 1709 they obtained a charter, and 82 leading Presbyterians were chosen members. To this society Dr. Daniel Williams, founder of the Williams Library of London, left several legacies for foreign missions, among them an estate yielding £50 a year, to be paid "a twelvemonth after the Society have actually sent three missionaries to foreign parts." Accordingly, in 1741, John Sargent was sent to the Red Indians on the Housatonic; in 1742, Azariah Horton to the same on Long Island; in 1743, David Brainerd to the same on Delaware and Susquehannah; in 1748 John succeeded David Brainerd;—all through the Synod of New York, who, in 1751, enjoined "all their members to appoint a collection in their several congregations once every year" —their beginning of foreign missions. In 1757 the Scottish Society bought land in South New Jersey, called the Brotherston tract, for an Indian reserve.

In 1774 the Synod of New York asked the Society to send two natives of Africa who had been converted to Christ "on a mission to propagate Christianity in their native country." The negroes were trained in the college of New Jersey for the coast of Guinea. The war of the American Revolution prevented this. In 1771 the first Red Indian minister who visited Great Britain, Samson Occom, raised £10,000 for the Indian school of Mr. Wheelock of Lebanon, Connecticut, among the Oneida Indians. His visit caused great interest. Of the above sum £2000 was raised in Scotland, and invested by the Scottish Society at 5 per cent. The Foreign Mission funds seem to be spent by this Society, now reorganised, on the Blantyre Mission of the Established Church of Scotland in East Central Africa.

In 1744, under the influence of Whitefield and the

revivals, several ministers in the west of Scotland united to form that Prayer Concert "that our God's kingdom may come," which, as commended by Jonathan Edwards in New England, prepared William Carey and his contemporaries for the formation of the first English Missionary Society in 1792. Following that came the London Missionary Society, now preparing to hold its centenary.

Members of the various Presbyterian Churches in the United States, encouraged by the success of the movement in London, and not then ready any more than the Church of Scotland to use the Church as a missionary organisation, founded in 1796 the New York Missionary Society, which in 1818 became merged in the United Foreign Missionary Society, composed of the Presbyterian, Reformed Dutch, and Associate Reformed Churches. The object, no longer confined to the Indians of North America, covered "Mexico, South America, and other portions of the heathen and antichristian world." President Monroe[1] used the new society as the State almoner for the civilisation of the Indians. The work was practically confined to what is now happily regarded as a Home Mission of the American Churches, when it was transferred to the American Board for Foreign Missions. The Synod of Pittsburgh, which had always been foremost in missionary zeal, in 1831 formed the Western Missionary Society, which became merged six years after in the great Board of the Presbyterian Church. This society it was which first led the Presbyterians of America to seek the conversion of India, while caring for the negroes of what is now Liberia, and the first to look "eventually" to Central Africa as a principal field of its intended operations.

In May 1834 John C. Lowrie and William Reed sailed in the "Star" from Philadelphia, and in due time the former founded the famous Lodiana Mission. It was a momentous step, full of hope for the future of India and Central Asia. John Lowrie, followed by John Newton, first opened up to the gospel of Christ the Punjab, its

[1] See Dr. Ashbel Green's *Historical Sketch of Domestic and Foreign Missions in the Presbyterian Church, U.S.A.* Philadelphia, 1838.

Sikhs and Mohammedans. The Free Church of Scotland had been urged to open a mission at Lahore when it became a British capital, but Dr. Duff followed the more catholic course of giving the American Mission such ordained converts as Gopinath Nundy and Goluk Nath, of the latter of whom he wrote in 1848:—"Through him our Institution is diffusing the light of the gospel among the warlike Sikhs, who so lately contested the sovereignty of India with Britain." The successors of these pioneers have proved worthy of them in the prayerful zeal and the far-seeing energy with which they have followed up the wars and annexations of the British Government, and in the apostolic charity with which they have invited and co-operated with the Anglicans of the Church Missionary Society. Associated with Dr. Lowrie was the Rev. James R. Campbell of the Reformed Presbyterian Church of America. Allahabad, and the region of North India between that and the frontier at Peshawur, became remarkable for the labours of saints and scholars like Owen and Walsh, Janvier and Loewenthal, Morrison and Forman.

We have not yet named the greatest of all American missionaries, that we might trace the course of the Presbyterian occupation of the Punjab and Hindustan. Adoniram Judson is surpassed by no missionary since the apostle Paul in self-devotion and scholarship, in labours and perils, in saintliness and humility, in the result of his toils on the future of an empire and its multitudinous peoples. He took possession of Burma for Christ when only a strip of its coast had become the nucleus of the eastern half of the British Empire of India; and he inspired his native country to found two great missionary societies.

Samuel John Mills, born in the year of the independence of his country, and consecrated by his mother to the service of God as a missionary, when at Williams' College, Massachusetts, gathered together his fellow-students behind a haystack daily to pray for self-surrender to the Lord's call to go to the uttermost parts of the earth. At Yale University he continued the propaganda. At the Theological College of Andover he met with Judson. There, in 1810, Judson drew up the memorial, signed by himself, Mills, Nott, and Newell, asking the General Association of Massachusetts "whether they may expect patronage and support from a missionary society in this country, or must commit themselves to the direction of a European society." The result was the formation of the American Board of Commissioners for Foreign Missions in 1812. Mills found his career and early death on the west coast of Africa. Judson, becoming a Baptist on the voyage to India, was sent by William Carey to Burma, with the consequent establishment of the American Baptist Missionary Union in 1814.

During two of the thirty-seven years of Judson's apostolate in Burma, 1844 and 1845, he enjoyed the friendship and help of the British Commissioner of Tenasserim. That was Captain Durand of the Bengal Engineers, a scion of the Dukes of Northumberland, who had sailed and been shipwrecked along with Dr. Duff off Dassen Island, and had been private secretary of the Governor-General, Lord Ellenborough. After learning to love Judson as he all his life admired Duff, Durand became one of the heroes of the first Afghan campaign. The close of the Mutiny saw him successively one of the first members of the Council of India, foreign secretary, member of the Governor-General's Council, and Lieutenant-Governor of the Punjab, where an accident, all too soon for the empire, ended the stainless and chivalrous career of the Christian soldier, Major-General Sir Henry Marion Durand, K.C.S.I., C.B. It is such a man who wrote the first and noblest, if the briefest, biography of Adoniram Judson,[1] and impassioned but discriminating sketches of Ann Hasseltine and Sarah Judson, whom also he knew. The foe against which Judson equipped himself with the panoply of God was Buddhism, professed at the present day by seven millions out of the eight who occupy the now British province, which in its independence he influenced from Moulmein to Ava. In the foul prison of that capital he lay for nine-

[1] In the *Calcutta Review* for 1850, then edited by Dr. Duff. The article is reprinted by his son in vol. ii. of *Durand's Life* (1883).

teen months, in three or five pairs of fetters, that he might win the land for Christ, as he did win much of it for Christian Britain. This is the first testimony, of the most upright soldier-statesman next to Henry Lawrence the writer has known, to the missionaries sent by evangelical America for the conversion of India:—

"Are we to suppose truth less powerful than falsehood? Are we to despair of her coping with an opponent, which the Hindu Pantheon and the Brahmanical fallacy trod down into the dust? We must be of very different mettle, and actuated by very different views from the Burman apostle, Adoniram Judson, if for a moment so faint-hearted a feeling lodge in our breasts. He, from the dawn to the close of his eventful career, could contemplate the millions still under the yoke of Buddhist error with the hope and the assurance of ultimate victory for the cause of truth. Strong in this hope, like a good soldier of the Cross, he unfurled his standard on the enemy's ground; and though in the contest it was at times struck down, yet the standard-bearer's heart and courage were proof, and the banner triumphing in such hands over every struggle, soon rose and floated again in the breath of Heaven. We may well say with the Psalmist, 'How are the mighty fallen in the midst of the battle!' But in this instance, though the mighty are fallen, the weapons of war are not perished. A champion of the Cross, and a notable one too, has indeed, after waging a seven-and-thirty-years' conflict against the powers of darkness, fallen at his post; but he has fallen gloriously, leaving a well-furnished armoury to his seconds and successors in the fight—weapons sound of temper, sharp of edge, and gleaming brightly with the light of Heaven. He was indeed a mighty champion—mighty in word—mighty in thought—mighty in suffering—mighty in the elasticity of an unconquerable spirit—mighty in the entire absence of selfishness, of avarice, of all the meaner passions of the unregenerate soul—mighty in the yearning spirit of love and of affection—above all, mighty in real humility, in the knowledge and confession of the natural evil and corruption of his own heart, in the weakness which brings forth strength—mighty in fulfilling the apostolic injunction, 'Whatsoever ye do, do it heartily, as to the Lord, and not unto men'—mighty in the entire, unreserved devotion of means, time, strength, and great intellect to his Master, Christ."

That eulogy is from the pen of the high official who saw its subject at work night and day, and it is within the truth. Yet this stern soldier, whose enemies complained of no fault in him, save the severity of his judgments, wrote of the three remarkable companions of Judson's life and toil:—"To our mind there is no comparison whatever between what the missionary has to bear and what his wife has to endure in the American Baptist Mission on the Tenasserim coast."

Contrasting the character, methods, and results of the work of Judson with that of Xavier, Durand, who was no sectary, wrote—

"The isle of Sancian saw Xavier expire, with *In te, Domine, speravi; non confundar in æternum* on his lips. Three centuries have passed since this hope was uttered with his dying breath by one of the noblest heroes of the Cross. Of his labours which, under any aspect, were truly gigantic, what now remains? Where are the churches which he founded? We will not ask where are the Scriptures which he translated, for that he considered neither his duty nor his calling; but where is there anything to indicate that the spoken word, the seed sown three centuries ago, struck root, and grew, and continues to bear fruit? His success was sudden, meteor-like, and transient, as that of one of earth's conquerors. It was too much based upon the gross superstition of his hearers, to which his own deep enthusiasm and fanaticism made no vain appeal:—he conquered them with their own weapons rather than with the dogmas of his own creed.

"Far different has been the success of the seven-and-thirty years of Judson's continuous unflinching labour. His career has not been marked by the alleged sudden conversion of tens of thousands of idolaters. Princes indeed listened, but did not bow their heads to the truths of the gospel. Brilliant success nowhere attended him. Yet it may be permitted us to doubt whether Judson has not laid the foundation of a fabric, which, instead of vanishing in the course of the next three centuries, will, should earth last, grow into the stately proportions of an extensive and solid spiritual temple."

When, in 1820, Judson first surveyed the splendid pagodas and extensive ruins of the once famous city of Pah-gan where, eight centuries before, the mingled atheism and devil-worship of the Buddhists was first disseminated by Shen-ah-rah-han, the Christian apostle exclaimed—

"'We looked back on the centuries of darkness which are passed. We looked forward, and Christian hope would fain brighten the prospect. Perhaps we stand on the dividing line of the empires of darkness and light. O shade of Shen-ah-rah-han! weep over thy fallen fanes; retire from the scenes of thy past greatness! But thou smilest at my feeble voice;—linger, then, thy little remaining day. A voice mightier than mine—a still small voice—will erelong sweep away every vestige of thy dominion. The Churches of Jesus will soon supplant these idolatrous monuments, and the chanting of the devotees of Budh will die away before the Christian hymn of praise." "True, Judson," adds Durand, "and those Christian hymns of praise will ascend heavenward, either in your own pure rendering of the words of the sweet psalmist of Israel, or in the poetical versions and original compositions of the talented being, the second partner of your labours and trials."

Before death parted them, and she was laid to rest in the green islet of St. Helena, Sarah Judson wrote the lines which sent her husband back to the conflict, and which thus conclude—

> "Then gird thine armour on, love,
> Nor faint thou by the way—
> Till the Budh shall fall, and Burma's sons
> Shall own Messiah's sway."

When Judson himself revisited his native land, and was about to return to finish his service in Burma, voiceless with emotion he wrote at Boston a farewell address which should be the priceless heritage of American Christians. "At one moment the lapse of thirty-four years is annihilated; the scenes of 1812 are again present." But where, he asked, are "my early missionary associates—Newell, and Hall, and Rice, and Richards, and Mills? Where are the intervening generation who moved among the dark scenes of Rangoon, and Ava, and Tavoy? With what words shall I address those who have taken their places—the successors of the venerated and beloved—of the generation of 1819?"—

"In that year American Christians pledged themselves to the work of evangelizing the world. They had but little to rest on, except the command and promise of God. The attempts then made by British Christians had not been attended with so much success as to establish the practicability, or vindicate the wisdom, of missionary enterprise. For many years the work advanced but slowly. One denomination after another embarked in the undertaking, and now American missionaries are seen in almost every land and every clime. Many languages have been acquired; many translations of the Bible have been made; the gospel has been extensively preached; and Churches have been established, containing thousands of sincere intelligent converts. The obligation, therefore, on the present generation to redeem the pledge given by their fathers is greatly enhanced. And it is an animating consideration that, with the enhancement of the obligation, the encouragements to persevere in the work, and to make still greater efforts, are increasing from year to year. Judging from the past, what may we rationally expect during the lapse of another thirty or forty years? Look forward with the eye of faith. See the missionary spirit universally diffused, and in active operation throughout this country—every Church sustaining, not only its own minister, but, through some general organization, its own missionary in a foreign land. See the Bible faithfully translated into all languages—the rays of the lamp of Heaven transmitted through every medium, and illuminating all lands. See the Sabbath spreading its holy calm over the face of the earth—the Churches of Zion assembling, and the praises of Jesus resounding from shore to shore; and though the great majority may still remain, as now in this Christian country, 'without hope and without God in this world,' yet the barriers in the way of the descent and operations of the Holy Spirit removed, so that revivals of religion become more constant and more powerful.

"The world is yet in its infancy. The gracious designs of God are yet hardly developed. 'Glorious things are spoken of Zion, the city of our God.'"

The writer of that prayer-prophecy broke forth — "I wish with my own voice to praise God for the proofs which He has given of His interest in missions. Pray for me and my associates and the missionary work." What a rebuke is this to the little faith of the Churches at the close of the first missionary century! But the answer has assuredly come to that longing aspiration in a way that Judson knew not, when he declared himself ready to go to Ava again and risk his life once more if he could only have an article of toleration inserted in the British treaty with the king. First Pegu and then all Burma fell under Christian sway, and toleration reigned from the Bay of Bengal to the confines of China and even over Siam. Christian governors succeeded Durand—Arthur Phayre, beloved by every American in Burma, Sir Rivers Thomson, Sir Charles Aitchison, Sir Charles Bernard, and the present provincial ruler. The Karens have poured into the Church by families and villages; the Burmans follow more slowly. But the census revealed 120,768 native Christians in Burma three years ago, of whom those under Judson's society had increased at the rate of 43 per cent in ten years. "One soweth and another reapeth," and both shall rejoice in the harvest since, on 27th June 1819, Judson wrote in his journal, "Moung Nan, the first Burman convert, was baptized."

When the other early missionaries of the American Board, Hall and Nott, were driven from Calcutta in 1812 they took ship to Bombay, relying on the Christian reputation of the governor, Sir Evan Nepean. After warning them off, the discussions in England on the first charter of toleration in 1813 led him to temporise, and they were with difficulty permitted to take up the great mission to the Marathas of Western India, for whom Carey had just prepared his translation of the New Testament, besides Grammar and Dictionary. In places like Kalyan, seat of a Nestorian bishopric and scene of the martyrdom of four Romish Christians, and away inland to Ahmednuggur, the missions of the American Board have done a work which extorted the praise of the governor, Sir Bartle Frere, as it had met with the support of Sir Robert Grant, the hymn-writer, and led the present ruler of the Presidency, Lord Harris, to publicly declare when last year he opened some of the mission buildings:—"I do not think I can too prominently say that our gratitude towards this American Mission has been piling up and piling up all the years of this century." Again, "I take this public opportunity of conveying, on behalf of the Government of Bombay, our most grateful thanks for the assistance the people of the United States are rendering in pushing forward the cause of education in India. The conjunction of the efforts of the two countries out here is a happy augury that their joint efforts may be put forth in other directions also."

In the older Presidency of Madras the present Governor, Lord Wenlock, when opening the Arthur G. Watts Memorial of the American Lutheran Mission at Guntoor this year, spoke thus from the neutrality point of view:—"Our cousins in America are not, as we are, responsible for the welfare of a very large number of the human race; but seeing our difficulties and knowing how much there is to do, they have not hesitated to put their hands into their pockets to assist us in doing that which is almost impossible for any government to achieve unassisted. They go out themselves, their wives, and their sisters; they enter into all parts of the country, they spend a very large amount of money, and they spend their time and their health in promoting the welfare of those who are in no way connected with them in an extremely kind and generous manner, not only in Kistna district, but in other parts of the Presidency. In all districts I find our American cousins joining with us in improving the system of education and in extending it wherever it was wanted. To their efforts we owe a very great deal. It must be recognised that their great object is the advancement of the Christian religion."

In the North-Western Provinces, in Lucknow, the late Dr. Badley founded the Christian College of the American Episcopal Methodists on a site granted by the State near the sacred mound of the Residency, which is for ever associated with memories of the double siege, and of Henry Lawrence's death. The Lieutenant-Governor, Sir Auckland Colvin, as his last public act, opened the building, declaring that ever since his arrival in India he had witnessed with much satisfaction the aid given by missionaries to the British Government in educational and philanthropic enterprises. He eulogised the Episcopal Methodist missionaries, whom Dr. Duff invited to take up the evangelisation of Oudh just before the Mutiny of 1857, for their consistent and large-hearted policy and their widely beneficent plan for the improvement of all classes of the people. He pointed with satisfaction to the union of the American and the British flags which he saw around the new hall. The proceedings finished with the national anthem.

In the most populous of all the provinces of India, Bengal, with its seventy millions of human beings, the Lieutenant-Governor, Sir Charles Elliot, made at the Himalaya sanatorium of Darjeeling a statement which marks the advance in a wise toleration secured by British rule in the East, when reporting for the first time that the number of Christians in his jurisdiction had increased from 122,000 to 189,000 in the ten years ending 1891. He described missionaries of all Churches as forming "an unrecognised and unofficial branch of the great movement which alone justifies British rule in Southern Asia. The officers of Government have to treat all alike in religious matters, and to show no more consideration for one faith than for another, though they know right well that the only hope for the true development and elevation of the peoples lies in the evangelisation of India. Only the missionaries are carrying on that work, filling up what is deficient in the efforts of the Government."

The revival of foreign missionary enthusiasm created by the visit of Judson was renewed by that of Duff in the year 1854. The Scots missionary and orator had completed the reorganisation of the missionary administration of his own Church, and was about to return to Bengal for the last time, when Mr. George H. Stuart induced him to spend four months in America. Beginning with a vast meeting in Philadelphia, he spent the weeks from February to May in a campaign which extended from Louisville and St. Louis north to Chicago and Canada, and closed with New York. Then in the perfection of his powers, still under fifty years of age, the greatest missionary statesman Christendom has seen, whether as organiser, teacher, or orator, produced an effect on the Churches which continues to this hour. All was gathered up and directed to a practical end in the first Union Missionary Convention of America, fruitful parent of many ecumenical assemblies in the subsequent forty years. On the roll of the Convention are found the names of between two and three hundred representatives of the Evangelical Churches and Missions, notably those of the Reformed (Dutch) Church. The five resolutions passed, after frank and harmonious conference, embody the principles of the missions which are evangelising India and the non-Christian world, as these had not been stated since in 1805 Carey, Marshman, and Ward drew up the covenant of Serampore.[1] On reporting the proceedings to his own Church, Duff declared, "When these men of all ages and denominations came together and began to speak of Christ's work—the work of the evangelisation of the nations—it was astonishing what a spirit of love sprang forth into vivid manifestation. One venerable man said, 'It is the dawning of the millennium.' May that spirit speedily pervade the entire ecclesiastical firmament of the New World, and reach every corner of a sadly divided and distracted old Christendom!" Summoning America and Britain alike to form the United States of the World—united for its evangelisation—he had said to this Convention of 1854, "Let us arise and march together as one mighty phalanx to the spiritual conquest of the nations."

At this time evangelical America, through forty-two Churches and Societies, is spending a million sterling a year on foreign missions of all kinds. Its contribution to the conversion of the non-Christian world is a missionary battalion of 3500 men and women directing 11,500 native helpers, of whom 1250 are ordained, and supervising 26,000 churches in the mission fields. Of its foreign representatives 1250 are ordained missionaries, 250 are lay missionaries, and 850 are women, besides missionaries' wives, who make up the American force of 3500. These are trained and sent forth by the evangelical majority of the Christians of the west. The whole Church membership of the United States numbers twenty-one millions, and the last census reveals their Church property at a value of more than 646 millions of dollars, or 129 million pounds sterling. How much of the one million of this given by

[1] See *Short History of Missions*, page 166 of 3rd edition. Edinburgh, 1890.

the evangelical Churches for foreign missions goes to India does not clearly appear, but these are their organisations now at work in India proper, Burma, and Ceylon, side by side with those of Great Britain and Ireland.

UNITED KINGDOM OF GREAT BRITAIN AND IRELAND AND ITS COLONIES.	UNITED STATES OF AMERICA.
Baptist Missionary Society.[1]	* Baptist Missionary Union.
,, Zanana Society.	* Free Baptist Missionary Society.
* Canadian Baptist Telugu Missions.	
* London Missionary Society.	* Board of Commissioners for Foreign Missions.
Church Missionary Society.	
,, Zanana Society.	
Propagation of the Gospel Society.	
,, Ladies' Association.	
Oxford Mission.	
Cambridge Mission.	
* Society of St. John the Baptist.	
Dent Mission.	
Local Church of England.	
Free Church of Scotland.	* Presbyterian Church (North).
,, Woman's Society.	* United Presbyterian Church.
Established Church of Scotland.	Reformed (Dutch) Church.
,, Ladies' Association.	Reformed Presbyterian Church.
* United Presbyterian Church of Scotland.	German Evangelical Missionary Society in the United States.
* Presbyterian Church of England.	
* Welsh Calvinistic Mission.	
* Presbyterian Church of Ireland.	
* Canadian Presbyterian Church.	
Original Secession Church of Scotland.	

[1] Including Carey's Society of 1792, and the General Baptist Society founded by Pike in 1816, happily amalgamated before the Centenary of the former.

* These Societies report woman missionaries, but not separate organisations for woman's work.

UNITED KINGDOM OF GREAT BRITAIN AND IRELAND AND ITS COLONIES.	UNITED STATES OF AMERICA.
* Wesleyan Missionary Society.	Episcopal Methodist Church. ,, Woman's Society. Free Methodists.
Society of Friends. Bengal Evangelical Mission.	American Evangelical Lutheran. ,, Lutheran Church Board. Faith Mission (Berar). Kurku Mission (Central Provinces).
Chinsurah Zanana Mission. Society for Promoting Female Education in the East. Zanana Bible and Medical Mission.	American Women's Union Zanana Mission. American Episcopal Mission (Calcutta).

OTHERS.

Indian Home Mission.
Bethel Santal Mission.
Strict Baptist Mission.
Australian Baptist Missions.
Foreign Christian Mission.
East Bengal Aborigines' Mission.

Basel German Evangelical Mission.
Danish Lutheran Missionary Society
German Evangelical Lutheran (Gossner's).
Hermannsburg (Hanover) Mission.
Leipzig Evangelical Lutheran Mission.
Swedish Evangelical Lutheran Mission.
Episcopal Moravians or United Brethren.

Christo Somaj (Calcutta).
Independent Mission (Calcutta).
Christian Disciples (Calcutta).
Private Mission (Jamtara, Santalia).

* This Society reports woman missionaries, but not a separate organisation for woman's work.

These sixty-four organisations, great and small, are reported on as working in India, Burma, and Ceylon, at the end of the year 1890, by the Calcutta Missionary Conference, which has taken a detailed census of the Protestant Missions there in the five years 1851, 1861, 1871, 1881, and 1890.[1] Of the sixty-four the United States of America conduct eighteen, and Germany and other European and isolated agencies, seventeen. Except by one lady in Calcutta the Episcopal Church of America has not yet entered on the evangelisation of India.

The greatest of all the blessings which the evangelical Churches of America have conferred on the people of British India is that of healing their sick women, and thus powerfully showing the practically imprisoned inmates of the zanana and hareem, and the multitudes of widows so many of whom have never been wives, that to them the kingdom of God has come. Till recently Great Britain could not thus do what the liberal educational system of the United States had long enabled woman medical missionaries to begin. If Carey's colleague, Dr. Thomas, was the first medical missionary to the East in 1790,[2] and in 1798 the Dutch Dr. Vanderkemp, an Edinburgh student, began his mission to the Hottentots and Kafirs which extorted the admiration of Henry Martyn, it was Dr. Duff's educational system which in 1834 really founded medical missions in India.[3] He first induced his students, Bengali men and now women, to take a full medical qualification then in Great Britain and now in the Indian Universities, and started on their beneficent action the great hospitals and dispensaries of the Government of India. But long opposed by the teaching and licensing bodies in the United Kingdom, Christian women, yearning to relieve the misery, spiritual and bodily, of the millions of their sisters in the East, by teaching them of Christ the

[1] See the comparative results in the *Statistical Tables*, 1890, published at Calcutta by the Baptist Mission Press in 1892.

[2] In 1740 the Moravian Brethren sent five medical men to Persia, but unsuccessfully.

[3] See his *Life*, vol. i., chapter 8.

healer, were driven to America or Switzerland for training. Of the women missionaries sent out by America, no nobler has lived and died for the women and children of India than Mary Seelye, M.D. She worked alone in the dense population of Calcutta, and the gigantic work killed her in the midst of her success. The same fate befell other solitary and unaided workers—establishing the lesson that it is more true of women than of men, and more true of medical than of other missionaries, that they must go forth at least two and two. Now no evangelical mission in India is complete without those skilled and spiritual ministrants to the secluded half of the population of India, whom the example of America has led the medical schools of Great Britain and India itself to train and send forth to the highest calling that women can follow.

The story of one family and one mission will best illustrate the nature and the fruit of the co-operation of the Christians of America with those of the United Kingdom in the conversion of India. The family are the Scudders of four generations; the mission is that of the Reformed (Dutch) Church to Arcot in South India.

Five years before the death of Schwartz, or on 3rd September 1793, just a century ago, John Scudder was born at Freehold, New Jersey, and became one of the first physicians in New York. After a spiritual conflict with doubt of extraordinary intensity he found peace and power, and became one of the most active members of the Presbyterian Church in the city. While waiting in the anteroom of a lady patient, he took up a paper on "The Conversion of the World, or the Claims of Six Hundred Millions, and the Ability and Duty of the Churches respecting them." He had been moved by the self-surrender of Judson and the other young men of his own age ten years before, but had put the call from him. Now he at once offered himself to the American Board. In 1819 he sailed from Boston to Ceylon, where he was ordained and joined Newell; in 1836 he made the city of Madras the centre of his Tamil work, and he died when on sick leave at Wynberg, Cape Colony, in 1855. No stronger, more versatile, or more successful missionary pioneer ever evangelised a people as healer, preacher, teacher, and translator, in season and out of season. He lived in praying and working till, although he knew it not, he realised his ambition even in this world, "to be one of the inner circle around Jesus." Such a man had sons and children's children like himself to the fourth generation.[1] There was not a town in South-Eastern India which had not heard the gospel of Christ from his lips. There was not a village to which the publications of his Tamil press had not penetrated, while his descendants worked by his side and took up his mantle. His son, Silas, born in Ceylon in 1833, was, like them all, the subject of his father's daily prayer—"Make him a Christian and make him a missionary." The boy resisted, determined to make a fortune as a physician in New York, where he founded the Women's Hospital. But prayer prevailed, and he went out as a medical missionary to Arcot, where the Governor of Madras, Lord Napier and Ettrick, took Mr. Seward and many a visitor to see one of the most remarkable institutions under his administration. Like so many of the best men and women of all callings in India, he died of overwork.

It was in 1850 that John Scudder's eldest son, Henry Martyn Scudder, M.D., born in Ceylon in 1822, made a tour from Madras city in the neighbouring districts of Arcot. There, where Ziegenbalg had opened a school in 1716, where Sartorius ended his toils, and Kiernander taught before he went to Calcutta, and Schwartz landed in 1750, while Jean de Britto had carried on an offshoot of the Jesuit mission of Robert de Nobilibus, Scudder found a million and a half of human beings who had never heard the name of Jesus Christ. He sought and obtained permission to make the centre of a new mission in the northern district the city of Arcot, immortalised in history as the capital of the Nawabs of the Karnatic, captured and defended by Clive, as Orme and Macaulay so vividly

[1] See the early list in Dr. Corwin's *Manual of the Reformed Church in America* (1879), 3rd edition.

describe. Following the slow and sure method of the Scottish and American Presbyterians, Henry Martyn Scudder, his colleagues and successors, "never baptize any one, be his proficiency in knowledge ever so great, unless there is reason to believe that he is the subject of regeneration, and fit to enter the Church."[1] In that light this latest review of forty years' mission work in North Arcot should be read:[2]—

"It is a little more than forty years since Rev. Dr. Henry Martyn Scudder first pitched his tent in the North Arcot district, and laid the foundation of this mission. Forty years is but a brief cycle in a land so hoary with age as India, but we doubt whether any previous four decades have witnessed such stupendous changes. The material development of the district has been remarkable. Railways now penetrate the very heart of our mission field. Electric wires connect all our mission stations. Macadamised roads traverse the country in every direction. Magnificent bridges span the various rivers. Hospitals and dispensaries are established in all important centres. Houses of brick and tile take the place of those of mud and thatch in our towns. Clean streets and whitewashed walls show the observance of sanitary laws.

"Nor has the intellectual progress of the people been less marked. It is hard to believe, as one sees the vast number of schools that now exist of all grades, the growing number of natives who know English, the increasing circulation of papers and magazines, that all this has come about within the last forty years. And yet such is the fact. The social and moral changes have likewise been great. Superstitious customs that have been more powerful than law are gradually disappearing; Christian ideas on all subjects are spreading; the native mind is being formed on a new model. Natives of all castes travel freely by rail, attend the same school, and even read from the same book. Sudras contend with Brahmans for the highest government posts.

"Toward the accomplishment of these results our missionaries have contributed no small share. Besides preaching the gospel they have identified themselves with nearly every enterprise that has had for its object the amelioration of the people. They have been foremost in

---

[1] Dr. E. C. Scudder's paper, read to the Allahabad Missionary Conference of 1871.

[2] *Sixty-First Annual Report of the Board of Missions of the Reformed Church in America*, June 1893.

the extension of medical work. They were the pioneers of female education. They have encouraged and helped to promote sanitary reform. They have been the ready friend of the poor and oppressed.

"But what is there to show in the way of direct results? In 1861, ten years after he had entered the district, the founder of the mission was permitted to begin the annual report as follows:—'This mission, which sprang from a slender shoot, is by the culture of the Great Husbandman becoming a tree with boughs and flowers and fruit. This day we number nine missionaries, one native pastor, six churches, six catechists, four readers, six teachers, and 796 nominal Christians, of whom 232 are communicants. See what the Lord has wrought! We gaze upon His stately steppings and wonder and adore. He has transcended all our expectations.' But what emotions of joy would fill our brother's soul could he visit the mission to-day! While the number of missionaries remains about the same, we are able to report eight native pastors, sixty-two catechists, seventy-five readers and teachers, twenty-three churches, 124 congregations, 1881 communicants, 122 schools with 4517 pupils, 1809 of whom are girls, and a Christian community of 6504 souls.

"To free the Hindu from the shackles that Brahmanism has imposed upon him, and build him up so that all his faculties, moral, intellectual, and physical, shall receive development, is the work of the missionary. It is plain that the first step toward the new life must be conversion, but we use the word in no narrow sense. It is a conversion from what is false to what is true, from what is degrading to what is ennobling, from what is earthly and sensual to what is heavenly and spiritual. But while the work starts with conversion, it does not end there. That is simply the beginning which is to lead up to the true ideal, viz. character, the end of all being—the character of Christ, which is the character of God. We are aware that ours is no easy task. But we have yet to find any solid work for God that is easy. Nor do we expect to realise our hopes in a single generation. Neither reason nor revelation warrants us in expecting such a result. We are building not simply for the present, but for the future.

"Although we preach the gospel of peace, the world does not at first receive it as such. Every soul won for Christ is a conquest. We ask our friends to cultivate with us the grace of patience. It is greatly needed in the world to-day, and by no people more than by Americans. We assume that the rate at which we travel and erect buildings or make fortunes must have its counterpart in the work of missions too, and hence the impatience for immediate results. Listen to the weighty words of one of England's greatest preachers. 'Architects and builders adjust their work to the temper of the day, but the

Eternal Workman heeds not the varying moods and fashions of His creatures, but, in spite of the demand for rapid production, is at this hour as slow and as sure in His work as at any past time in history. A mission is essentially a work in which man counts for little although his active exertion is imperatively necessary. When this is felt, it will be felt also that an order, so to describe it, upon a given mission for so many converts at least, within such and such a time, is an indefensible thing.'"

Columbus found America when he was looking for India, and he persisted in the conviction that it was India he had found. So let it be; let us believe that the instinct of the great missionary admiral was true, as his America is used by the Spirit of God to carry life and light and joy to each of the great peoples of British India, to the Burmans and Karens of the north-east; to the Hindus, Mohammedans, and Sikhs of the martial north and north-west; to the Marathas of the western coast and plateau; to the Telugus of the eastern and central districts; to the Tamils of Arcot and Madura in the south; and to the villages of the depressed peoples who are everywhere pressing into the kingdom, from the Pariah serfs of Madras to the Choorha peasants of Sialkot.

VIII

THE METHODS OF THE EVANGELICAL MISSION TO INDIA

"*God so loved the world, that He gave His only begotten Son, that whosoever believeth in Him should not perish, but have everlasting life. For God sent not His Son into the world to condemn the world; but that the world through Him might be saved.*"—ST. JOHN iii. 16, 17.

WHAT is the India to which, with a patient faith and sometimes halting obedience, the Churches of the British Empire and of the United States of America are teaching Christianity? It is the land of three hundred millions of Hindus, Buddhists, Mohammedans, and Animists, all at variance with each other, and each dissatisfied with himself, all "vain in their imaginations and their foolish hearts darkened." Because the gospel of Christ is "the power of God unto salvation to every one that believeth" the missionary preaches that gospel to India as Paul did to Rome. There is a school of thinkers, somewhat disproportionately represented in the civil service of India, who loftily patronise the Christian missionary as on the same superstitious level with the votary of every religion, and declare that "England's prime function in India is at present this, to superintend the tranquil elevation of the whole moral and intellectual standard."[1] Even the positivist, the agnostic, and the eclectic, who believe death to end all, admit that the Hindu may be made

[1] Sir Alfred C. Lyall's *Asiatic Studies, Religious and Social*, 2nd edition, 1884.

better by the Christian morality. When Horace Hayman Wilson wrote his work on *The Religious Sects of the Hindus* he stored in the Bodleian Library of Oxford his collection of authorities as "libri execrandi." When Professor Max Müller published his first volumes of *The Sacred Books of the East* he was constrained to admit their ethical defects and even abominations. No one, Christian or Comtist, will seriously differ from the apostle Paul in his picture of Roman idolatry and lust, or will refuse to accept it as equally true of the Musalmans, polytheists, and demonolaters of India. The best that can be said of the best of them fills the true Christian with an infinite pity and a practical determination to reveal to them "the Desire of all nations."

MEDITATIONS OF A HINDU PRINCE[1]

All the world over, I wonder, in lands that I never have trod,
Are the people eternally seeking for the signs and steps of a God?
Westward across the ocean, and northward ayont the snow,
Do they all stand gazing, as ever, and what do the wisest know?

Here, in this mystical India, the deities hover and swarm
Like the wild bees heard in the tree-tops, or the gusts of a gathering storm;
In the air men hear their voices, their feet on the rocks are seen,
Yet we all say, "Whence is the message, and what may the wonder mean?"

A million shrines stand open, and ever the censer swings,
As they bow to a mystic symbol, or the figures of ancient kings;
And the incense rises ever, and uses the endless cry
Of those who are heavy-laden, and of cowards loth to die.

For the destiny drives us together, like deer in a pass of the hills.
Above is the sky, and around us the sound of the shot that kills;
Pushed by a Power we see not, and struck by a hand unknown,
We pray to the trees for shelter, and press our lips to a stone.

---

[1] From *Verses Written in India* (1889) by Sir Alfred Lyall.

The trees wave a shadowy answer, and the rock frowns hollow and grim,
And the form and the nod of the demon are caught in the twilight dim;
And we look to the sunlight falling afar on the mountain crest,
Is there never a path runs upward to a refuge there and a rest?

The path, ah! who has shown it, and which is the faithful guide?
The haven, ah! who has known it? for steep is the mountain side,
For ever the shot strikes surely, and ever the wasted breath
Of the praying multitude rises, whose answer is only death.

Here are the tombs of my kinsfolk, the fruit of an ancient name,
Chiefs who were slain on the war-field and women who died in flame;
They are gods, these kings of the foretime, they are spirits who guard our race,
Ever I watch and worship; they sit with a marble face.

And the myriad idols around me, and the legion of muttering priests,
The revels and rites unholy, the dark unspeakable feasts!
What have they wrung from the silence? Hath even a whisper come
Of the secret whence and whither? Alas! for the gods are dumb.

Shall I list to the word of the English, who come from the uttermost sea?
"The secret, hath it been told you, and what's your message to me?"
It is nought but the wide-world story how the earth and the heavens began,
How the gods are glad and angry, and a Deity once was man.

I had thought, "Perchance in the cities where the rulers of India dwell,
Whose orders flash from the farland, who girdle the earth with a spell,
They have fathomed the depths we float on, or measured the unknown main—"
Sadly they turn from the venture, and say that the quest is vain.

Is life then a dream and delusion, and where shall the dreamer awake?
Is the world seen like shadows on water, and what if the mirror break?
Shall it pass as a camp that is struck, as a tent that is gathered and gone
From the sands that were lamp-lit at eve, and at morning are level and lone?

Is there nought in the heaven above, whence the hail and the levin are hurled,
But the wind that is swept around us by the rush of the rolling world?
The wind that shall scatter my ashes, and bear me to silence and sleep
With the dirge, and the sounds of lamenting, and voices of women who weep.

Yes, it is the wide-world story of hereditary tradition, of primitive revelation which, in its divine fulness, power, and sanctions, Christianity proclaims for the conversion of India — "God so loved the world, that He gave His only begotten Son." To deliver in all its purity and completeness such a message, and to make it effectual with such men as the inheritors of centuries of ignorance of God or hostility to His Son, requires, first of all, that every missionary be like the first martyr, "full of the Holy Ghost and wisdom," "full of faith and power" (Acts vi. 3, 8). Before all methods is the man who is to work them. If the missionary be of the right spiritual temper, he will devise or apply with efficiency the method which God designs him to use.

The classical passages regarding the call and qualifications of men and women to be missionaries are Ephesians iv. and 1 Corinthians xii. and xiii. The Lord, having instituted the sacrament of commemoration and of consecration, and having proclaimed His command to teach all nations, on His ascension, "gave some men as evangelists," or "teachers" as it is in the parallel passage. The five signs of the true Christian missionary are these:—

(1) The missionary must be conscious of the call of Christ and the manifestation of the Holy Spirit for whatever "diversities of operations," as in 1 Corinthians xii. and 6, are given to him by God. This excludes every secondary motive however good in itself, and forbids every unworthy aim. The love of knowledge, the desire to travel, eagerness for early marriage, a legitimate hope of position or reputation, or even of pleasantly convenient work, are as much excluded as simony and hypocrisy, as

seeking a livelihood or a mere respectable profession. To use a mediæval phrase, the missionary must be Christ-intoxicated.

(2) The missionary must, in his training and his work, "covet earnestly the best gifts." He must qualify himself for the highest state of efficiency. At college he must study to the full measure of his powers and win, like Henry Martyn, the highest honours for the glory of his Master, while he feels that such honours are "a shadow," and prays that they be not a temptation. If not a college man, but an artisan, he must be master of his craft and rejoice in his art, that by teaching it in the spirit of the Carpenter's Son he may bring Christian communities to the birth and make nations of them.

(3) The missionary must follow the "more excellent way" of love as described in the golden passage that follows 1 Corinthians xii. He is to deal with the dark races, the majority of mankind, so as to be a means of bringing them out of darkness, and must not only love them, in his own degree, with the love of Christ, but must sympathetically show the patience, the tenderness, the wisdom of the Master, that his spiritual children may as soon as possible be made to walk on their own feet, and govern themselves, to be apostles to their countrymen. Less easy still, the missionary has to prove that, although a good temper towards his brethren is so difficult that it would seem practically to be the spiritual grace most seldom attained, he has learned apostolic charity in all its breadth of humility, self-sacrifice, and geniality. Ziegenbalg wrote in 1710—"I would humbly propose to the Protestant Churches to supply us with learned students in divinity, and send them here to be instructed in the Indian languages—men truly fearing God and hating covetousness, free from the inveterate ecclesiastical itch of ruling over God's inheritance." A century later Carey, Marshman, and Ward, in their Missionary Covenant which the brotherhood carried out through all their lives, made this the highest of the eleven points of which they wrote—"We think it right to

fix our serious and abiding attention." Judson's request to America was for "humble, quiet, persevering men; men of sound sterling talents, of decent accomplishments and natural aptitude to acquire a language; men of an amiable, yielding temper, willing to take the lowest place, to be the least of all and the servants of all; men who enjoy much closet religion, who live near to God and are willing to suffer all things for Christ's sake without being proud of it. These are the men we need!"

(4) The missionary must learn habits of order in his person, his study, his mission, and of business in keeping accounts, so as to economise the gifts of Christ's distant people, and in utilising time alike for work, rest, and recreation. In the great mission fields of the world want of common sense comes next to want of charity as an obstruction to the kingdom of Christ.

(5) The missionary, so called and so possessed of the Spirit of Christ, will complete the apostolic life and character thus—"We will give ourselves continually to prayer and to the ministry of the Word." The Serampore Covenant had this as its tenth point—"That we be constant in prayer and the cultivation of personal religion, to fit us for the discharge of these laborious and unutterably important labours. Let us often look at Brainerd, in the woods of America, pouring out his very soul before God for the perishing heathen, without whose salvation nothing could make him happy." And all this is as true of the members of the organisations—Churches and Societies—which select and accredit the missionaries as of those who go. Every true man and woman among them learns the fact that the highest spiritual development and enjoyment is in the work of foreign missions. Andrew Fuller, first and best of secretaries, wrote in 1789, when he joined Carey: "Before this I did little but pine over my misery, but since I have betaken myself to greater activity for God, my strength has been recovered and my soul replenished." Sutcliffe, their colleague, when dying, exclaimed, "I wish I had prayed more," or, as Fuller who often quoted this, paraphrased it, "I wish I had prayed

more for the outpouring of the Holy Spirit to attend the labours of our friends in India; I might have witnessed more of the effects of their efforts in the conversion of the heathen."

It is on prayer and sacrifice in Christendom, but, above all, on the personal spirituality and zeal of every missionary whom it sends forth now, that the future of the Church of India and the East depends. If the history, literature, and mental and moral character of the peoples of India demand Christians of the highest gifts of faith and intellect, the Spirit of God has richly granted a succession of such, while illustrating the law of the kingdom that weak things are chosen to confound the mighty. Carey, from the first, sought help in the record of David Brainerd, and willed to go to the scattered savages of the Pacific Ocean. God sent him to Bengal, as He had sent the Pietist scholars, Ziegenbalg, Schultze, and Schwartz, to South India. Since the martyrdom of Stephen, of Paul, and of Peter, no period of Church history and no region of the unevangelised world shows such a succession of great missionaries as the first century of the English-speaking conversion of India.

To follow the order of time, and mention only the holy dead, let the memory dwell on these names—Carey and Ward, Marshman and his wife, and Mack; David Brown and Claudius Buchanan, Martyn, Corrie, and Thomason; Heber and Cotton; Judson and the three women who were his true helpmeets, and Mason; Duff and Lacroix; John and Isabella Wilson; John Anderson, Stephen Hislop and Ion Keith-Falconer; Mullens and John Hay; Noble and George M. Gordon; Scudder and Newton; Caldwell and French. Every reader can add to the list, especially the names of women, matrons and maidens, and some not professional missionaries, who ministered to Christ in the persons of His flock in India. On them, too, as on all the servants who shall complete the number of God's chosen ones, and be with Christ where He is, the divine benediction is spoken and the apostolic record is written: "Prophets—who through faith subdued kingdoms, wrought righteousness, obtained promises," "of whom the world was not worthy." But wise and honest rulers of the world, like Lord Lawrence, bear to them this testimony: "Notwithstanding all that the English people have done to benefit India, the missionaries have done more than all other agencies combined."

The training of the best young men and women for missions to non-Christians, especially to the civilised and caste-bound millions of British subjects in the East, and the selection of the best of these, form the highest functions of Churches, committees, and secretaries. Where, as under Presbyterianism, the Church is itself the missionary society of which every communicant and child is a member, the missionary candidate is fully trained. He is, intellectually, the product of three or four years' study at one of the national universities, crowned by a degree, and of four years' thorough mastery of the Bible in the two original languages, of apologetic and systematic divinity, of the history of the Church, and of practical home mission and preaching work. Seven or eight years of such a course, severely tested, and guarded from the temptations of spiritual routine, have produced the men who have made the pioneers and the most successful messengers to the Brahmanical, Buddhist, and Mohammedan communities.

Nearly the same period of study, in which four or five years of medicine and surgery take the place of the Arts course and of Hebrew, qualifies the most successful medical missionaries who are ordained. The Universities of Cambridge, Oxford, and Dublin, liberalised, train the Anglicans and Nonconformists similarly, though with less theology and scholarship, for the Societies. Such full instruction as is common to ministers of all the Churches is better for the future missionary than that of special institutes, although these are necessary for unordained and artisan agents. For India, of all the world, the choicest of English-speaking youth are wanted. Such are never disappointed; the more accomplished they are for the conflict, the more they experience the joy of the true warrior for Christ. It is not such who return to cover their own discredit by childish criticism. Ever since the evangelical Churches of Christendom united, once a year on St. Andrew's Day and during the last week of November, in solemn intercession before God on behalf of missions, and especially that the Lord would thrust forth labourers into His harvest, India, China, and Japan, Africa and Oceania, have received from the United Kingdom and the United States hundreds of the student volunteers who, as when Judson and his followers reproached the Church of their day, are pressing to be sent to the front of the battle faster than there are faith and self-denial to send them.

The one aim—that Christians shall make Christians, and the best agent—the most efficient missionary spiritually and intellectually, being secured, the question of methods is easier of solution. Methods must follow the example and the command of Christ, under the providential guidance of the Holy Spirit. It is in the present stage of the Church's action in the non-Christian world, and especially in India, far more important to trust the missionaries it has sent, and to follow the evolution of Providence without weariness in well-doing or fickleness and faithlessness in council, than to be guided by critics, destitute alike of experience, charity, and responsibility, however plausible their profession.

Before He sent out the Twelve to the lost sheep of the house of Israel and the Seventy, "Jesus went about all the cities and villages teaching and preaching and healing" (St. Matthew ix. 35). These three words reappear in all the records of His last missionary charge, but amplified as if to leave unfettered the course of God's providence and the manifold activities of His Spirit in enabling His followers to do greater works than His own when upon earth. St. Matthew's is the widest—

(1) Disciple all nations: Μαθητεύσατε πάντα τὰ ἔθνη.

(2) Teaching them to observe all things whatsoever I have commanded you: Διδάσκοντες αὐτοὺς τηρεῖν πάντα ὅσα ἐνετειλάμην ὑμῖν.

(3) Preach the gospel to the whole creation, is Mark's: Κηρύξατε τὸ εὐαγγέλιον πάσῃ τῇ κτίσει.

(4) Ye are witnesses, is Luke's: Ὑμεῖς ἐστε μαρτύρες.

The conversion of India has been carried on for a century by methods springing out of the application of the example and the words of the Lord applied to its very different peoples at successive times. Seeking the supernatural conversion of the individual, the first missionaries naturally adopted the two methods essential and common to all Christian evangelising—they (1) translated the Bible into the language of the people, and they (2) preached its message in that language. Familiarity with the vernacular should be, and now is, insisted on in the case of every missionary even though his work be mainly through English. In his memorable paper on Preaching to the Hindus, read to the General Missionary Conference of India held at Allahabad in 1871, Dr. John Wilson, declaring the evangelisation of India to be in some respects the greatest distinctive enterprise yet attempted by the Church of Christ, defined preaching in India as "the proclamation of the gospel in many forms," and the mother tongue of the masses as the key to every form. English has rapidly become an alternative vernacular language with thousands, as temporary missionaries to the educated classes happily know. If there are now any absolute anti-Anglicists they must answer the question —Why did the wisdom of God choose the Greek language for the New Testament? But all must have the vernacular key to the heart of India, while the few wield that of the vernaculars themselves, the classical tongues and literatures of the Brahman, the Parsee, the Buddhist, and the Mohammedan.

(3) Teaching follows quick on translating and preaching. The children of converts must be taught, but the missionary soon finds that it is only the young whose conscience is quick and whose intelligence is active. While neglecting no inquirer, he learns to work for the coming generation, for the future as for the present. While earnestly seeking to persuade the individual he quickly realises that he is laying the foundation of a Church, of a spiritual community, of a nation. Then he is arrested by caste,

and by the impossibility of reaching one-half of the whole people except through their fathers and husbands. A generation passes before the door of the zanana or the hareem is open even to the missionary's wife. Translating, preaching, and teaching the men is followed in the development in the Church of India by (4) specially trained women visiting the women in their own homes. The individual becomes the family, and the families form churches and communities. Then the evangelical mission glides into (5) the new method of healing as, like the Lord, it goes about all the cities and villages. Again, it is the men who are first reached in this complex Indian society, but for them the State provides such help in the cities that medical missions in India seek more and more the neglected villagers. Last of all, Great Britain wakes up, as America had before done, to the sufferings of the other sex, and the great necessity is woman medical missionaries, as we enter on the second century. Of 170 medical men with a full British qualification in the mission fields of the world only 50 are in India. Of the 20 of these who are women 16 are in India, and every year is adding to the number. The gift of the United States of America to the women of India is far greater than that.

(6) The literary method, as it may be called, the use of the press to supply pure reading to the young Christian Church, while it is the first resorted to for the translation of Holy Scripture, has been the latest so far as the publication of good books for men, women, and children is concerned. Through the Christian Literature Society, the fruit of the Sepoy War of 1857-58, Dr. Murdoch, encouraged by Lord Northbrook when Governor-General, has produced and published school and reading books in most of the languages of India. To provide good text-books in the various vernacular languages for a vast juvenile population is a very difficult matter. For the forty years since Dalhousie's action this was left, as in the West, to private enterprise. But neither morally nor educationally has this been satisfactory. Accordingly, seventeen of the best experts in Bengal, of whom only four

are Europeans, now form a central text-book committee, independent alike of authors and publishers, and these advise the Government Department, who publish an authorised list. The plan for middle schools has proved so successful that it has been extended to high and primary schools. The result is that there is a rush of books for adjudication, of which one-half are declared unsuitable for schools. For more than half a century the Calcutta School-Book Society has most usefully served as the chief medium for distributing books, but Sir Charles Elliot, the Lieutenant-Governor, amalgamated it with the Society for the Diffusion of Useful Literature, which receives an annual grant of Rs. 2800. No man has done more during a long lifetime for pure literature in India, Ceylon, and China than Dr. Murdoch. The Scottish missions in Africa, no less than in India, and even in China, and wherever they are established, are always marked by the practical features of the educational and industrial training of the converts. Scotsmen are teachers and are captains of labour, so that their missionaries create Christian communities and form them into Christian nations.

Perhaps the most apparently remarkable result of the hundred years of foreign missions is seen, on their literary side, in the reduction of the languages of the peoples to writing and grammatical form, and in the translation of the Bible. When Carey settled at Serampore, and the Derby editor, William Ward, became his printer colleague, the Bible was translated into only 30 languages, beginning with the Latin. He himself, with his other colleague, Marshman, and their college of pundits, made or edited nearly 40 more. To-day the Bible is sold for a trifle in 330 languages—a gain of 300 in a century. What that involves and means the greatest secular philologers are not slow to confess. But the spiritual results it is impossible to over-estimate. The time has not yet come when the native Christians themselves shall produce translations of the Bible more idiomatic and national than those made and periodically revised by foreign missionary scholars, for the Wiclif and Tyndale of the Church of India have not yet arisen. But not a few Hindu and Mohammedan converts have enriched the ethically barren literature of their people with works that will live, such as Imad-ud-din Lahiz, D.D., with twenty-seven works in Hindi, Hindustani, and Persian; Baba Padmanji and Ganpatrao Navalkar in Marathi; Lal Behari Dey, in Bengali; and many more in Tamil, Kanarese, and Malayalam, while the publications in English as the *lingua franca* of the educated classes are innumerable.

The evangelical missionaries in India have recently defined their own methods after the experience of a century. In 1889 thirty-six of the British, American, and Danish agents of nine of the principal organisations at work in South India, and four native clergymen, forming the Madras Missionary Conference, sent "an open letter to the Churches" of the West. This communication, extending to sixteen widely-printed pages, must be put at the head of all the literature on the subject up to the present time, in ripeness of experience, calmness of judgment, wisdom of suggestion, accuracy of facts, and catholicity of spirit. A description of modern Hinduism, its popular worship and as a system of thought, followed by a sketch of the present condition of the people, leads up to these conclusions:—The conditions of mission work in India are intricate and peculiarly difficult; the elements with which Christianity has to contend are most various and powerful; the present time, marked not only by disintegration and social unrest, but by struggles after reform, pathetic and hopeful even in their comparative failure, calls for every possible sacrifice and for wise and varied effort for the salvation of India. "Since the Spirit of God still abides in the Church, it is not shut up to a mere imitation of methods used in bygone days by men, however saintly, successful, or illustrious. God is with us also, inspiring and guiding us as He guided our fathers; and by placing us in such new untried conditions God means us, and the Church through us, to learn new lessons and apply new methods. As missionaries in India for the specific purpose of making all its people the disciples of Jesus Christ, we judge of all methods by the degree in which they contribute, whether ultimately or immediately, to the attainment of this great end. Our methods, as might be expected, are various, and as far as possible, the gospel of Christ is presented to every section of the community." The work now being done is grouped as follows:—

I. MISSION WORK AMONG THE CHILDREN.
- Boys' Schools.
- Girls' Schools.
- Mixed Schools for Boys and Girls.
- Sunday Schools for Boys and Girls.

II. MISSION WORK AMONG YOUNG MEN.
- Higher Education in Schools and Colleges.
- Bible Classes for Young Men.
- Special Addresses (English) to Young Men.

III. MISSION WORK AMONG THE MASSES.
- Evangelistic preaching in streets and halls.
- Evangelistic preaching in circles of villages.
- Evangelistic tours and visits to Hindu festivals.
- House-to-house visitation.

IV. MISSION WORK AMONG WOMEN.
- Zanana teaching.
- Special Evangelistic meetings for Women.
- The work of Bible Women.

V. MISSION WORK AMONG THE SICK.
- Medical mission work by means of Hospitals and Dispensaries.
- Medical mission work in Zananas.
- Visitation of the Sick in Hospitals.

VI. MISSION WORK BY CHRISTIAN LITERATURE.
- The Bible Society.
- The Religious Tract Society.
- The Christian Literature Society.
- Sale of Bibles and other books by Colporteurs and at Depôts.
- Distribution of Tracts and Handbills.
- Reading Rooms.

VII. WORK AMONG NATIVE CHRISTIANS.
Preaching and pastoral oversight.
Sunday Schools for Christian Children.
Meetings for united prayer.
Young Men's Christian Associations.
Institutions for the training of Mission Agents.

"In all these methods there is no rigidity, nor do we hold the view that we have reached finality. We welcome wise suggestion whether coming from without or within. Of the methods now employed, we thankfully affirm that every one of them has been owned of God in the salvation of Hindus. To recent criticisms of Indian mission work in which its failure has been alleged, we do not think it needful to reply, since the Church of Christ in India is visible enough.

"In educational attainments, and in morality, the rapidly increasing Christian community is well known to be in advance of all other sections of the people of India. Though we gratefully acknowledge the success which has been gained, we attach but little importance to count of heads, believing that the moral test is higher than the arithmetical. The kingdom of God cometh not with observation, and to us there are many signs, subtle and unobtrusive, which assure us, more certainly than any figures on a register, that the Gospel of Christ 'wins its widening way.'

"We have noted an outcry in some quarters against the work of higher education, but knowing its value in India at the present time, we are convinced that Providence points out most clearly the duty of effectively maintaining it. The withdrawal from the mission field of this agency, which after all absorbs but a small fraction of our numerical strength, would leave a blank, for the filling up of which no hostile critic has yet made any practical suggestion.

"While we place the spiritual gifts of all mission agents, their conversion to God, their evident call to and spiritual fitness for Christian work, above all other qualifications, we desire also to lay stress on those other attainments without which Christianity receives only an imperfect representation. Since the work of European missionaries in India must continue mainly to be that of teaching, inspiring, moulding and shaping the Christian community, and guiding its methods of work as well as of preaching to non-Christians, we are convinced that men possessing the highest spiritual and intellectual gifts must always be sent forth, and that any reduction of the number of such men would be a calamity.

"In India, the question of the salary of Europeans has not been raised. We deem it unnecessary to refer to it beyond stating that in our opinion the allowances now granted are by no means excessive, but fairly reasonable, and that they are in no way superior on the average to what it is thought prudent and even necessary that ministers should have at home. No class of Englishmen in India, not even excepting artisans, receives such small allowances as the missionaries of the great Societies."

The most hopeful movement in Western Christendom is due to a new sense of responsibility for the non-Christian peoples. The section which both in and outside of the Churches corresponds to the Pietists of last century, no longer satisfied with Home Missions alone, or selfishly wrapt up in frames and feelings which stop short of active service and catholic intercession, seeks the conversion of the dark races. Africa and China chiefly rejoice in the results. India, with its unique Brahmanical and Musalman problems, its claims as a British dependency, and its advantages for assaulting the strongholds of Asiatic unbelief, has not yet shared proportionally in the new missionary activity. To some the evangelisation of its peoples through the disintegration and destruction of their hoary religious and social systems, seems to have suffered from the spiritual but inexperienced critics. Missionaries in India are doing the Church's most difficult work with fine courage, intelligent faith, and devoted obedience, and they expect the faithful intercession, the loyal support, and the loving sympathy of those whose representatives or substitutes they are. It is the whole Church which is working through them. While resenting criticism which, alike in its terms and its spirit, is of the kind condemned by the Lord in His untempered disciples, the missionary Churches and Societies have used it to review their methods in the conversion of the peoples of India. More particularly in England, the Church Missionary Society, representing two-thirds of the Church of England, the Wesleyan Missionary Society, and the London Missionary Society, have thus vindicated their position and their agents.

The discussion of the past four years has narrowed itself to what has been called Educational Missions, to the administration of which the Presbyterian Churches in Scotland have been called by national character and historical providence, though the English Baptist, Carey, led the way in this as in all the chief methods. In 1888 the Free Church of Scotland sent out two deputies to report on the missions begun by Duff and Wilson in India. In 1889 the Established Church of Scotland, which twenty-five years before had been roused by Dr. Norman Macleod's report of his visit, published the opinions of eighty-four experts on this subject. Dr. Macleod's last words to his Church were these,—"The special characteristic of the Scottish nation and the special gift of the Scottish Church seem to be in the pathway of education. . . . If the non-religious schools and colleges be left alone they will eventually leave the bulk of the educated portion of the natives either without any faith in God or without any fear of God. Whereas, if Christian schools and colleges flourish alongside of secular ones, this demoralising effect will be checked, for a true and influential and reverent faith will then be seen to be compatible with the highest education."

Of these experts the most authoritative is Sir William Muir. He declares [1] that he values the Christian colleges for their results in "immediate conversion to the faith,"

[1] See *Educational Missions in India*. Revised Special Report to the General Assembly of the Church of Scotland, May 1890, p. 213.

and that it would be a calamity for India if these were withdrawn. But, besides that, "the country has by them been inoculated with Christian sentiment," and it was the Scots schools and colleges which first called forth the sympathies of Hindus towards Occidental learning, and in doing so gave them a bent towards Christianity. "It is our duty to maintain them," concludes one who, while he is himself at the head of all Arabic scholars in the English language, has, during half a century's career in the highest offices in India, England, and Scotland, been identified with the evangelical and evangelistic school. An authority of a similar type is the great Marquis of Dalhousie's cousin, the Hon. Sir Henry Ramsay, C.B., who has spent his life as an official in the Himalayan province of Kumaon. He has seen the result of the labours of Dr. Duff, not only in Bengal but in Kumaon, and all over the North-Western Provinces, during an experience of fifty years. "The truths of Christianity and salvation through Jesus Christ alone have been made known widely; faith in Hinduism has been shaken, and the superstitions connected with it are only maintained through the influence of old pundits and leading men who have had no school education." At the head of all the purely evangelistic missionaries in North India is the Rev. Robert Clark, of Amritsar, of the Church Missionary Society. Like Sir Henry Ramsay, he has seen results as few have lived to see them. He would strengthen the missionary colleges instead of giving them up, and would encourage those who are in charge of them. The non-Christian teachers in them he would not prematurely discontinue. "There are many good Hindu and Mohammedan teachers who have been trained in Christian truth, and are doing as good service to us as ever Hiram's carpenters and servants did in the building of the Temple in the days of David and Solomon."

But of all the more recent experts consulted, the authority of none stands so high as that of the late Lieutenant-Governor of the Punjab, Sir Charles U. Aitchison, LL.D. One of the first to enter the Bengal Civil Service by competition, after a brilliant training in the

Theological as well as the Arts Faculty, he was selected by Lord Canning and placed above many of his seniors as Foreign Under-Secretary on the close of the Mutiny campaigns. His cautious judgment, his high character, and his unique experience, made him for the next quarter of a century the trusted guide of every Governor-General (except the author of the Second Afghan War) in the foreign policy of our Indian Empire. Like the Lawrences and the rest of the old Punjab school, he never concealed his own belief, which he adorned by unceasing private support of all good objects, native and British, of whatever reformed sort. No man in India in the last forty years has had such a career, or has so well borne its honours in all modesty and meekness. His opinion, on whatever side of this question, might be accepted as the most influential. This is how he writes:—"God forbid that I should undervalue preaching and evangelising. I believe India is only waiting for some native St. Paul to turn by thousands to the Lord. But the more active you are in your schools the better you will be prepared for that day when it comes. Even now, as a matter of fact, although statistics of conversion are no true test of the value of missionary work, the most numerous converts and the best are made in the schools." "It is more than ever the duty of the Church to go forward in its educational policy:"—

"In my judgment the value of educational missionary institutions, in the present transition state of Indian opinion, can hardly be overrated. The importance of mission schools and colleges is even greater now than when Duff initiated his education policy, and converted a reluctant General Assembly to his views. His argument then was, that Hinduism is so wedded to a cosmogony demonstrably false, that Western education of any kind became a direct missionary agency, effective at least in overthrowing the false religions. Experience has amply justified his views—so much so that, in the work of destroying the heathen beliefs, the Government secular schools, the railways and the telegraphs, have done as effective work as the missionaries themselves. Educated Hindu society is honeycombed with unbelief, and the great question of the day in India is, What shall take the place of the broken gods? Hence a growing Buddhist optimism. Hence the revival of Vedantic deism. Hence the Brahmo Somaj and other theistic societies. Hence, too, the inquiry and searching into the Christian Scriptures, which go on in India to an extent which those who ignore missions have no conception of. Now, if ever, is the Church's opportunity. If the breach that has been made is filled up—if, in place of Hinduism we have agnosticism, or even a positive but unchristian theistic belief with which physical science is not necessarily in antagonism—the Christian Church will have to do all the sapping and mining over again; while, instead of the crumbling old fortresses of heathenism, we shall have in front of us strong fortifications, held and defended with weapons of precision forged in our own arsenals. It is of primary importance now, just at this time when the Government of India itself is looking anxiously round for some means of supplementing the deficiencies of its own secular system of education, to get hold of the youth of India and impregnate them with Christian truth. They are the generation in whose hands the immediate future of India will lie, and the importance of bringing them under direct Christian influences is beyond all calculation. We want institutions like the Cambridge Mission College at Delhi, the American Mission College at Lahore, and the Established Church and Free Church Institutions at Calcutta multiplied over the country."

Among the other writers on this side were such missionaries of other Churches as Dr. Mackichan, of Bombay; Bishop Caldwell, of the Society for the Propagation of the Gospel; Mr. Rouse, of the Baptist Society; Dr. William Miller, of Madras; Dr. E. W. Parker, of the American Methodist Episcopal Society; and Dr. Shoolbred, of the United Presbyterian Mission. The evidence is completed by translations from two native newspapers. The *Arya Patrika*, weekly organ of the Lahore Arya (Theistic) Somaj, writes thus:—"Education work may be very expensive, but the missionary knows that there is no other work so helpful in gaining converts. The Indian mind has well-nigh shaken off the torpor of ages, and will no longer receive as gospel truth what it has not first thoroughly examined." The *Oudh Akbar* (Lucknow), a non-Christian vernacular paper, has "never known missionaries compel any one to become a Christian, yet would not be at all surprised if Bible teaching should create a tendency in our Indian youths to embrace

Christianity in the absence of any moral training in our homes."

The General Assembly of the Established Church of Scotland resolved to maintain its educational institutes in India on the same principles as heretofore, and to make them thoroughly efficient; but it also resolved "to make more direct efforts toward the training of a native ministry for India."

Of the two Free Church of Scotland's deputies Professor Lindsay, D.D., spent a complete year in India, travelling over its length and breadth south of the Punjab, and inspecting many missions besides the Scottish. The Report[1] shows an amount of common sense, a knowledge of business, a fertility of resource, and a kindly frankness rare in such literature. Every detail of a vast organisation, financial and property as well as educational and spiritual, is considered. The Free Church of Scotland controls the expenditure of £100,000 a year on purely Foreign Missions, of which £70,000 is raised in Scotland, and the rest is derived, chiefly in India, from European and native contributions, and from fees and grants-in-aid. The four Indian colleges now meet all their expenditure locally, only the ordained missionaries' salaries being sent out, and these partly from endowments. But the colleges have been in the past the centres from which converts, at first Brahmans by birth, have carried the new light into the surrounding villages and districts, and into the missions of other Churches and societies, which took up new provinces as these were annexed to the Empire. Has this later process, now marked as "evangelistic," not been restrained by spending too much of the available funds on the "educational" work? Has proportional attention been paid to the aboriginal tribes, Santal and other? Have the missionaries not continued so long to concentrate their energies on the great cities as to neglect the multitudinous villages? Where the village people

[1] *The India Mission and the Free Church of Scotland:* being Report of the Deputies to India in 1888-89, Opinion of the Missionaries in 1890, and Minute of the Foreign Missions Committee 1891.

are cared for, have not the so-called educational and the evangelistic sets of missionaries failed to assist each other?

The General Assembly referred the Report to their India missionaries for criticism. Thirty of these—almost the whole number—preachers in the native languages, and medical men as well as teachers in the English colleges, sent home a joint-letter, agreeing in many of the practical conclusions, but remarking "a certain hesitation or ambiguity" which appeared to them to run through the whole Report. Does it mean that "the Scottish Church somehow blundered into the course of bringing its missionary work to bear on the Hindus, strictly so called, though it judged correctly that in dealing with them education was the best, or perhaps the only efficient method it could use"? Or is this intended to be the general tenor of the Report? "There was a providential guidance of the Scottish Church when she resolved to deal with that great central core of the people of India on which Christianity had made almost no impression," in 1830. "The work, which is chiefly preparatory in its proper nature, has providentially developed so as to leave scarcely any time or strength to those engaged in it for that other side of the work which is its indispensable complement." The two, educational and evangelistic, "are in no sense opposed, but are necessary parts of one united whole. Each is to be so conducted as to take advantage of or help the other." Many of the missionaries individually write on the same lines; while Mr. A. H. L. Fraser, the able civilian who is a Commissioner in the Central Provinces, makes a powerful contribution to the discussion, leading to the same conclusion.

The Free Church of Scotland's General Assembly in 1891 closed the discussion by a series of resolutions which were admitted to be at once just to the historic past of the Scots Missions in India, and adequate to the needs of the present order of things, while they express the unanimous opinion of the older missionaries of all classes and methods there:—

"(1) That the Church was wisely guided when, in reliance on Divine help, it resolved, through the agency of Christian educational mission work, to deal with that great central core of the people of India on which Christianity had, up to that time, made small impression; that this educational work always deserved, and still deserves, the support of the Church; and that missionaries who are engaged in that work ought to have the sympathy and the prayers of every one who has at heart the cause of Christ in India.

"(2) That this educational work, as the missionaries have all along insisted, always needed, and now more than ever needs, to be supplemented and completed by the simple earnest proclamation of saving truth, and by earnest personal dealing with individuals, carried on in the districts more immediately under the influence of the *præparatio evangelica* of the educational work; and that the two sides of the work should always be in visible connection with each other.

"(3) That, as the evangelistic side of the work has not been developed *pari passu* with the other, the committee regard it as necessary, while in no way sanctioning anything that may tend to impair the efficiency of the educational work, specially to foster the evangelistic operations, and therefore resolve, in accordance with minute 119 of January 1887, still to limit to the present amount the resources spent on the educational institutions, and to devote to the evangelistic side whatever increase of contributions may be received, and any saving that may be effected in connection with educational work without detriment to its efficiency."

In the division of labour, as well as of area, which is more than ever desirable in the non-Christian regions of the world, and especially in India, the two Scottish Churches, and the United Presbyterian Church also as it develops in Rajpootana, will thus keep the lead in evangelising the educated classes, and in training native ministers and teachers, by the educational method. China is already calling for such a method, and its application to Africa on industrial lines has wrought the best results in the creation of native churches and the formation of many of the Kafir people into Christian communities.

Sir Charles Bernard, formerly a Government Secretary and Chief Commissioner in India, suggested in this discussion the best practical means for meeting any lingering objection to educational missions drawn from the present neutral university system of India. So long as missionaries like Duff, Wilson, and Bishop Cotton controlled the text-books and regulations of the University Syndicates, the Christian colleges had fair play. Let the missionary organisations now unite to form a Christian university, such as Government would legislatively establish, just as the Punjab University was created from the other side, to test purely Oriental learning. The cost of an examining university which made Christian teaching compulsory, while securing a high average standard in all secular subjects, need not be great at first, and could be met by fees, and ultimately by endowments, as the Christian Church continues to grow in numbers, and its native members to distance their Hindu and Mohammedan fellows in influence, position, and wealth, which they are fast doing. Union in a complete form, with the independence of the affiliated colleges, would thus be secured. A Christian university would solve the difficulties, and remove most of the objections of inexperienced people to educational-evangelistic missions.

What Dr. John Wilson and his colleague, Robert Nesbit, wrote[1] from Bombay, when approving of the despatch of 1854 which created the university system, more than ever demands observance by their successors: The despatch "will aid the missionary institutions in that department of their labours which embraces secular knowledge. But missionaries and their supporters must vow before God and man not to dilute or diminish their religious instruction in their seminaries on this account. . . . The evangelistic feature of our educational establishments must be preserved."

The present writer, while still in the inexperience of youth forty years ago, but after two years' residence in Bengal, was not friendly to the educational method of missions. But the study of India on the spot for twenty years thereafter, and the careful observation of all the facts and controversies since, have led him to this con-

[1] *Life*, page 531, first edition, London (John Murray).

clusion: The most powerful method for the conversion of India, and through India, of Southern Asia, is that of educational-evangelising directed by spiritual men and supplemented by preaching and healing. Some of the ablest and most hard-working missionaries in the East are the educational. While they ought to be stronger, like their predecessors, in their influence on the university syndicates, to withdraw their colleges from affiliation would be to confess defeat and abandon the most hopeful youth of India to unmitigated antichristian influences. The pressure of the university may be such, that the present staff in each college is too busy to bring to bear on the students the same personal influence and individually persuasive appeals, by which their predecessors led into the Kingdom the earlier generation of remarkable converts. The remedy is to be found in strengthening the staff of each college for this end rather than in appointing outsiders to do evangelistic work among the students. It is the personal fascination exercised by the able Christian teacher that the Spirit of God uses to draw his students to Christ. What Wilson and Nesbit wrote in 1855 should be pondered now—"For our systematic Biblical reading and lecturing we can maintain a due place by insisting on the *conditions* of our missionary institutions. It is a fact that the eagerness for graduation is a *temptation* to many young men to confine their attention to the studies prescribed by the universities. But what would be the consequence if, instead of opposing that temptation, we were to withdraw from the arena?[1] What would soon

[1] The Jesuits, who always seek the control of education, have vigorous aided colleges in Bombay and Calcutta. The present Pope has appealed to Latin Christendom for a wide extension of educational institutions as a means of proselytism. On the 27th June 1893, a Papal Encyclical was issued on the subject of the institutions for native Catholic clergy in India. The Pope demonstrates the necessity for the appointment of native priests, especially in cases where missionaries are unable to penetrate into the interior in countries such as Japan and China. The Encyclical adds that the Vicars Apostolic had received authority to found colleges in India, and had arranged for

be the character of the universities themselves? What would soon be the state of the educated mind of India which rules the native world? What—? I may go on for hours suggesting most lamentable consequences."

each diocese to have its own Consistory, but want of means prevented the full realisation of the scheme. On the other hand, the British Government and various Protestant societies were constantly expending money in establishing colleges. The Pope concludes by exhorting the Catholics of Europe to co-operate with him in the work of founding Indian seminaries.

IX

THE RESULTS OF CHRISTIAN MISSIONS TO INDIA

"*Then saith He unto His disciples, The harvest truly is plenteous, but the labourers are few.*"—ST. MATT. ix. 37.

THE imagination of the most Christian as well as that of the most scientific student of India has always failed to realise comparatively the relation, in point of magnitude and density, of the vast Peninsula of India[1] and its peoples to the rest of the world and of the human race. Till Christendom, and especially its English-speaking majority, *knows* the facts, the duty laid upon it of preaching the gospel to every creature cannot be adequately faced. Geography is the most valuable of the allies of Foreign Missions, which have done, in return, so much for the development and elevation of the most interesting and comprehensive of all the sciences. Missionary geography is, however, only beginning to win for itself that place in the education of the public and the Sunday schools, in the curriculum of the universities and theological colleges, and in the instruction of the Church in prayer-meetings and preaching, which it must hold before Christian people, "lifting up their eyes,"[2] share the Lord's infinite compassion and self-devoted service for the multitudes "scattered abroad as sheep having no shepherd."

[1] See *The Geography of British India: Political and Physical* (Student's Manual). John Murray, 1882.

[2] St John's Gospel, iv. 34-38.

As the most cautious and reliable figures showing the area and population of the globe, we take those submitted by Mr. E. Ravenstein, F.R.G.S., to the British Association at Leeds in September 1890. We bring them down to September 1893:—

THE WORLD'S POPULATION IN 1893.

	Population.	Average to a Sq. Mile.	Increase per Decade. Per Cent.
Europe . .	381,200,000	101	8·7
Asia . . .	854,000,000	57	6
Africa . .	127,000,000	11	10
Australasia . .	4,730,000	1·4	30
North America .	95,250,000	14	20
South America .	38,420,000	5	15
	1,500,600,000[1]	31	8

CULTIVABLE AREA OF THE GLOBE (in square miles).

	Fertile Region.	Steppe.	Desert.	Total.[2]
Europe . .	2,888,000	667,000	...	3,555,000
Asia . . .	9,280,000	4,230,000	1,200,000	14,710,000
Africa . .	5,760,000	3,528,000	2,226,000	11,514,000
Australasia .	1,167,000	1,507,000	614,000	3,288,000
North America .	4,946,000	1,405,000	95,000	6,446,000
South America .	4,228,000	2,564,000	45,000	6,837,000
Total . .	28,269,000	13,901,000	4,180,000	46,350,000

The Church will enter on the twentieth century in a few years, with the population increased to 1587 millions. At the same rate in the year 1950 there will be 2332 millions, and in the year 2000 there will be 3426 millions. In the year 2072, or only 180 years hence, there will be 5977 millions. That seems far to look forward, but in the history of the Church, as of the human race, it is a short period. One hundred and eighty years ago William III.

[1] Exclusive of 300,000 in the Polar Regions.

[2] Exclusive of the Polar Regions, 4,888,800 square miles.

was still king, and Foreign Missions from English-speaking people could not be said to exist. The longer every Christian delays to take a part in the evangelisation of the dark races, the greater becomes the difficulty of bringing in the increasing peoples. War, famine, and other checks to the growth of population may reduce the normal increase of eight per cent every ten years, as the coming century goes on, but all the political and historical facts are against this probability up to the time we have mentioned, when economic law as to population occupying all the cultivable area must affect the result, unless checked by new discoveries of applied physics.

How are these fifteen hundred millions of human beings divided as to religious belief and worship? Here we have less scientific certainty, on the whole, though not for the peoples under Christian governments. Estimates hitherto published have been repeated year after year, and so fail to take account of the extraordinary increase given to the Reformed Churches by two causes—the superior spawning-power of, and the rapid colonising extension over fertile waste lands by, the English- and German-speaking peoples during the past century. Taking into account the latest figures of the census of the whole British Empire, of the United States of America, and of the principal countries of Europe, as made and published in the years 1890-92, and adding to them an estimate up to 1893, we have this as the result, in round numbers :—

CHRISTIANITY AND WORLD-RELIGIONS, 1893.

Reformed Church	200,000,000
Roman Catholic	195,600,000
Greek and Eastern	105,000,000
Professing Christians	500,600,000
Jews	8,000,000
Mohammedans	180,000,000
Heathens	812,000,000
Non-Christians	1,000,000,000

The Human Race = 1,500,600,000.

Since Carey's *Enquiry,*[1] written in 1786, the proportion of Christians in the doubled population of the world has risen from one in six to one in three.

What are the two hundred millions of the Reformed Church, historically called Protestants and professedly evangelical, doing for the conversion of the thousand millions of non-Christians? We do not take into account their efforts, vigorous and necessary, especially in the lands of Asia and North Africa occupied by the Eastern Churches for whom Americans do much, nor any labours for Christians by Christians of a purer faith and life. Leaving out of account also the many wives of missionaries who are represented statistically in their husbands, Rev. J. Vahl, President of the Danish Missionary Society, gives us these results.[2] We accept them as the most accurately compiled, and as almost too cautiously estimated where estimate is unavoidable. In Turkey and Egypt only work among the Musalmans is reckoned.

	1890.	1891.
Income (English Money)	£2,412,938	£2,749,340
Missionaries	4,652	5,094
Do., unmarried ladies	2,118	2,445
Native ministers	3,424	3,730
Other native helpers	36,405	40,438
Communicants	966,856	1,168,560

We abstain from estimating in detail the results for 1892, as they are about to appear, and still less for the year 1893, but experts can do this for themselves. This only we would say, that the number of native communicants added in those two years has been very large, especially in India. Allowing for that, we should place them now

[1] *An Enquiry into the Obligation of Christians to use Means for the Conversion of the Heathens, in which the Religious State of the Different Nations of the World, &c., are considered.* Leicester, Ann Ireland, 1792. Reprinted in Facsimile. London, Hodder and Stoughton, 1891.

[2] *Missions to the Heathen in* 1890 *and* 1891 *: A Statistical Review.* Copenhagen, Fr. Bertelsen, 1893.

at 1,300,000, which gives a native Christian community of 5,200,000 gathered out of all non-Christian lands.[1]

Dean Vahl's statistics are drawn from the reports of 304 mission societies and agencies in 1891, beginning with Cromwell's New England Company, for America, in 1649. On the following page the details are summarised from seventeen lands of Reformed Christendom. The amount raised in 1891 by the 160 Mission Churches and Societies of the British Empire was £1,659,830, and by the 57 of the United States of America £786,992. Together the two great English-speaking peoples spent £2,446,822 on the evangelisation of the non-Christian world. The balance, or £302,518, was contributed by Germany and Switzerland, Netherlands, Denmark, France, Norway, Sweden, Finland, and in Asia.

The figures which start out of the tables of the world's population and area are those of Asia, contrasted with each of the other five divisions of the globe. The great majority of unevangelised human beings, for each of whom Christ died, are there. At least eight hundred millions of these toil on its nine and a quarter millions of fertile square miles, or roam over its four and a quarter millions of miles of steppe. In Asia what is the relative position and what the consequent claims of India and its peoples?

The last decennial census of British India, taken in February 1891, revealed the following as the divisions of the 287¼ millions of our fellow-subjects there according to religious belief or custom.[2] To the Christians in *British* India must be added those in the small *French*

[1] In the case of the ordinary civil population the number of adult men is multiplied by five for the total. Communicants being of both sexes the number is, for missionary purposes, multiplied by *four*. The *Church Missionary Intelligencer* for September 1893 would multiply by 3½.

[2] Sir W. W. Hunter's chapter ix. of his great work on *The Indian Empire, its Peoples, History, and Products*, 3rd edition, 1893, should be consulted for fuller details and percentages, as well as on all Indian facts.

World-Summary of Evangelical Foreign Missions.

	Income (English Money).		Missionaries.		Unmarried Female Missionaries.		Native Ministers.		Native Helpers.		Native Communicants.		Mission Soc. and Agencies.	
	1890	1891	1890	1891	1890	1891	1890	1891	1890	1891	1890	1891	1890	1891
	£	£												
1. England	1,020,417	1,228,211	1522	1608	794	944	1932	1968	16,469	18,166	262,645	281,627	70	73
2. Scotland	176,039	193,257	218	234	148	175	42	42	1,837	2,033	23,749	25,160	17	16
3. Ireland	16,934	17,074	17	20	8	10	2	8	124	127	539	763	2	2
4. Netherlands	24,232	25,869	147	150	...	...	31	31	236	253	84,966	85,240	13	17
5. Germany	122,808	129,542	485	504	101	126	72	75	2,973	3,171	88,161	92,768	18	18
6. Switzerland	48,698	52,356	142	148	2	3	39	37	617	640	11,859	12,575	3	3
7. Denmark	5,863	6,472	8	10	2	2	3	3	20	24	233	250	3	3
8. France	12,753	18,386	41	39	8	7	19	21	218	241	9,124	9,937	2	2
9. Norway	25,505	27,674	52	56	22	27	20	22	1,149	1,187	20,905	23,616	4	6
10. Sweden	20,718	22,795	48	48	25	25	3	6	45	38	174	195	7	7
11. Finland	3,903	3,800	6	5	...	1	...	...	...	23	87	170	1	2
12. United States of America	717,466	786,992	1301	1513	911	1004	938	1158	6,983	8,654	183,861	346,699	55	57
13. British North America	55,523	64,170	113	127	61	70	40	34	460	346	12,244	12,734	12	16
14. West Indies	62,856	73,420	335	316	5	5	75	91	337	370	152,303	158,294	11	13
15. Asia	16,029	15,624	18	20	8	10	19	23	311	332	3,966	3,966	16	29
16. Africa	43,616	44,942	92	176	9	18	96	100	471	516	38,627	40,946	12	14
17. Australia	39,578	38,756	107	120	14	18	103	111	4155	4,317	73,418	73,580	18	26
Summa	2,412,938	2,749,340	4652	5094	2118	2445	3424	3730	36,405	40,438	966,856	1,168,560	264	304

and *Portuguese* India, making the total 2,601,355 thus divided:—

CHRISTIANS IN ALL INDIA, 1891.

Native Reformed	648,843
Syrian Jacobite (say)	300,000
Syrian and Roman Catholic	1,594,901
European and American Evangelical . .	57,611
In all India	2,601,355

RELIGIONS OF BRITISH INDIA, 1891.

	British Provinces.	Native States.	Totals.	
Hindu	155,171,943	52,559,784	207,731,727	Hindu
Musalman	49,550,491	7,770,673	57,321,164	Musalman
Animistic	5,848,427	3,432,040	9,280,467	Animistic
Buddhist	7,095,398	35,963	7,131,361	Buddhist
Christian	1,491,458	792,714	2,284,172	*Christian*
Sikh	1,407,968	499,865	1,907,833	Sikh
Jain	495,001	921,637	1,416,638	Jain
Zoroastrian	76,952	12,952	89,904	Zoroastrian
Jew	14,669	2,525	17,194	Jew
Minor and Unspecified	20,645	22,326	42,971	Minor and Unspecified
Grand Total	221,172,952	66,050,479	287,223,431	

These figures show that Christians have increased by 316,033 in the Provinces, and 105,713 in the States, total 421,746, since the census of 1881, and that their advance has been 22·65 per cent, compared with a growth of only 13·1 per cent in the entire population.[1] Even after allowing for a somewhat stricter registration in 1891 the result remains very remarkable. The Christians of India outnumber the Sikh nation. The Christians are found in the several Provinces and States in these proportions:—

[1] We follow the analysis published by Sir Theodore C. Hope, K.C.S.I., C.I.E., formerly member of the Governor-General's Council, in his *Church and State in India.* London, S.P.C.K., 1893.

British Provinces.		Native States.		Total India.
Assam . .	16,820	... ...	...	16,820
Burma and Andamans . .	121,223	Shan States .	154	121,377
Bengal . .	190,816	Bengal States .	1,655	192,471
North-West Provinces . .	58,424	North-West Provinces States .	77	58,501
Punjab and Quetta	56,582	Punjab States and Kashmer .	539	57,121
Ajmer-Merwara .	2,683	Rajpootana .	1,855	4,538
Bombay, Sindh, and Aden .	161,766	Bombay States and Baroda .	8,885	170,651
Central Provinces	12,970	Central India and C.P. States .	6,335	19,305
Berar . . .	1,359	Haidarabad .	20,429	21,788
Madras and Coorg	868,815	Madras States .	714,651	1,583,466
		Mysore . .	38,134	38,134
Totals	1,491,458		792,714	2,284,172

About two millions of the Christians are natives of India, and only a quarter of a million are Europeans and Eurasians. Of the native Christians nearly two-thirds live in the British Provinces, and fully one-third in the territories of native princes. The whole of the religious establishments of this great body of native Christians, eight-ninths of all Christians in India, are self-supporting, and unconnected with the State—indeed, practically ignored by it.

In 1891 the Europeans numbered 168,000, and the mixed class of Eurasians about half of these, thus divided—

	Europeans.	Eurasians.
British troops . . .	70,953	...
,, Officers with sepoys .	3,617	...
Civil establishments . .	10,524	8,190
Railway establishments .	6,093	9,093
Non-officials . . .	76,813	62,559
	168,000	79,842

For the troops and civil service Government provides an ecclesiastical establishment under the Charter of 1813, considerably increased by its successors, costing £216,231 [1] a year. In 1891 there were 241 chaplains and 100 aided clergy for the 247,842 Christians of pure and mixed British descent, in the proportion of 215 Anglicans, 22 Presbyterians, 28 Wesleyans, and 76 Roman Catholics. In many stations the missionaries to the natives supplement this establishment where it is lacking in strength or evangelical purity. What a powerful influence for good or evil are these Christians of the dispersion in India! What is true of Christendom is still more certain of British and American Christians in India and non-Christian lands—were each a living epistle of Christ the conversion of India and of the World would be at hand.

We now confine our attention to the Reformed Native Churches. Four times in the past forty years the Calcutta Missionary Conference has compiled and published statistical tables of Protestant or evangelical missions in India, Burma, and Ceylon. Dr. Mullens—who afterwards, when secretary of the London Missionary Society, became one of the earlier martyrs to the coast climate of East Africa—began the work in 1851, and repeated it in 1861. The rate of increase in the number of native Christians in that decade was 53 per cent. In the next decade it rose to 61 per cent, and in that from 1871 to 1881 it was 86 per cent. From 1881 to 1890, it was 53½ per cent for nine years. The compilers of the tables for 1881-1890 [2] deal with a period of nine years only, in order to bring the results into line with the more general returns of the Imperial census, for purposes of comparison. The figures accordingly show, in great detail, the number of native Christians, of native communicants, of native Christian boys and girls at school and college and Sunday school, of women under instruction in zananas, and of missionary

[1] Or tens of rupees, RX.

[2] *Protestant Missions in India, Burma, and Ceylon. Statistical Tables*, 1890. Calcutta Baptist Mission Press, 1892.

churches, societies, and agents of all kinds and both sexes, at the close of 1890.

Then there were 559,661 native Protestant Christians in India, and 89,182 in Burma, or 648,843 in all. The increase is thus seen:

India proper in 1851 .	91,092	In 1890 . .	559,661
Burma in 1861 . .	59,369	In 1890 . .	89,182

In forty years 468,569 converts in India, and in thirty years 29,873 converts in Burma, that is, 498,442 in all, or about half a million, have been added to the Christian Church. The strictest test, however, is not the strength of the whole community bearing the Christian name, but the number and rate of increase of communicants. These stood as follows:—

India proper in 1851 .	14,661	In 1890 . .	182,722
Burma	...	In 1890 . .	33,037

In 1851, all of Burma that Great Britain held was the two coast strips of Arakan and Tenasserim, where Judson had laboured chiefly for the future. It was afterwards that Lord Dalhousie conquered fertile Pegu, and only the other day that Lord Dufferin added the Upper Kingdom. It may be said with truth that the number of native Christian communicants connected with the evangelical Churches of Great Britain, America, and Germany has grown in forty years from 15,000 to 215,759 in 1890, or at the present time to above a quarter of a million. No statistics can show the growth of these native Christians in wealth, in social position, and in official and professional influence. They are pushing out the Brahmans, many of them being simply Christian Brahmans, by character, by ability, and by intelligent loyalty, till the Hindu press confesses the fact with apprehension, and the local Blue-books report it continually to Parliament. The Christians have wives educated up to their own level, while polygamy and the hideous sexual customs, which legislation can hardly ameliorate from the outside, continue to depress the Hindu and Musalman communities.

Perhaps the most interesting fact in these Tables is expressed in the three lines which state that of 19,298 adult baptisms in the year 1890, only 15 were of Buddhists, from 200 to 250 of Mohammedans, about 28,000 of demon-worshippers, and some 16,800 of Hindus of all castes. Even in tolerant and neutral British India the Mohammedans are still the forlorn hope of the missionary campaign. The number of our Buddhist subjects on the Himalayan slopes and in Burma is comparatively small, but every year shows an advance in the work of the Moravian, the Scottish, and the American missions among them.

The medical returns show 97 foreign or European and 168 native Christian medical missionaries, with 166 hospitals and dispensaries.

In the nineteen years ending 1890 the number of women workers, foreign and Eurasian, in India has increased from 370 to 711, and of native Christians from 837 to 3278. These taught 7302 girls and 1784 orphans in 166 boarding schools, 62,414 girls in 1507 day schools, and so many as 32,659 women in houses or zananas.

WOMAN'S WORK IN INDIA, 1890.

	Female Agents.		Boarding-Schools.			Day-Schools.		Zananas.	
	Foreign and Eurasian.	Native Christian.	Schools.	Pupils.	Orphans.	Schools.	Pupils.	Houses.	Pupils.
Church of England . .	223	988	60	2599	432	411	15,129	11,109	4,361
Presbyterian	112	515	20	788	152	324	12,814	1,612	2,959
Congregationalist . . .	88	390	18	662	108	188	9,554	11,782	4,120
Baptist	108	810	15	705	229	99	5,276	3,244	2,465
Methodist	113	616	32	1738	555	364	11,687	7,898	14,358
Lutheran	2	136	10	407	128	18	1,859	298	21
Zanana B. & M. Mission.	56	161	2	47	1	54	2,191	8,995	3,063
Miscellaneous	59	162	9	356	184	49	3,904	585	812
	711	3278	166	7302	1784	1507	62,414	40,513	32,659

This is exclusive of the medical work of fully-qualified women. That and the educational work of both men and women must tell powerfully on every new generation when we find these grand totals :—

Year.	Under Missionary Instruction—Males and Females.
1851	64,043
1861	75,995
1871	122,372
1881	196,360
1890	299,051

Besides these, 135,565 attended Sunday schools in 1890, and 8698 in Burma, against 61,668 in the year 1881.

The staff of missionaries (male) has stood as follows in successive periods :—

Year.	Foreign Ordained.	Native Ordained.	Foreign Lay.	Native Lay.
1851	339	21	...	493
1861	479	97	...	1266
1871	488	225	...	1985
1881	586	461	72	2488
1890	868	797	118	3491

The hopeful feature of that table is the increase of native ordained missionaries from 21 to 797 in forty years. Adding together the numbers of workers of every kind, male and female, there were 9263, of whom 3491 were native men and 3278 native women, while 986 were foreign men and 711 were foreign women, exclusive, generally, of missionaries' wives. Since 1890 the increase of woman and medical missionaries has been still more marked, while the healthy tendency of all the Societies, especially the American, is to solve the question of "cheap missions" by largely increasing the number of native catechists placed under each white overseer.

The results of the missionary census of Ceylon show that it has not yet recovered from the intolerance of the Portuguese and the policy of the Dutch.[1] The rate of increase up to 1881 seems to have been arrested by a Buddhist revival, prompted to some extent from America and Europe. In that year the native Christian community numbered 35,708, cared for by the Church of England, the Wesleyan and the Baptist Societies, and the American Board. In 1890 the returns do not show more than 25,000, or fewer than in 1871, of whom 9000 were communicants. There were 40,000 boys and girls in the mission schools.

Evangelical Christendom sent to Christianise the Indian Empire 868 ordained and 118 non-ordained men (not reckoning their wives), and 711 unmarried women, or 1697 missionaries, at the end of the year 1890. Allowing for the normal rate of increase during the subsequent three years, there are now 1800 foreign missionaries to 300,000,000 of British subjects, or one missionary—man or woman—to about every 167,000 of the population. The number of ordained men is smaller than that of the specially-trained covenanted civil servants who rule and administer the country. The number of men and women together is less than half of the British officers who command the native troops; is only a fourth of the British

[1] See Miss C. F. Gordon-Cumming's *Two Happy Years in Ceylon* (3rd ed., 1892). So soon as the priests of Buddha in Ceylon realised that the scholarly missionaries, Gogerly and Spence Hardy, "were no longer satisfied with a merely nominal profession of the foreign creed in order to obtain Government employment, but insisted on a radical conversion, they roused themselves to resist their progress by violently antagonistic preaching from village to village." This was legitimate enough, and a testimony to the truth of Christ. But Miss Gordon-Cumming shows the impetus given to Buddhism by the so-called Theosophists under Colonel Olcott, the American, and Sir Edwin Arnold, and she convicts the Government of encouraging Buddhism on a system like that which resulted in the India Mutiny of 1857, and the extinction of the East India Company.

military garrison which keeps the peace of Southern Asia. Each Church of the United Kingdom and the United States may contrast the nine hundred male missionaries sent to the three hundred millions specially entrusted to our care, with the number of its own congregational and professorial clergy. Nor is the smallness of the number sent to India the only reproach. Were each of the eighteen hundred entrusted with funds for the training of many more native catechists, teachers, and village preachers, with medical subordinates for dispensaries and the zananas, the problem of a cheap organisation of missions would be solved. Each of India's seventy-five cities with a population above fifty thousand, of its 2035 municipal towns with a population above five thousand, and of its 715,500 villages, would be brought within the direct influence of the Christian Church in as many decades as at present seems likely to occupy centuries.

The British Indian empire occupies only one-fifteenth of the area of the habitable globe, yet it contains one-fifth of the human race. One-tenth of these live in cities, nine-tenths in villages. Mr. J. A. Baines, the commissioner, who took the census of India—the greatest scientific enumeration of human beings ever made—gives us the remarkable table on page 209 as its accurate result.[1]

The inquirer, who would learn *how little* evangelical Christians are doing for the conversion of the peoples of India, should contrast with that table the decennial statistics of Protestant missions at the same time which we have summarised, Province by Province and State by State. After Dr. Mullens published the statistics of 1851 this was done by Mr. Macleod Wylie, the Calcutta judge, in *The Urgent Claims of India for More Christian Missions.*[2] Then the number of Protestant missionaries in India was 403, and that was threefold more than in 1831, near the close of Carey's apostolate of forty-one years. He who

[1] See his Paper in the *Journal of the Royal Statistical Society for March* 1893, pp. 1-43.

[2] Published under the name of "A Layman in India," by W. H. Dalton, London, in 1853. Second edition.

INDIA: ITS AREA AND POPULATION IN TOWNS AND VILLAGES, 1891.

1	2	3	4	5	6	7	8
			Persons per		Percentage of		
						Net Increase of Population since 1881.†	
Province, State, or Agency.	Area in Square Miles.	Population in February 1891.	Square Mile.	Village.*	Urban Population.	Total.	Urban.
Madras	141,189	35,630,440	252	578	9·56	15·58	10·75
Bombay	77,275	15,985,270	207	635	19·49	13·71	} 10·29
Sindh	47,789	2,871,774	60	686	11·92	18·97	
Bengal	151,543	71,346,987	471	301	4·82	6·89	7·37
North-West Provinces	83,286	34,254,254	411	384	12·70	4·55	2·24
Oudh	24,217	12,650,831	522	494	7·60	11·09	5·82
Punjáb	110,667	20,866,847	188	548	11·56	10·74	7·93
Upper Burma	83,473	2,946,933	35	246	12·60	..	..
Lower "	87,957	4,658,627	53	236	12·35	24·67	7·86
Central Provinces	86,501	10,784,294	125	299	6·85	9·61	7·11
Assam and North Lushai Land	49,004	5,476,833	112	318	1·86	11·30	10·37
Berár	17,718	2,897,491	163	464	12·45	8·41	8·49
Coorg	1,583	173,055	109	348	8·96	−2·94	−7·36
Ajmér-Mérwára	2,711	542,358	200	581	21·87	17·72	22·44
Quetta, Aden, and Andamans	80	86,958	..	..	..	..	..
Total British Provinces	964,993	221,172,952	229	383	9·22	9·70	8·50
Haidarabád	82,698	11,537,040	139	539	9·45	17·18	11·09
Baroda	8,226	2,415,396	294	693	20·02	10·54	7·02
Mysore	27,936	4,943,604	177	274	12·67	18·09	13·55
Kashmér	80,900	2,543,952	31	287	7·77	..	..
Rajpootána	130,268	12,016,102	92	363	12·73	20·22	12·22
Central India	77,808	10,318,812	133	297	9·34	9·92	7·27
Bombay States	69,045	8,059,298	117	475	14·61	16·35	12·67
Madras "	9,609	3,700,622	385	1703	4·73	10·63	0·85
Central Province States	29,435	2,160,511	73	207	1·79	26·36	12·09
Bengal States	35,834	3,296,379	93	174	0·50	18·30	8·85
North-West Province States	5,109	792,491	155	309	13·02	6·84	2·01
Punjáb States	38,299	4,263,280	111	212	10·71	10·42	6·77
Fort Steadman (Shán) Outposts)	..	2,992	..	..	..	..	..
Total Feudatory States	595,167	66,050,479	111	338	10·38	15·52	12·32
Total India	1,560,160	287,223,431	184	372	9·48	10·96	9·40

* Places of under 10,000 inhabitants, including the smaller towns.

† Excluding tracts and towns not enumerated in 1881 as well as in 1891.

would learn *how much* the Christian Church has done in India in the forty years since Wylie wrote, will give God thanks that the native evangelical community has increased sevenfold, and that one in three is now a member of the Church against one in six in 1851. If such a rate of progress were continued, the most cautious of experienced missionaries and divines, Dr. John Robson of Rajpootana and Aberdeen, remarks,[1] "The Protestant Church would absorb the whole population of India about the middle of the twenty-first century."

But the comparative success of these fifty years only increases the responsibility and the reproach of the majority of the hereditary Christians of Great Britain and America—two-thirds—who are still doing nothing to bring India and the non-Christian world to Christ. At last each of the great Native States, even the fanatical capital of Haidarabad, Deccan, has been occupied by a missionary or two, with results which, from Travankor to the most ancient and caste-bound principalities of Rajpootana, encourage manifold effort. But there are many of the smaller States into which no preacher, teacher, or healer has yet entered, although in some cases the chief is known to be a student of Scripture, while in others he becomes a convert to Islam. There are many British and American Christians able enough, if they were in earnest, to take each one of these Native States—Mohammedan, Hindu, or Buddhist—and provide for its evangelisation within their own lifetime or that of their children. Nepal alone, attempted by the Jesuits nearly three centuries ago, is shut to the gospel, as Kashmer was till Elmslie, the Scots medical missionary, forced a free entrance for all. From Sikkim and Leh, though not yet from the borders of Assam and the North-Western Provinces, attempts have long been made upon the sealed region of Thibet, now opening up.

It is in directly British Provinces, however, like Bengal and that of the Ganges and Jumna valleys, that the

[1] *Hinduism and its Relations to Christianity.* New edition. Edinburgh (Oliphant), 1893.

Christians of America and Britain have most lamentably failed in their duty. The Lieutenant-Governor of Bengal, Sir Charles Elliot, publicly rejoiced that the number of Christians in his jurisdiction had advanced from 122,000 to 180,000 in ten years. But Bengal has a non-Christian population greater than those of the United Kingdom and France combined, greater than that of the whole United States of America at this hour. It is, in plain language, the scandal of British Christians, at least, that the rich, fertile, and healthy division of the Province, Bahar, whence Buddhism overran the East from Ceylon north to Mongolia, and where the Hindus kept the Mohammedan invaders in check, has only thirty missionaries, of whom one-half are women, for twenty-five millions of souls, including two hundred thousand in its fanatical capital, Patna. Macleod Wylie's urgency is still justified after fifty years, for we have more knowledge, more resources, more liberty, and a far larger population to whom the gospel must be preached for a witness, and for their turning from darkness to light:—

"The duty of the Church of Christ indeed is so plain, that he who runs may read it. Who hath hindered that we should not obey? Have we love for Christ? that will constrain us. Do we honour Christ? His last commands will bind us. Do we desire to promote his glory? That will impel us. Do we mourn over all who know Him not? Then pity for them will compel us,—yes, all heavenly affections, all scriptural convictions, all obligations of duty, will force us to shake off the lethargy and selfishness of bygone years, to awaken all our powers in proclaiming 'the glorious gospel of the blessed God,' and to do this *now*, for 'now is the accepted time, now is the day of salvation.' Much more would I say for India, but words fail to express her woe, or to expose the Christian's shame for past neglect of her. I feel that it is wise to cease from man and to look to Jesus. With His infinite power, He can sway the hearts of those with whom all entreaties fail. He can raise up men of faith and holiness, constraining them to labour for Him, and at last He will give victory to truth. The cause of missions is His own peculiar cause, for He is the friend of sinners. He came not only to call them to repentance, but also to give His life for them, and He now pleads for them in glory. Oh that he would speedily look down upon India, send showers of blessings, give us thousands of labourers in this plenteous harvest, and cause His Gospel to triumph in every place! To Him be the praise and dominion for ever."

On the 5th day of January 1893 the Reformed missionaries in India, assembled at Bombay in the third great Decennial Conference, sent this message to the Churches of Christendom:—

"Overwhelmed by the vastness of the work contrasted with the utterly inadequate supply of workers, earnestly appeal to the Church of Christ in Europe, America, Australasia, and Asia, we re-echo to you the cry of the unsatisfied heart of India. With it we pass on the Master's word for the perishing multitude, *Give ye them to eat.* An opportunity and a responsibility never known before confront us.

"The work among *the educated and English-speaking classes* has reached a crisis. The faithful labours of godly men in the class-room need to be followed up by men of consecrated culture, free to devote their whole time to aggressive work among India's thinking men. Who will come and help to bring young India to the feet of Christ? *Medical missionaries* of both sexes are urgently required. We hold up before medical students and young doctors the splendid opportunity here offered of reaching the souls of men through their bodies. The *women of India* must be evangelised by women. Ten times the present number of such workers could not overtake the task. Missionary ladies now working are so taxed by the care of converts and inquirers already gained, that often no strength is left for entering thousands of unentered but open doors. Can our sisters in Protestant Christendom permit this to continue? India has fifty-seven millions of *Mohammedans* —a larger number than are found in the Turkish Empire, and far more free to embrace Christianity. Who will come to work for them?

"Scores of missionaries should be set apart to promote the production of *Christian literature* in the languages of the people. *Sunday Schools,* into which hundreds of thousands of India's children can readily be brought and moulded for Christ, furnish one of India's greatest opportunities for yet more workers. *Industrial Schools* are urgently needed to help in developing a robust character in Christian youths, and to open new avenues for honest work for them. These call for capable Christian workers of special qualifications.

"The population of India is largely rural. In hundreds and thousands of villages there is a distinct mass-movement toward Christianity. There are millions who would speedily become Christians if messengers of Christ could reach them, take them by the hand, and not only baptize but lead them into all Christian living. Most of these people belong to the *depressed classes.* They are none the less heirs to our common salvation, and, whatever admixture of less spiritual motives may exist, God Himself is stirring their hearts and turning their thoughts toward the things which belong to His kingdom.

"In the name of Christ, and of these unevangelised masses for whom He died, we appeal to you to send more labourers at once. May every Church hear the voice of the Spirit saying, 'Separate me Barnabas and Saul for the work whereunto I have called them'! In every Church may there be a Barnabas and Saul ready to obey the Spirit's promptings!

"Face to face with two hundred and eighty-seven millions in this land, for whom in this generation you as well as we are responsible, we ask, Will you not speedily double the present number of labourers? Will you not also lend your choicest pastors to labour for a term of years among the millions who can be reached through the English tongue? Is this too great a demand to make upon the resources of those saved by omnipotent Love? At the beginning of another century of missions in India let us all 'expect great things from God—attempt great things for God.'

"For the reflex blessings to yourselves, as well as for India's sake, we beseech you to *hear what the Spirit saith unto the Churches.* The manifestation of Christ is greatest to those who keep His commandments, and this is His commandment—

GO YE INTO ALL THE WORLD, AND PREACH THE GOSPEL TO EVERY CREATURE."

it thirty years of his life and much of his fortune, has made an analysis of the list of graduates sent out by that one college, which, though governed by the Free Church of Scotland, represents a union of all the evangelical missions in South India. Of 650 native graduates now living, 100 are Christians. Only seven are Mohammedans, and of the rest two-thirds are Brahmans, and one-third non-Brahman Hindus. Yet of the general population from which the college draws its students, Christians form less than a fiftieth, while the Christian graduates are between a seventh and a sixth.

The political prospects of the conversion of India, in producing amongst its races, in territories covering the extent of Europe, a sense of nationality and the capacity for self-government, arise legitimately out of the consideration of their evangelisation. Even the Mohammedans have learned submission to "the powers that be ordained of God," and hold aloof from the pretensions of the National Congress to an impossible form of representative government. Many of the native Christians take their place in that movement. From the first, Christianity, identified with liberty as well as submission to lawful authority, has been the political friend of the natives of India of every religion. It was Lord William Bentinck who, in the early Duff era, opened the subordinate service to them freely. It was Macaulay and Charles Trevelyan, associated with these two in 1830-35, who opened the covenanted Civil Service on the broad basis of the equal treatment of all classes of the Queen's natural-born subjects, and the Queen-Empress confirmed that in the Imperial Proclamation. Justice has been done as Cæsar and Akbar never did it. The native Christians and the many "almost Christians"

quite unexpectedly. We found the young men sitting thoughtfully at their desks with their Bibles before them, the teacher sitting below at his table giving the lesson and questioning them on it. In England we may call such men 'heathen,' but I never saw more reverent attention at a Bible class anywhere, or more complete evidence of sustained interest than in these classes, where nine-tenths of the scholars profess Hinduism."

in the National Congress, having succeeded in opening the consultative Legislative Councils to a wider number nominated by public bodies like the Universities and Chambers of Commerce, will do well to turn their attention to social reforms springing out of Christian and humane principles. That the Bengalees, Tamils, and Marathas of the coast, whose intellectual and moral growth is arrested by their sexual and social customs, should aspire to govern the martial and the Musalman races of Hindustan and the Dekkan, is suicidal[1]—until all are Christians.

Then, in matters ecclesiastical as well as political, and through the ecclesiastical, the millions of India may, according to their own genius, have learned to follow the settlement and the growth of the Christian Churches and powers of Europe. The Church in the Punjab[2] and in Burma will be different from the Church

[1] The Hindu-Mohammedan riots in Rangoon and Bombay in 1893 and elsewhere are a commentary on this.

[2] When Dr. Norman Macleod was dying, in 1872, he described a dream which filled him with happiness: "I have had such a glorious dream! I thought the whole Punjab was suddenly Christianised, and such noble fellows, with their native Churches and clergy." Contrast this picture, from Mr. Bateman's Report of the C. M. S. Narowal Mission, Punjab, with the experience of the great missionaries of the Middle Ages of Europe, like Anskar, Olaf, and Otto of Bamberg. "The site of the new church, seated for 300 worshippers, with cloisters on three sides of a square where 2000 more are accommodated—the whole ground measuring an acre and a quarter—was given by the Hindu owners. The Mahant (or abbot) of Narowal was the first to make over his share. He had been a pupil in the mission school in the days of Dr. Bruce, and he pointed out to us that the ground which he was giving had held the pegs of Dr. Bruce's tent the first time (more than 30 years ago) that any missionary had encamped at Narowal. The other owners, five in number, were Sikhs, in no way under the orders of the Mahant. They too freely gave their shares for the Christian church, only stipulating that they should remove the timber before doing so. The deed of gift has been signed and registered in the ordinary legal manner, but it was thought fit first of all in the Bishop's presence to go through the Punjabi form of bestowal and consecration to sacred uses. So the Hindus met the

in Bengal, Madras, or the Konkan of Bombay. Even the most opportunist of English statesmen, Lord Palmerston, learned so much from the Mutiny as to declare to a deputation headed by the Archbishop of Canterbury in 1859, "We seem to be all agreed as to the end. It is not only our duty, but it is our interest to promote the diffusion of Christianity as far as possible throughout the length and breadth of India."

When our Lord selected and sent forth the Twelve, first of all, on a mission confined to their own Jewish countrymen, He "appointed other Seventy also, and sent them two and two before His face unto every city and place whither He Himself would come" (St Luke x. 1). Representatives of the missionaries of the kingdom to all peoples in all ages, they returned again with joy, saying, "Lord, even the devils are subject unto us through Thy name." Let all true Christians, of the younger branch of the Indo-European family, who having inherited their faith rejoice in their duty to their elder brethren in India,

Christians on a high mound which had been a fort in days gone by, and which now stands in the middle of the site in question. The donors were introduced to the Bishop, and declared to him that freely and in the fear of God they were making the property over to the Christian community, and then the leading man poured out a bottle of oil on the spot, and the others distributed sugar to everybody there. The Bishop was then presented with a spade of most business-like proportions, and his lordship turned the first sod much to the astonishment of the spectators, who, however, soon followed suit, and there was hardly a Christian from 3 years old to 70 who did not ply that same spade in turn." The church was opened in 1893, the Hindu abbot lending his temple bell to summon the Christian worshippers. After the dedication service followed the confirmation of 38 catechumens and Communion. Of the former a spectator writes :—"It was a wonderful sight. Side by side with the poor outcast labourer and the Hindu convert knelt the rich landowner, the miserable superstition of the one and the severe Mohammedanism of the other were alike things of the past, and the proud ex-Mohammedan and outcasted *Choora*, having looked into the face of Jesus the Elder Brother, looked on one another and found they too were one in Christ Jesus. It was an object lesson, and one on the learning of which depends the unification of India."

take heart from the Lord's own experience while they, like the Seventy, are faithfully toiling: "I was beholding ('Εθεώρουν) Satan as lightning fall from heaven . . . . Blessed are the eyes which see the things that ye see."

Every British Christian, every one who speaks the English language, has a solemn mission from God for the conversion of India.

XI

INTERCESSION AND THANKSGIVING

"*Hear Thou in heaven Thy dwelling place, and do according to all that the stranger calleth to Thee for; that all people of the earth may know Thy name, to fear Thee.*"—1 KINGS viii. 43.

THESE forms of Missionary Intercession and Thanksgiving belong to the whole Catholic Church. Some have been prepared by Bishop Lancelot Andrewes, and in more recent times by Archbishop Sumner and by Bishop Cotton when Metropolitan of India. Others have long been used by the Church Missionary and Propagation of the Gospel Societies.

I. INTERCESSION.

SUBJECTS OF DAILY MISSIONARY INTERCESSION AND THANKSGIVING.

Sunday—The whole World.
Monday—The whole Church of Christ.
Tuesday—India and the East.
Wednesday—Africa.
Thursday—Oceania.
Friday—The Jews.
Saturday—The Christian Dispersion—Missionaries, Emigrants, Sailors, Soldiers, and our Countrymen abroad.

Let us pray for OBEDIENCE TO THE LORD'S COMMISSION :—

Almighty God, who by Thy Son Jesus Christ didst give commandment to the holy Apostles, that they should go into all the world and preach the gospel to every creature: Grant to us whom Thou hast called into Thy Church a ready will to obey Thy Word, and fill us with a hearty desire to make Thy way known upon earth, Thy saving health among all nations. Look with compassion upon the heathen that have not known Thee, and on the multitudes that are scattered abroad as sheep having no shepherd. O heavenly Father, Lord of the harvest, have respect, we beseech Thee, to our prayers, and send forth labourers into Thine harvest. Fit and prepare them by Thy grace for the work of their ministry: give them the spirit of power and of love and of a sound mind; strengthen them to endure hardness; and grant that by their life and doctrine they may set forth Thy glory, and set forward the salvation of all men; through Jesus Christ our Lord. *Amen.*

Let us pray for INDIA, BURMA, and CEYLON :—

O God, who hast made of one blood all nations of men to dwell upon the face of Thy whole earth, and who didst send Thy blessed Son to preach peace to them that are afar off and to them that are nigh, grant that all the people of Hindu, Buddhist, and Mohammedan lands may feel after Thee and find Thee; and hasten, O Lord, the fulfilment of Thy promise to pour out Thy Spirit upon all flesh.

O Lord God, who rulest in the kingdoms of men and givest them to whomsoever Thou wilt, we present our humble supplications before Thee in behalf of India. We acknowledge Thine overruling Providence in having given India unto us for a possession. Make us faithful, we beseech Thee, in so great a trust. Give us a spirit of true compassion for the multitudes in that land, who yet walk in darkness and the shadow of death. Suffer them no longer to bow down to idols which their own hands have made. Lead them from the corrupt worship of false gods to worship Thee in the beauty of holiness. Have pity on their blindness, their misplaced confidence, their mistaken zeal, their self-inflicted sufferings. Teach them the pure mystery of the Incarnation of Thy blessed Son. Deliver them from their dread of the powers of darkness. Raise up among them, O Lord, teachers of Thy truth, who may lead them to embrace the holy faith of Thy Church; for Thy mercy's sake, through Jesus Christ our Lord. *Amen.*

Let us pray for MOHAMMEDANS :—

O Lord Jesus Christ, may it please Thee to have mercy upon Mohammedans, and bring them to confess Thee as the Word consubstantial with the Father. Reveal Thyself to them as the Lord of Glory manifest in the flesh. Cleanse the thoughts of their hearts by the inspiration of Thy Holy Spirit. Mould their dispositions in conformity with Thine own gentleness and meekness; for Thine own mercy's sake, who art, with the Father and the Holy Ghost, one God, world without end. *Amen.*

Let us pray for CHINA AND JAPAN :—

O Lord, who hast taught us that the heathen shall fear Thy Name, and all the kings of the earth Thy majesty, when Thou shalt build up Zion and make Thy glory to appear; fulfil, we beseech Thee, Thy word that these shall come from far, and these from the west, and these from the land of Sinim. Make all Thy mountains a way, and let Thy highways be exalted, for the feet of them that bring good tidings of good, that publish salvation; through Jesus Christ our Lord. *Amen.*

Let us pray for AFRICA :—

O God, who hast promised to Thy Son the heathen for His inheritance, and the uttermost parts of the earth for His possession, hear our prayers for the long benighted races of Africa. Make wars to cease among them; give the slaves their liberty, and bid the oppressed go free; send the light of life to dispel all darkness and ignorance; and grant that Thy Church, now spreading over those wide lands, may lengthen her cords and strengthen her stakes, and be, of Thy mercy, the peaceful home where all may be one in Thee. Grant this for Jesus Christ's sake. *Amen.*

Let us pray for OCEANIA :—

May it please Thee, good Lord, to prosper the work of Thy Church in the far-off isles of the sea; that a new song may be sung unto Thee and Thy praise from the ends of the earth; through Jesus Christ our Lord. *Amen.*

Let us pray for THE CONVERSION OF ISRAEL :—

O merciful God, long-suffering and gracious, have pity upon Thine ancient people Israel. Take away the veil from off their hearts. Remove from them all ignorance and hardness of heart and unbelief, that they may look on Him whom they have pierced, and mourn. Enable them, O heavenly Father, to receive as their King Him whom Thou hast exalted to be a Prince and Saviour for them. Grant this, O Lord, for the sake of the same Thy Son Jesus Christ our Lord. *Amen.*

Let us pray for INQUIRERS sincerely convinced of the truth of the Christian faith :—

O Lord Jesus Christ, we pray for those among the heathen who know Thy Name, but fear to confess Thee before men. We beseech Thee to carry on the work Thou hast begun in them, that they may be obedient to the faith. Lord, they believe, help Thou their unbelief. Be pleased in mercy to reveal Thyself to them so that they may be ready to give up all for Thy sake, and rejoice if they are counted worthy to suffer shame for Thy Name. May the Holy Spirit descend on all missionary schools and colleges, and baptize the many thousands of young souls who are daily instructed from Thy holy Word. May they walk while they have the light, lest darkness come upon them. May they yield themselves up to Thy command, and enter into the full light and liberty and peace of Thy kingdom, who art, with the Father and the Holy Ghost, one God over all, blessed for ever. *Amen.*

Let us pray for CATECHUMENS:—

O Lord God, remember the Catechumens who in various lands are under instruction preparatory to their baptism: have mercy upon them; strengthen their faith; purify their hearts; and plant therein Thy fear, Thy truths, and Thy commandments: prepare them to be a habitation of the Holy Ghost; and grant that they may receive the washing of regeneration for the remission of their sins to the glory of Thy name; through Jesus Christ our Lord. *Amen.*

Let us pray for the spiritual progress of DISCIPLES:—

We yield Thee humble thanks, O heavenly Father, for all whom Thou hast called from among the dark peoples to the knowledge of Thy grace and faith in Thee. Grant that they may daily increase in Thy Holy Spirit more and more; and that, using all diligence to be rightly instructed in Thy holy Word, they may grow in the knowledge and love of our Lord Jesus Christ, and may live godly, righteously, and soberly in this present world, until in the end they obtain everlasting life, through Jesus Christ our Lord. *Amen.*

Let us pray for STUDENTS preparing for missionary work:—

Almighty and eternal God, we humbly pray Thee, let Thy special blessing abide on all colleges where Thy servants are preparing as students for the ministry of Thy Word in foreign parts. Raise up, we beseech Thee, a due supply of men and women, moved inwardly by the Holy Ghost, and truly called, according to the will of our Lord Jesus Christ. Take from them all pride and self-conceit, and every unworthy motive. Enlighten their minds, subjugate their wills, purify their hearts, and so fill them with Thy Spirit that they may go forth animated with zeal for Thy glory and love for the souls of men; and may Thy Holy Word so burn within their hearts that they may speak and heal with that resistless energy of love which will melt the hearts of sinners. And grant to their teachers, that, being patterns of holiness, simplicity, and self-denial, they may wisely and patiently train up the ministers and missionaries of Thy Holy Church. Hear us, O Lord, for the sake of Jesus Christ our Saviour. *Amen.*

Let us pray for THE CHURCH IN THE UNITED STATES OF AMERICA:—

O Almighty God, who from Thy throne dost behold all the dwellers upon earth, we thank Thee for that Thou hast given to the sections of the Catholic Church in Great Britain and Ireland sister Churches in the United States of America. Let the dew of Thy blessing descend evermore on them, and make them rich in every fruit of the Spirit. Grant that between their members and ourselves the communion of saints may be maintained to Thy glory, and to the edifying of the body of Christ in love, May the hearts of the fathers be so turned to the children, and the hearts of the children to their fathers, that peace and love may be multiplied among nations, and that the world may receive thereby a blessing from on high, through Jesus Christ our Lord. *Amen.*

Let us pray for MISSIONARIES:—

O most merciful Saviour and Redeemer, who wouldest not that any should perish, but that all men should be saved and come to the knowledge of the truth, fulfil Thy gracious promise to be present with those who are gone forth in Thy name to preach the gospel of salvation to distant peoples. Be with them in all perils by land or by water, in sickness and distress, in weariness and painfulness, in disappointment and persecution. Bless them, we beseech Thee, with Thy continual favour; and send Thy

Holy Spirit to guide them into all truth. O Lord, let Thy ministers be clothed with righteousness, and grant that Thy word spoken by their mouths may never be spoken in vain. Endue them with power from on high; and so prosper Thy work in their hands, that the fulness of the Gentiles may be gathered in, and all Israel be saved. Hear us, O Lord, for Thy mercy's sake, who livest and reignest with the Father and the Holy Ghost, ever one God, world without end. *Amen.*

Let us pray for THE QUICKENING OF ZEAL IN CHRISTIANS:—

O Lord, our Saviour, who hast warned us that Thou wilt require much of those to whom much is given; grant that we, whose lot is cast in so goodly a heritage, may strive together the more abundantly, by prayer, by almsgiving, and by every other appointed means, to extend to others what we so richly enjoy; and as we have entered into the labours of other men, may we so labour that, in their turn, other men may enter into ours, to the fulfilment of Thy Holy Will and our own everlasting salvation. *Amen.*

Prayer to be used by MISSIONARY COMMITTEES AND SECRETARIES:—

Almighty God, our heavenly Father, who hast purchased to Thyself an Universal Church by the precious blood of Thy dear Son, we give Thee hearty thanks that it hath pleased Thee to call us to the knowledge of Thy grace and faith in Thee, and to appoint our lot in an age and country where the true light shineth. We bless Thee that Thou hast awakened us in some measure to feel our responsibilities. We praise Thee for what we have seen and heard of the power of Thy word among the heathen; we adore Thee for Thy many servants who have gone out from amongst us to toil, and suffer, and die in making known Thy salvation; and we thank Thee that Thou dost allow us, unworthy sinners, to unite together in this work of faith and labour of love.

We humbly confess our past lukewarmness in this Thy service, notwithstanding these Thine inestimable benefits and mercies. For our Lord Jesus Christ's sake forgive us our past negligences, and so endue us with Thy Holy Spirit that we may more earnestly seek Thy glory in the salvation of souls.

Grant us, we beseech Thee, Thy very present help at our meetings. We ask, most gracious God and Father, for a constraining sense of the love of the Lord Jesus, and for wisdom to direct us in all our endeavours. Increase upon us the spirit of power, and of love, and of a sound mind. Give us faith and courage; give us zeal and patience; give us a single eye to Thy glory, and help us to bear and to forbear. The silver and the gold are Thine, O King of kings! Supply us with what is needful for our great work, and make us faithful stewards of Thy bounty for proclaiming the unsearchable riches of Christ.

We pray also for all who are united with us in the direction of this sacred cause. May Thine especial blessing rest upon Missionary Committees, with their Secretaries, throughout the world. Bestow on them the help that we feel so needful for ourselves. Enable them to maintain the unity of the Spirit in the bond of peace, and ever to find favour in the sight of all with whom they may have to do.

Especially we beseech Thee to look, O most merciful Father, upon our Missionary brethren. Draw out our hearts towards them more and more; and while they are bearing the burden abroad, give us grace to help and succour them by our sympathy and prayers at home. Bless every letter written to them from this place, and all our intercourse with them. We pray for them that they may be filled with Thy Spirit. Grant that the same mind may be in them which was also in Christ Jesus. Let them never lose their first love. Raise them above the cares of this world. Help them to deny themselves and to endure all things for the elect's sake. Give them the tongue of the learned. Clothe them with humility. Teach them to follow peace with each other, and with all men. Support them under spiritual distresses, temptations of the adversary, bodily sickness, domestic anxieties, and hope deferred. And so confirm Thy word from their lips by the power of the Holy Ghost, that through them multitudes may be turned from darkness to light, and from the power of Satan unto Thee, our God.

We praise Thee, O Thou God of all grace, for the Converts, the Native Catechists, and the Native Ministers, whom Thou hast granted to us in our several missions. As Thou hast raised the Native Churches thus far, bring them, we pray Thee, to full ripeness and perfectness of age in Christ. Pour out upon them Thy Holy Spirit. Stablish, strengthen, settle them, and so enlarge their liberality, that they may both maintain Thy Word among themselves, and may make it known to the regions beyond them, till all the peoples hear the glad tidings of Thy love and praise Thee.

Give us a constant sense of Thy presence; and may all our undertakings be begun, continued, and ended in Thee, to the honour of Thy great name, for the sake of our Lord and Saviour Jesus Christ. *Amen.*

II. THANKSGIVING.

Let us give thanks for THE PROGRESS OF THE GOSPEL:—

Thou art worthy, O Lord, to receive power
And riches and wisdom and strength,
And honour and glory and blessing:
Blessed be Thy glorious Name,
That Thy word hath sounded forth,
Not only in Jerusalem, and Antioch,
In Athens and in Rome,
In London and in New York;
But in every place the faith of Christ
Is spread abroad.

All glory be to Thee.

For Thy good soldiers in every age,
Striving lawfully, enduring unto the end;
For the wisdom of doctors,
The zeal of evangelists,
The eloquence of prophets,
The love of pastors.
For the praises of babes, the ministry of women,
The purity of the young, the fervour of the aged,
For all the signs of Thy presence,
All the marks of Thy Cross:
All glory be to Thee.

For the light of Thy everlasting gospel,
Sent to every nation, and kindred, and tongue, and people,
Shining so long amongst ourselves;
For Thy Church, the pillar and ground of the truth,
Against which the gates of hell have not prevailed;
For Thy gracious word of promise,
That they that be wise shall shine
As the brightness of the firmament,
And they that turn many to righteousness
As the stars for ever and ever:
All glory be to Thee.

The Lord is gracious and merciful,
Long-suffering, and of great goodness.
The Lord is loving unto every man,
And His mercy is over all His works.
All Thy works praise Thee, O Lord,
And Thy Saints give thanks unto Thee.
They show the glory of Thy kingdom,
And talk of Thy power,
That Thy power, Thy glory, and mightiness of Thy kingdom,
Might be known unto men;
Thy kingdom is an everlasting kingdom,
And Thy dominion endureth throughout all ages.
All glory be to Thee.

Great and marvellous are Thy works,
Lord God Almighty;
Just and true are Thy ways,
Thou King of Saints.
Who shall not fear Thee, O Lord, and glorify
Thy Name?
For Thou only art holy;
For all nations shall come and worship before Thee;
For Thy judgments are made manifest.

All glory be to Thee.

After this I beheld, and, lo, a great multitude,
Which no man could number,
Of all nations, and kindreds, and people, and tongues,
Stood before the throne, and before the Lamb,
Clothed with white robes,
And palms in their hands;
And cried with a loud voice, saying,
Salvation to our God, which sitteth upon the throne,
And unto the Lamb.
Hallelujah!
For the Lord God Omnipotent reigneth.

Glory be to the Father, and to the Son, and to the Holy Ghost;

As it was in the beginning, is now, and ever shall be, world without end. Amen, Amen.

X

THE PROSPECTS OF THE CONVERSION OF INDIA

"*He said unto them, I beheld Satan as lightning fall from heaven. Behold, I give unto you power . . . over all the power of the enemy.*" —St. Luke x. 18, 19.

The prospects of the conversion of India, in the same sense, historically, as that of the Roman Empire and that of the Northern Nations, depend on the faith and labour of the Church entering in at every door opened by British power and administration. Never in all its history has Christianity had such facilities. The danger is that, in its representatives, the Church trusts too much to its providential environment, uses too little its supernatural weapons. There is an intolerance that is demanded by Christ of His followers, and is understood and admired by the Asiatic of other faiths. By such, Gibbon rightly judges, the missionaries of Christ in the first two centuries conquered the Roman Empire. The want of it neutralised all the toil and the heroism of the Nestorian and the Roman monks in Asia. Brahmanism has defeated Buddhism and checked Mohammedanism in India, and it is quite ready to extend to orthodox Christianity a compromise like that which it learned from the Syrians and the Jesuits when it developed the Vishnu worship of Krishna.[1] Sir M. Monier-Williams, after personal study

[1] See Dr. John Muir's introduction to his *Religious and Moral Sentiments from Sanskrit Writers* (Williams & Norgate), 1875, and

on the spot, in his *Modern India and the Indians* (1878), while too inclined to advocate compromise, shows that "the chief impediment to Christianity among Indians is not only the pride they feel in their own religion, but the very nature of that religion. For pantheism is a most subtle, plausible, and all-embracing system, which may profess to include Christianity itself as one of the phenomena of the universe. An eminent Hindu is reported to have said, 'We Hindus have no need of conversion; we are Christians, and more than Christians, already.'"

The temptations to unconscious compromise on the side of the Reformed are not absent. In India itself the missionaries have sometimes recognised caste, and have been too content with a low level of faith, zeal, and self-sacrifice on the part of the converts. In Britain, America, and Germany, the cry for results that can be tabulated and for success that is evident, the preference of methods which produce immediate fruit in individuals to those which work for the destruction of Brahmanism itself and the creation of Christian nations, are of this subtle nature. Both are required, each for a different class, yet some of the supporters of missions attack the latter as no experienced missionary ever does. The wisest preacher of our age,[1] expounding the confession of apparent failure by the man who laid the foundation of the Church of all the nations, Paul, in his greatest letter from Rome to the Philippians, (ii. 20, 21), warns the most zealous that the followers of the Cross have no right, *in their own day*, to look for the recognition of success. Only in heaven shall we know which are the lost causes and which the victorious.[2]

The prospects of the conversion of India are brighter

Mr. C. H. Tawney on "The Bhagavad-Gita and Christianity" in the *Calcutta Review* for January 1876, vol. lxii.

[1] See the late Dean Church's Sermons, xvii.

[2] For a curious estimate, marked by a mixture of rashness and wisdom, read *Christian Missions to Wrong Places, among Wrong Races, and in Wrong Hands*, by A. C. Geikie, D.D. (London, 1871), in the light of the facts of 1893.

than the faith and the obedience of the Church. Men who landed in India, as the writer did, forty years ago, and have watched the divine drama unrol its scenes, till the present hour; men like the great pioneers of the century, of whom Caldwell was the last—may record this as their least hopeful testimony: "To be almost a convert is the highest point many well-disposed Hindus have reached at present. They are timidly waiting for a general movement which they will be able to join without personal risk; but the time may any day come when masses of them will become not only almost, but altogether followers of Christ."[1] Yet, looking up and abroad from the circumstances of the hour to the wide contrasts of a period of forty years, we have authoritatively stated results which make this seem rather the testimony of pessimism. We who began our Indian career in 1853, who witnessed the Mutiny of 1857, took part in the reorganisation of the administration in 1858–1861, and rejoiced in the increase at that time of missionary efforts, would have pronounced it incredible that, ten years before the end of the nineteenth century, there would be more Christians than Sikhs in India, and that the rate of increase of native Christians in the martial races of the Punjab, Mohammedan and Hindu, would be three hundred per cent every decade.

	1881.	1891.	Increase.
Sialkot District	253	9711	9458
Gujranwala ,,	81	2246	2156
Gurdaspur ,,	157	2069	1912
Amritsar ,,	241	959	718
Lahore ,,	760	1397	637
Ambala ,,	224	453	229
Lodiana ,,	179	305	126
Rawalpindi ,,	110	214	104
Jalandhar ,,	66	136	70
Gurgaon ,,	26	86	60
Jhelum ,,	48	106	58
Simla ,,	210	262	52

[1] Bishop Caldwell *On Reserve in communicating Religious Instruction to non-Christians in Mission Schools in India.* Madras, 1879.

We can better record some signs of the present transitions of the peoples of India from the power of darkness into the kingdom of the Son of God's love, through repentance and the forgiveness of sins.

The aboriginal or præ-Aryan peoples of India, entered in the census of 1891 as "Animistic," and numbering nine and a quarter millions, were returned by a more correct classification twenty years before as seventeen and a half millions, exclusive of those in Madras and the Feudatory States. Allowing for these, and adding the casteless tribes and those semi-Hinduised, one-fifth of the whole population, or fifty millions, from the Chooras of North Punjab to the Pariahs of South India, are in the same position for rapidly receiving Christianity as the Kafirs and Negroes of Africa and the islands. It is among these chiefly that Christianity has, all along, won its numerical successes. Till Carey and Duff began the slow sapping and mining processes among the now two hundred millions of the Brahmanical and Musalman cults, these only were evangelised. In the last forty years they have been instructed, organised, and consolidated with a care unknown in the parishes of Christendom. The result is seen in South India, in the Telugu country, in Chota Nagpore, in Santalia, and in the more recent labours of the Established Church of Scotland and the Church Missionary Society in the Punjab districts of Sialkot and Goojrat. This is a marvellous table of the results of evangelical Christianity in forty years, not to be equalled by any period of Church history:—

FORTY YEARS' PROGRESS OF EVANGELICAL CHRISTIANITY IN SOUTH INDIA.

	1851.	1861.	1871.	1881.	1890.
Foreign Ordained Agents	147	201	196	217	262
Native do.	21	97	225	461	767
Foreign and Eurasian Lay Preachers	..	..	..	72	118
Native Lay Preachers	498	1,266	1,985	2,488	3,491
Native Christians	91,092	138,731	224,258	417,372	559,661
Native Communicants	14,661	24,976	52,816	118,325	182,722

Historically, in every province, as the pioneering stage of sowing, and weeding, and watching is passed, similar and even greater results proportionally are being worked out every year. Where the missionary is weak in his enthusiasm and toil, or where, in yielding to the pressure of his Church, he snatches at wholesale baptisms, falling into the snare of the Jesuits without their sacramentarian excuse, he then suffers from inability to instruct the baptized, and schism and apostasy are the consequence.[1] But all over India the aboriginal and the casteless, the down-trodden and the famine-stricken, the serf and the poor, are pressing into the Church by families and villages, till the Church fails to do its duty to the inquirers on the one hand and to the new disciples on the other. If the methods of the Reformed were those of the sacramentarian, or if the Reformed Church doubled its missionary staff at once, the next decennial report would show a fourfold increase.

The hundred and fifty millions of caste Hindus still present to Christendom an unbroken front, or very little broken, apparently. But that it is disintegrating under the combined influence of Western civilisation and Christian truth its own leaders allow, and their methods of meeting the assault confess. Eclectic, elastic, willing to absorb every belief and cult that will tolerate its social system, Brahmanism presents a greater difficulty than classical Paganism, if only because of caste. But the caste principle itself is so weakened, that an educated Hindu may now be anything, do anything, believe anything, and go anywhere, if only he remains nominally within the fold. Formerly Brahmans could not so far resist the influence of the Spirit of God, under Christian teaching, as to remain in Hinduism, because the system rejected them with indignation: now it tempts them by concessions. The deistical Brāhma Somāj, which has passed through many stages of development since the writer's friend,

[1] See, for one painful warning, the report of the Narowal Mission, Punjab, by the C. M. S. able missionary, Rev. Rowland Bateman, and the *Church Missionary Intelligencer* for August 1893, pp. 628-9.

Keshub Chunder Sen, reached his nearest point to Christ in 1868, and is now represented by the thoughtful Pertab Chunder Mozoomdar, consists of only three thousand four hundred members. But it has kept, and it keeps far more back from the profession of faith in Christ than it helps out of idolatry. The later Arya Somāj, which admits all castes to the new caste created by its Brahman founder, Dayānand Saraswati, as Sikhism did, takes its forty thousand members back to the Veds. Dr. John Robson, whose book is the wisest brief exposition of *Hinduism and its Relations to Christianity*,[1] on going back to Rajpootana after an absence of twenty years, pronounces the Arya Somāj one of the most redoubtable antagonists of Christianity, but "it is one of the most powerful disintegrations of old Hinduism, and may thus do a work in clearing the way for Christianity."

Under the pressure and example of vernacular-preaching missionaries Hinduism seems to have entered on new methods of self-defence. A universal Hindu conference—*Bharat Dharma Mahamandal*—was lately held at Benares, including many Hindu ladies of high family. A select committee of pundits brought up a report on "the deterioration of the Hindu religion." To an immense crowd at each of the four corners of a great pavilion four pundits read a copy of the report, after which a salute of one hundred *sankha*, or blasts from the conch shell, was given. These were the practical conclusions of the report:—

"First, all the dharmasova and all the priests of the Hindu temples will offer prayers at a fixed time to the Supreme Power, so that the sonaton dharma be saved from the deplorable state to which it has come down, the day for general prayer being fixed on the 9th of sukla nabami of Aswin; second, to establish provincial dharma mandal all over the country, such as are established in Bengal and Lahore, and to establish a central maha mandal; third, to send a upadeshakas to all parts of Hindustan, who should preach sonaton dharma; fourth, to publish Sanskrit books containing all rules of apadharmas, and to publish a series of moral and educational Sanskrit books; fifth, to establish schools for Sanskrit education."

---

[1] Edinburgh, 1893.

That is, the pundits appoint a day of united prayer, the employment of evangelists, the circulation of their religious tracts and scriptures, and the establishment of Hindu mission schools. So the Brahmanical revival goes on after a half-hearted fashion, for while caste has a side hostile to all reform from without, it disintegrates from within, and prevents the formation of an united front against the enlightened assailant.

The ablest and most eloquent of all the Brahman converts of the Free Church of Scotland is a distinguished Pleader, Kali Churn Banerji, LL.B. His own opinion and his report of the prevailing Hindu view of the advance of Christianity were recently stated in an address to the Calcutta Missionary Conference on the "Organised Opposition to Christianity in India":—

> "The opposers of Christianity no longer attack Christianity, but set themselves to show that Christians are not worthy the confidence of the Hindu people. The enemy are attempting to spread abroad the following ideas—1, With the exception of zanana workers, the missionaries are exercising no influence in the country, and not worth noticing. 2, Missionaries are not the opponents of the national faith, but the opponents of national institutions, enemies to India patriotism. 3, The general influence of missions upon the life and customs of the people is not helpful, but injurious to the country. Besides this, numbers of the Hindus systematically attempt to co-ordinate Hinduism with Christianity, and do all they can to entice missionaries and Christians to admit by word or deed that Christianity and Hinduism are each systems of religion of high authority and excellence. This is done by copying the methods of the Christian propaganda, preaching, publishing tracts, etc. etc. These forms of opposition to Christianity, so far as they go, are very encouraging to Christians, and indicate that they have the whole matter in their own hands. And if the non-Christians have nothing more serious to present in opposition, all that is needed is for the missionaries to be true to their colours and India will be theirs."

If there is a New Hinduism there is also the beginning of a New Islam under the influence of the Christian propaganda and Western rule. In British India alone Mohammedans, now fifty-eight millions in number, are constrained to learn toleration. Under the "neutral" rule of Great Britain, as they term it, the later generation of Islam are becoming rationalists, like the Mutazala sect of freethinkers, that thus they may justify reforms such as will bring their children abreast of the progress which is changing all around them. They hold that the Shariat Law of Islam is common law which must advance with new conditions. They teach that the Koran has only a temporary authority on moral questions. On the one hand the more thoughtful of the old school are represented by Nawab Mushin-ul-Mulk, of Haidarabad, who exclaims, "To me it seems that as a nation and a religion we are dying out. . . . Unless a miracle of reform occurs we Mohammedans are doomed to extinction, and we shall have deserved our fate. For God's sake let the reform take place before it is too late."[1] On the other, Syed Amir Ali Sahib, a judge of the High Court in Calcutta, who represents the young men influenced by English culture but hostile to Christian influence, wrote his book *The Spirit of Islam* to assist "the Moslems of India to achieve intellectual and moral regeneration under the auspices of the great European Power that now holds their destinies in its hands." That apologist for the Mohammedanism of the Koran, who tries to explain away its sanctions of polygamy and concubinage, the "disgusting ordeal" of the temporary husband (Sura II. 230), and slavery, and only substitutes an imaginary Islam of his own, congratulates his co-reformers "that the movement set on foot is conducted under a neutral government." Christians must wish them well.

Meanwhile Christianity has won greater triumphs from Islam in India than even experts had believed. The Rev. Maulvi Imad-ud-din, D.D., a lineal descendant of the famous Mohammedan saint Qutub Jamal, who again is a descendant of the ancient royal house of Persia, was invited to attend the "World's Parliament of Religions" at Chicago, and to read a paper. He declined the invita-

[1] See Rev. Edward Sell's remarkable article on "The New Islam" in the *Contemporary Review* for August 1893.

tion to attend, but sent a paper, written by himself in Urdu, and translated into English by Dr. Henry Martyn Clark. His subject is "Christian Efforts amongst Indian Mohammedans; being an Account of the Effects of the Teaching of the Bible amongst the Mohammedans of India, together with a Consideration of the Question how many of them have become Christians, and why." The writer and the paper are alike remarkable :—

"I was at one time a Mohammedan, though by the grace of God I am now a Christian. I know my forefathers by name for the last thirty generations. They were all Mohammedans, and amongst them have been some renowned champions of the faith of Islam. I was born in the town of Panipat, near Delhi, about the year 1830, and from my earliest youth my stedfast desire was to learn all things concerning Mohammedanism, and to spend my life in its defence and in its propagation. I was sent at the age of sixteen years to Agra for my education, and there I was taught in matters concerning the faith of Islam by men of light and learning and note amongst Mohammedans, and in order that my secular education should not suffer, I at this time entered as a student in the Government College at Agra, and in that institution I remained five years. Having completed my curriculum in Oriental learning, I passed out of the College with credit, having obtained my degree and testimonials with honour. From boyhood until the year 1860, I most earnestly and true-heartedly observed all the precepts of Mohammedanism in their minutest details with much pain and weariness, and I dived also into the waters of Sufiism and tested it. For three years I preached in the Royal Jama Musjid of Agra, and for many years I preached in numberless mosques all over the country. I was a determined opponent of the Christian faith, but I found nothing in Mohammedanism from which an unprejudiced man might in his heart derive true hope and real comfort, though I searched for it earnestly in the Koran, the Traditions, and also in Sufiism. Rites, ceremonies, and theories I found in abundance, but not the slightest spiritual benefit does a man get by acting on them. He remains fast held in the grip of darkness and death. As the result of much such painful experience and quite of its own motion my heart was no longer willing to submit to the profitless weariness of Mohammedanism, nevertheless I thought none the better of Christianity, nor did I cease to oppose it with all my might.

"In 1864 I met an aged, God-fearing, honourable English layman who was in Government service, and in conversation with him the talk happened to turn on the true faith—which one is it amongst the many faiths of the world? He contended the Christian faith is the true one; I maintained that there was not one that was true. All faiths, I held, were merely a collection of the thoughts and customs of men, and that nothing whatever was to be gained by following any of them, and I told him that this observation of mine was the result of years of painstaking and conscientious endeavour and inquiry. 'But,' said the gentleman, 'have you really honestly examined the Christian faith and have you found it lacking?' I said, 'Yes, I have, and I have found it false.' I lied. He replied, 'Is it *really* true, this that you say that you have examined Christianity and found it wrong?' Hearing the word 'true' from his mouth I was ashamed before God, and I said, 'Sir, I have not yet myself tested this faith, nor have I as yet read the Bible and informed myself concerning its principles, but having read all that the Mohammedan controversialists have to say against Christianity, on the strength of that I declare that this religion also is false,' and this really was the true state of the case. He said to me, 'And what answer will you give to God at the last day? He has given the light of reason to every one, and it is the duty of each man to use the reason God has so given. You have not yet exercised your reason concerning the faith of Christ; and yet you declare it to be false on the strength of the mere statement of others. This is to follow others blindly instead of honestly inquiring for yourself into the matter.'

"These words so pierced my heart that from that moment I gave myself up whole-heartedly to examine into the Christian faith. This I did unremittingly for two years, and having come to the conclusion that the religion of Christ is the true faith, I was baptized on April 29th, 1866. From that day to this, for nearly twenty-seven years, it has been my thought night and day how to rescue Mohammedans from the errors in which they are plunged; and by the grace of God I have written a number of books, big and little, for their benefit, twenty-four in all. These have been printed and circulated by the Punjab Religious Book Society. A number have passed through several editions, and all are at this time sold over the whole country. Now whatever seemed to me to be necessary to write for Mohammedans I have written. I am now engaged on a Life of Christ in Urdu. This will appear in a series of books, of which each will be published as soon as it is ready. The first book of the series has already appeared, the second is now ready for the press, and the third is being written.

"Even as the Lord has had mercy on me and has called me into His Church, in like manner has He shown His grace to many other

Mohammedans also, who too have now been or are being called by Him. I now wish to consider two questions: firstly, to what extent any result has been produced in the way of direct accessions to Christianity from amongst Mohammedans; and, secondly, how, if any, has this result been brought about?

"As regards the first point, let it be noted it is now some 100 years since Christian missions were commenced in India. Before that time Mohammedans spoke of the Christian faith in the terms of the Koran and Hadis Traditions in such a way that it was looked upon as degraded and erroneous by the people. Since the year 1800, when William Carey commenced work in a part of Bengal, things have gradually gone forward until now the Christian faith is discussed all over the land. Only forty-five years have passed since Christianity was introduced into the Punjab. When Carey landed in India, the condition of the land was such that from the standpoint of mere worldly wisdom it was simply impossible that the Christian religion should spread in this country. The Hindus and Mohammedans of that time were strong in their faith, most bigoted and hard of heart, and were firmly entrenched behind the citadel of their own pride and overweening self-sacrifice. Nevertheless, what worldly wisdom could not see was revealed to the eye of the Christian faith of Carey, to wit, that to Christ shall assuredly the victory be in this land. He will conquer in India now, even as He has conquered in other lands in the past. This, too, is the intense conviction nowadays of us Christians here, and our expectation from God is that some day our land will certainly be Christian even as Great Britain now is. However much our enemies, Hindus, Mohammedans, Dayanandis, and others, may oppose and revile, the time is most assuredly coming when they will not be found even for the seeking. We shall have only two sorts of people then—the people of God and the people of the world who serve their own lusts. The trend of national life amongst us is now setting swiftly and surely in this direction. Thus also has it ever been in the history of the past. Such also, as may be historically demonstrated, are invariably the results of education."

Maulvi Imad-ud-din then mentions the principal converts from Islam since Abdul Masih, who copied Henry Martyn's Persian New Testament in 1810, and was ordained by Bishop Heber. He gives the names with brief biographies of no fewer than 117 men of position and influence, of whom 62 became clergy and leading men in several of the India missions, and 57 are gentlemen occupying various positions, official and professional:—

"It is difficult to say exactly how many Mohammedans have become converts, for no separate list is kept in missions of converts from Islam ; all converts are entered alike in the Church of Christ. The figures in one of the Church Missionary Society Churches in the Amritsar district show that in forty years there have been 956 baptisms; amongst this number there are 152 Mohammedan converts. The register of the Baptist Mission at Delhi shows twenty-eight such converts. Nowadays there are Churches all over India, and in every Church there are baptisms from amongst Mohammedans. I have quoted the figures for two Churches ; from these it may be inferred as regards the others what baptisms take place from amongst Mohammedans. Amongst those baptized there are all sorts and conditions of men, rich and poor, high and low, men and women, children, learned and unlearned, tradesmen, servants, all kinds and classes of Mohammedans whom the Lord our God hath called are coming into His Church. . . .

"What may we learn from the things that I have stated? First, then, it is evident that learned Mohammedans are coming in larger numbers into the fold of Christ than the unlearned, because they are better educated ; and, secondly, that so far from the situation being devoid of hope, it is big with blessings. There was a time when the conversion of a Mohammedan to Christianity was looked on as a wonder. Now they have come and are coming in their thousands. Compared with converts from amongst Hindus, converts from amongst Mohammedans are fewer far. Where there are ten thousand from amongst Hindus, there are a thousand from amongst Mohammedans. This backwardness to come into the Church of Christ is but part and parcel of Mohammedan backwardness and sluggishness in all other matters. . . . Nevertheless, we may thank God that such numbers have become Christians from amongst them, and are now jealous for the faith, and are an example to their brethren still in Mohammedan darkness.

"It still remains to be considered in what way the results of which I have spoken in the first part of this paper have been produced. The hidden and real cause, of course, is the grace of God. He, according to His promises, is gathering into His Church from amongst all nations those that are being saved, even as He has done from the first (Acts xi. 47). The other causes are certain manifest things.

"The first is the freedom for individuals to follow their own beliefs which the British have conferred on India. This is a great blessing, which God has as yet withheld from the peoples under the sway of Mohammedan rulers. When tolerance and freedom obtain in those lands, there also will many become Christians.

"The second reason is that God has been pleased to send His blessing on the efforts, self-denial, and labours of loving-hearted, devoted saints of His in this land.

"The third reason is one which obtains especially in India, because of it learned Mohammedans are being converted to Christianity, and it is this: From 1850 till the present day, great discussions and continual strivings about things religious have gone on between Christians and Mohammedans. These began in Agra, and by means of these Mohammedans and others as well have not only learnt how to investigate faiths, but have been very greatly incited by these people to speak and think. So the hidden things of various faiths have been thoroughly brought to light. It is not necessary for Christians and Mohammedans now to engage in further controversy. All about Mohammedanism that it was necessary to say has been said, and whatever Mohammedans could do against Christianity they have done to the utmost. We may now truly say the battle has been fought out in India, not only between Christianity and Mohammedanism, but also between Christianity and all that is opposed to it in all the earth."

The supernatural power of Christianity, and the secondary influence of Western science and literature,[1] have thus been allowed, for the first time in the history of Asia, fairly to take their place side by side with all the agencies of the Hindu, the Mohammedan, and the aboriginal religious and social systems. The result is a revolution, silent, subtle, and far-reaching, which works in each successive generation with increasing force. Gradually the Hindus themselves, and still more a few of their leaders, are becoming conscious of a force and a pressure which is transforming their society, if not themselves, and which they can only blindly resist. Now it is the physical signs or instruments of the revolution which the mob attack; now it is the spiritual force behind the whole British influence which their leaders recognise with a sort of despair. The first of these forms of discontent was lately seen in a riot of profound significance which attracted no attention in this country. Into the filthiest and most

[1] See the very suggestive paper of Rev. F. E. Slater, Bangalor, on "Work among the Educated Classes in India," in vol. i. of the *Report of the Third Decennial Missionary Conference held at Bombay*, 1892-93.

superstitious city of India, Benares, waterworks were being introduced. The Brahmans had long boasted that the sacred Ganges would never suffer the indignity of being bridged, and yet two bridges far above the city had been thrown across it. At last the great Benares bridge itself spanned the mighty river, the Dufferin Bridge, and then came the waterworks. The Hindu mob rushed at water-pipes, steam-engines, telegraph wires, and railway stations, and would have attempted to destroy even the bridge but for the interference of the troops. They attacked the house of the most enlightened of their own religion, the Raja Shiva Prosad, C.I.E., considering him a traitor to his faith and city. The spiritual fermentation caused by education and positive Christian truth expresses itself in vain lamentations and yearning aspirations such as this, from Pundit Sivanath Sastri of the Sadhāran Brahmā Somāj :—

'Many religious movements are now agitating our country. Men's minds are now filled with doubts regarding those things which formerly commanded respect. When a hurricane drives the waters of the ocean along the beds of rivers, they swell and overflow their banks, and inundate the surrounding country. Thatched roofs of houses, trees, logs of wood, are found floating on the waters and drifting with the current. Here men and birds and beasts, in their struggle for life, get upon a log of wood, which sinks under their weight, and they are drowned. There, perhaps, some serpents are found coiling round the floating branches of a tree, and men, nevertheless, struggling to save themselves by catching hold of those branches. Such is the plight in which our countrymen are at present. A great flood has come and swept over the face of the country, carrying away the roofs of the edifices of past creeds and customs. Drowning men in their despair are catching at whatever they find nearest their hands. They are finding it difficult to obtain peace of mind. They cannot rest on any beliefs. What a mournful state of things it is! Peace and rest have become unattainable."

The working of this silent revolution may be traced in the position of the native Christians. The increase of the native Christians in numbers, and the positions which they are fast winning for themselves in every walk of life, and especially in Government service, are alarming the Brahmans. In Madras, where Christianity is oldest and strongest, we find the native Christian papers "anxiously awaiting the results of the census of 1891, for we anticipate a very large increase in the native Christian population." That of the Hindus and Mohammedans is 10½ per cent in the decade, while that of the Christians is known to have been 86 per cent. "If this increase has been kept up till 1891 it will be one of the most wonderful triumphs which Christianity has ever had in the world." Their native Christian Association has begun to issue pamphlets on the position and prospects of the community. The first on "Educational Progress among Hindus" called forth this comment from the *Hindu* on the Christians :—

"Some of their women are highly educated, and this fact coupled with the other—namely, that they have no caste restrictions—gives them an advantage which is not possessed by the Hindus. The Director of Public Instruction in his latest reports remarks, 'I have frequently drawn attention to the educational progress of the native Christian community. There can be no question that if this community pursues with steadiness the present policy of its teachers, with the immense advantages it possesses in the way of educational institutions, in the course of a generation it will have secured a preponderating position in all the great professions, and possibly, too, in the industrial enterprise of the country—in the latter because no section of the community has entered on the new departure in education with greater earnestness than the native Christians.' This rapid progress in education naturally gives them a corresponding claim on the patronage of Government, as it gives them also a share in other occupations of the country. Recently a native Christian barrister was appointed as Acting Administrator-General."

In South India alone there were 44,225 native Christians at school and college, or 61 per cent of boys and 28 per cent of girls of a school-going age, while the percentage of the Presidency as a whole is 23 of boys and 3 of girls. The native Christians are only a fortieth of the population as yet, but more than 8 per cent of the students attending college and of the graduates of the university are native Christians. The political bearing of this, from the Government's point of view, is evident. Christians are loyal, and not passively but actively so. The next generation of ruling men in India will have a supply of highly loyal and trained native Christians from which to draw for the ordinary ranks of the local services, as well as for help in any crisis which may come upon the Empire. Even *The Hindu* newspaper acknowledges that this community "in politics, industry, and the domestic and civil virtues, has special advantages enabling it to set an example to the Hindus."

No feature of the rapid progress of education in South India is so remarkable as the extent to which the native Christians are distancing the Hindu and Mohammedan communities from which they have sprung. The well-known missionary, Dr. William Miller, C.I.E., who has virtually created the Madras Christian College,[1] giving to

[1] See *Days of Grace in India* by Henry Stanley Newman, of the Society of Friends (Leominster). He writes: "The Christian College is a monument of large-hearted Scottish philanthropy. . . . We found Mr. Miller in the midst of a crowd of attentive students, to whom he was talking and giving instruction in that easy way which showed at once his marvellous power of winning boys and control over them. He has about one thousand students in the Institution, and is the soul and life of the whole, and the College is manned with an exceptionally good staff of competent professors and teachers. What would not some of the grouse-shooting billiard-playing gentlemen of England give for the honest joy and pleasure Miller finds in this work for Christ in the tropics! . . . The affection of these students for Mr. Miller is something beautiful, yet nothing but the power of God can make them Christian converts. Though only a small proportion of them actually make an open profession of Christianity, Mr. Miller tells me that there is an immense change going on in the feeling of the people in favour of Christianity. I inquired what proportion of the scholars were Christians. He replied there were about one hundred Christians to nine hundred Hindus. Who can measure the influence for good exerted upon these nine hundred Hindus, as they daily receive systematic scriptural instruction from Christian teachers in their respective class-rooms? Some may imagine they endure the Bible lesson for the sake of the privileges of the College. On the contrary, Mr. Miller says, 'The Bible lesson is one of the most popular lessons we have.' It happened to be the hour for Bible study when we visited the College. We entered one class-room after another with Mr. Miller,

APPENDIX

THE FINDING OF THE NESTORIAN TABLET

THE work of the Jesuit missionary, Alvarez Semedo, referred to on page 19, was translated into English and published in London in 1655.[1] It is now so rare that we append that part of chapter 31, "Of the Christian Religion planted many Ages since in China: and of a very ancient Stone lately discovered there, which is an admirable Testimonie thereof," which describes the finding:—

"When the *Tartars* conquered *China* there were many *Christians* who had sumptuous Churches, being much favoured by them, as appeareth by the relation of *Paulus Venetus*. Afterward when *Humvu* endeavoured to regaine the Kingdom, and made warre upon the *Tartars*, the *Moores* tooke part with the *Chinesses*, and lent them their assistance for the gaining of the Kingdom, and of the victory which they obtained, in acknowledgement whereof they were allowed to remaine in *China*, with libertie of their Religion and of their *Mosches*. The *Christians*

[1] "The History of that great and renowned Monarchy of China. Wherein all the particular Provinces are accurately described: as also the Dispositions, Manners, Learning, Lawes, Militia, Government, and Religion of the People. Together with the Traffick and Commodities of that Countrey. Lately written in *Italian* by F. Alvarez Semedo, a *Portughess*, after he had resided twenty two yeares at the Court, and other Famous Cities of that Kingdom. Now put into *English* by a Person of quality, and illustrated with several Mapps and Figures, to satisfie the curious, and advance the trade of Great *Brittain*. To which is added the History of the late Invasion and Conquest of that flourishing Kingdom by the Tartars. With an exact Account of the other affairs of *China*, till these present times. London: Printed by *E. Tyler* for *John Crook*, and are to be sold at his Shop at the Sign of the Ship in S. *Pauls* Church-yard, 1655."

inclined to the *Tartars*, and they being overcome in that warre, the *Christians* also were deprived of their *Estates*, and some being slain, others changing their Religion, others flying and hiding themselves in secret places, in a short time, all signe and memory of our Religion perished, so that it was not possible for us to discover anything, with all the diligence we used to that purpose.

"To conclude, we remained very disconsolate in the midst of so great darknesse, when it pleased *The only fountaine of light to draw us out of this obscuritie with a most clear Testimony, that the Gospel had flourished there many ages since: The thing fell out thus.*

"In the year 1625, as they were digging the foundation for to erect a certain building neere to the City of *Siganfu*, the Capitall Citie of the Province of *Xemsi*, the workemen lighted upon a table of stone about nine palmes long, and more than foure in breadth, and above one palme in thicknesse. The top of it, (that is, one of the extremities, or ends, of the length thereof,) endeth in the forme of a Pyramid, above two palmes in height, and above one palmes breadth at the Basis. On the plaine of this Pyramid, there is a well form'd *Crosse*, the extremities whereof end in flower-deluces, after the fashion of that *Crosse*, which is reported to have been found graved on the Sepulchre of the Apostle S. *Thomas* in the Towne of *Meliapor*, and as they were anciently painted in *Europe*, of which there are some yet to be seen at this day.

"This *Crosse* is encompassed, as it were, with certain clouds, and at the foot thereof were three Traverse lines, each consisting of three great letters, being all such as are commonly used in *China*, very fairly graven: with the same sort of letters is engraven the whole *Superficies* of the stone, as also the thicknesse thereof, the which notwithstanding differeth from the rest, in that some of the letters graven thereon, are forraine, neither were they knowne here at the first finding of it.

"Scarcely had the *Chinesses* discovered and cleansed this notable piece of Antiquitie, when excited by the fervour of their naturall curiosity, they ranne to the Governour to give him notice of it, who being much joyed at this newes, presently came to see it, and caused it to be placed upon a faire Pedestall, under a small Arch, sustained by pillars at each end thereof, and open at the sides, that it might be both defended from the injuries of the weather, and also feast the eyes of such as are true Lovers of venerable Antiquity. He caused it also to be set within the circuit of a Temple belonging to the *Bonzi*, not farre from the place where it was taken up.

"There was a wonderfull concourse of people to see this stone, partly for the Antiquity thereof, and partly for the novelty of the strange Characters, which was to be seen thereon: and as the knowledge of our Religion is at this day very much spread abroad in *China*, a *Gentile*, who was a great friend unto a grave Christian *Mandarine* named *Leo*, being present there, presently understood the mystery of that writing, and believing it would be very acceptable to his friend, sent him a copy thereof, although he was distant above a month and a halfes voyage, the *Mandarine* dwelling in the City of *Hamcheu*, whither our fathers had retired themselves, by reason of the former persecution, whereof we shall speak in its proper place. This copy was received with a spirituall *Jubilee*, and many exteriour demonstrations of joy, as an irrefragable Testimony of the *Ancient Christianity* in *China*, which had been so much desired and sought after: for no lesse was contained in this writing, as we shall shew anon.

"Three years after in the year 1628 some of our fathers went into that Province in the company of a *Christian Mandarine*, who had occasion to go thither. They founded a Church and house in the capitall City thereof for the service of our good God, that he, who was pleased to discover so precious a memoriall of the possession taken in that Country by his divine law, would also facilitate the restitution thereof in the same place. It was my good fortune to be one of the first, and I esteemed it a happy abode, in that I had the opportunity to see the stone, and being arrived I took no thought for any thing else. I saw it and read it, and went often to read, behold, and consider it at leisure, and above all, I did much admire, that being so ancient, it should be so entire, and have the letters so plainly and neatly graven.

"On the thicknes of the sides thereof, it hath many *Chinesse* letters, which containe many names of the *Priests* and *Bishops* of that time. There are also many other letters, which were not then knowne, for they are neither Hebrew nor Greek: and (for as much as I now understand) they containe the same names, that if peradventure some strangers might not understand the letters of the Countrie, they might perhaps be better acquainted with those of a forraigne extraction.

"Passing by *Cocchine* I came to *Cranganor*, where is the *Residence* of the *Archbishop* of *Costa*, to consult about these letters with father *Antoni Fernandes* one of our societie, who is very skilfull in the books and writings of those ancient Christians converted by S. *Thomas.* He told me the letters were *Syriack*, and the very same which are used there at this day."

Further accounts of the Nestorian Tablet will be found in Nieuhoff's narrative of the Dutch East India Company's embassy to the Emperor of China in 1655, Englished by John Ogilby in 1673 (2nd ed.), and in Du Halde's *Description of the Empire of China and Chinese Tartary*, of which an English translation appeared in two folios in 1741.

INDEX